The Philosophy of Natural Magic

AGRIPPA VON NETTESHEIM

The Philosophy of Natural Magic, A. von Nettesheim
Jazzybee Verlag Jürgen Beck
86450 Altenmünster, Loschberg 9
Deutschland

ISBN: 9783849675653

Translated by Lauron William de Laurence (1868 – 1936)

www.jazzybee-verlag.de
admin@jazzybee-verlag.de

Printed by Createspace, North Charleston, SC, USA

CONTENTS:

AGRIPPA. 1

SUBLIME OCCULT PHILOSOPHY. 1

PREFACE. 1

EARLY LIFE OF CORNELIUS AGRIPPA. 2

CORNELIUS AGRIPPA TO THE READER. 8

AGRIPPA TO TRITHEMIUS. 10

TRITHEMIUS TO AGRIPPA. 12

CHAPTER I. HOW MAGICIANS COLLECT VIRTUES FROM THE THREE-FOLD WORLD IS DECLARED IN THESE THREE BOOKS. 14

CHAPTER II. WHAT MAGIC IS, WHAT ARE THE PARTS THEREOF, AND HOW THE PROFESSORS THEREOF MUST BE QUALIFIED. 14

CHAPTER III. OF THE FOUR ELEMENTS, THEIR QUALITIES, AND MUTUAL MIXTIONS. 17

CHAPTER IV. OF A THREE-FOLD CONSIDERATION OF THE ELEMENTS. 18

CHAPTER V. OF THE WONDERFUL NATURES OF FIRE AND EARTH. 19

CHAPTER VI. OF THE WONDERFUL NATURES OF WATER, AIR AND WINDS. 20

CHAPTER VII. OF THE KINDS OF COMPOUNDS, WHAT RELATION THEY STAND IN TO THE ELEMENTS, AND WHAT RELATION THERE IS BETWIXT THE ELEMENTS THEMSELVES AND THE SOUL, SENSES AND DISPOSITIONS OF MEN. 25

CHAPTER VIII. HOW THE ELEMENTS ARE IN THE HEAVENS, IN STARS, IN DEVILS, IN ANGELS, AND LASTLY IN GOD HIMSELF. 26

CHAPTER IX. OF THE VIRTUES OF THINGS NATURAL, DEPENDING IMMEDIATELY UPON ELEMENTS. 28

CHAPTER X. OF THE OCCULT VIRTUES OF THINGS. 29

CHAPTER XI.HOW OCCULT VIRTUES ARE INFUSED INTO THE SEVERAL KINDS OF THINGS BY IDEAS THROUGH THE HELP OF THE SOUL OF THE WORLD, AND RAYS OF THE STARS; AND WHAT THINGS ABOUND MOST WITH THIS VIRTUE. 30

CHAPTER XII. HOW IT IS THAT PARTICULAR VIRTUES ARE INFUSED INTO PARTICULAR INDIVIDUALS, EVEN OF THE SAME SPECIES. 31

CHAPTER XIII. WHENCE THE OCCULT VIRTUES OF THINGS PROCEED. 32

CHAPTER XIV. OF THE SPIRIT OF THE WORLD, WHAT IT IS, AND HOW BY WAY OF MEDIUM IT UNITES OCCULT VIRTUES TO THEIR SUBJECTS. 35

CHAPTER XV. HOW WE MUST FIND OUT AND EXAMINE THE VIRTUES OF THINGS BY WAY OF SIMILITUDE. 36

CHAPTER XVI. HOW THE OPERATIONS OF SEVERAL VIRTUES PASS FROM ONE THING INTO ANOTHER, AND ARE COMMUNICATED ONE TO THE OTHER. 38

CHAPTER XVII. HOW BY ENMITY AND FRIENDSHIP THE VIRTUES OF THINGS ARE TO BE TRIED AND FOUND OUT. 38

CHAPTER XVIII. OF THE INCLINATIONS OF ENMITIES. 40

CHAPTER XIX. HOW THE VIRTUES OF THINGS ARE TO BE TRIED AND FOUND OUT, WHICH ARE IN THEM SPECIALLY, OR IN ANY ONE INDIVIDUAL BY WAY OF SPECIAL GIFT. 42

CHAPTER XX. THE NATURAL VIRTUES ARE IN SOME THINGS THROUGHOUT THEIR WHOLE SUBSTANCE, AND IN OTHER THINGS IN CERTAIN PARTS AND MEMBERS. 43

CHAPTER XXI. OF THE VIRTUES OF THINGS WHICH ARE IN THEM ONLY IN THEIR LIFE TIME, AND SUCH AS REMAIN IN THEM EVEN AFTER THEIR DEATH. 44

CHAPTER XXII. HOW INFERIOR THINGS ARE SUBJECTED TO SUPERIOR BODIES, AND HOW THE BODIES, THE ACTIONS, AND DISPOSITIONS OF MEN ARE ASCRIBED TO STARS AND SIGNS. 45

CHAPTER XXIII. HOW WE SHALL KNOW WHAT STARS NATURAL THINGS ARE UNDER, AND WHAT THINGS ARE UNDER THE SUN, WHICH ARE CALLED SOLARY. 47

CHAPTER XXIV. WHAT THINGS ARE LUNARY, OR UNDER THE POWER OF THE MOON. 49

CHAPTER XXV. WHAT THINGS ARE SATURNINE, OR UNDER THE POWER OF SATURN. 51

CHAPTER XXVI. WHAT THINGS ARE UNDER THE POWER OF JUPITER, AND ARE CALLED JOVIAL. 52

CHAPTER XXVII. WHAT THINGS ARE UNDER THE POWER OF MARS, AND ARE CALLED MARTIAL. 52

CHAPTER XXVIII. WHAT THINGS ARE UNDER THE POWER OF VENUS, AND ARE CALLED VENEREAL. 53

CHAPTER XXIX. WHAT THINGS ARE UNDER THE POWER OF MERCURY, AND ARE CALLED MERCURIAL. 54

CHAPTER XXX. THAT THE WHOLE SUBLUNARY WORLD, AND THOSE THINGS WHICH ARE IN IT, ARE DISTRIBUTED TO PLANETS. 54

CHAPTER XXXI. HOW PROVINCES AND KINGDOMS ARE DISTRIBUTED TO PLANETS. 55

CHAPTER XXXII. WHAT THINGS ARE UNDER THE SIGNS, THE FIXED STARS, AND THEIR IMAGES. 56

CHAPTER XXXIII. OF THE SEALS AND CHARACTERS OF NATURAL THINGS. 58

CHAPTER XXXIV. HOW, BY NATURAL THINGS AND THEIR VIRTUES, WE MAY DRAW FORTH AND ATTRACT THE INFLUENCES AND VIRTUES OF CELESTIAL BODIES...60

CHAPTER XXXV. OF THE MIXTIONS OF NATURAL THINGS, ONE WITH ANOTHER, AND THEIR BENEFIT. 60

CHAPTER XXXVI. OF THE UNION OF MIXED THINGS, AND THE INTRODUCTION OF A MORE NOBLE FORM AND THE SENSES OF LIFE..61

CHAPTER XXXVII. HOW, BY SOME CERTAIN NATURAL AND ARTIFICIAL PREPARATIONS, WE MAY ATTRACT CERTAIN CELESTIAL AND VITAL GIFTS...63

CHAPTER XXXVIII. HOW WE MAY DRAW NOT ONLY CELESTIAL AND VITAL, BUT ALSO CERTAIN INTELLECTUAL AND DIVINE GIFTS FROM ABOVE..64

CHAPTER XXXIX. THAT WE MAY, BY SOME CERTAIN MATTERS OF THE WORLD, STIR UP THE GODS OF THE WORLD AND THEIR MINISTERING SPIRITS...65

CHAPTER XL. OF BINDINGS; WHAT SORT THEY ARE OF, AND IN WHAT WAYS THEY ARE WONT TO BE DONE. 66

CHAPTER XLI. OF SORCERIES, AND THEIR POWER. 67

CHAPTER XLII. OF THE WONDERFUL VIRTUES OF SOME KINDS OF SORCERIES. 68

CHAPTER XLIII. OF PERFUMES OR SUFFUMIGATIONS; THEIR MANNER AND POWER...71

CHAPTER XLIV. THE COMPOSITION OF SOME FUMES APPROPRIATED TO THE PLANETS. 73

CHAPTER XLV. OF COLLYRIES, UNCTIONS, LOVE-MEDICINES, AND THEIR VIRTUES. 74

CHAPTER XLVI. OF NATURAL ALLIGATIONS AND SUSPENSIONS.....75

CHAPTER XLVII. OF MAGICAL RINGS AND THEIR COMPOSITIONS. 77

CHAPTER XLVIII. OF THE VIRTUE OF PLACES, AND WHAT PLACES ARE SUITABLE TO EVERY STAR. 78

CHAPTER XLIX. OF LIGHT, COLORS, CANDLES AND LAMPS, AND TO WHAT STARS, HOUSES AND ELEMENTS SEVERAL COLORS ARE ASCRIBED. 79

CHAPTER L. OF FASCINATION, AND THE ART THEREOF. 81

CHAPTER LI. OF CERTAIN OBSERVATIONS, PRODUCING WONDERFUL VIRTUES. 82

CHAPTER LII. OF THE COUNTENANCE AND GESTURE, THE HABIT AND THE FIGURE OF THE BODY, AND TO WHAT STARS ANY OF THESE DO ANSWER--WHENCE PHYSIOGNOMY, AND METOPOSCOPY, AND CHIROMANCY, ARTS OF DIVINATION, HAVE THEIR GROUNDS...84

CHAPTER LIII. OF DIVINATIONS, AND THE KINDS THEREOF. 86

CHAPTER LIV. OF DIVERS CERTAIN ANIMALS, AND OTHER THINGS, WHICH HAVE A SIGNIFICATION IN AUGURIES. 88

CHAPTER LV. HOW AUSPICIAS ARE VERIFIED BY THE LIGHT OF NATURAL INSTINCT, AND OF SOME RULES OF FINDING IT OUT. 93

CHAPTER LVI. OF THE SOOTHSAYINGS OF FLASHES AND LIGHTNINGS, AND HOW MONSTROUS AND PRODIGIOUS THINGS ARE TO BE INTERPRETED. 97

CHAPTER LVII. OF GEOMANCY, HYDROMANCY, AEROMANCY, AND PYROMANCY, FOUR DIVINATIONS OF ELEMENTS. 98

CHAPTER LVIII. OF THE REVIVING OF THE DEAD, AND OF SLEEPING OR HIBERNATING (WANTING VICTUALS) MANY YEARS TOGETHER. 100

CHAPTER LIX. OF DIVINATION BY DREAMS. 102

CHAPTER LX. OF MADNESS, AND DIVINATIONS WHICH ARE MADE WHEN MEN ARE AWAKE, AND OF THE POWER OF A MELANCHOLY HUMOR, BY WHICH SPIRITS ARE SOMETIMES INDUCED INTO MEN'S BODIES...103

CHAPTER LXI. OF THE FORMING OF MAN, OF THE EXTERNAL SENSES, ALSO THOSE INWARD, AND THE MIND; AND OF THE THREE-FOLD APPETITE OF THE SOUL, AND PASSIONS OF THE WILL. 106

CHAPTER LXII. OF THE PASSIONS OF THE MIND, THEIR ORIGINAL SOURCE, DIFFERENCES, AND KINDS. 109

CHAPTER LXIII. HOW THE PASSIONS OF THE MIND CHANGE THE PROPER BODY BY CHANGING ITS ACCIDENTS AND MOVING THE SPIRIT...109

CHAPTER LXIV. HOW THE PASSIONS OF THE MIND CHANGE THE BODY BY WAY OF IMITATION FROM SOME RESEMBLANCE; OF THE TRANSFORMING AND TRANSLATING OF MEN, AND WHAT FORCE THE IMAGINATIVE POWER HATH, NOT ONLY OVER THE BODY BUT THE SOUL. 111

CHAPTER LXV. HOW THE PASSIONS OF THE MIND CAN WORK OF THEMSELVES UPON ANOTHER'S BODY...113

CHAPTER LXVI. THAT THE PASSIONS OF THE MIND ARE HELPED BY A CELESTIAL SEASON, AND HOW NECESSARY THE CONSTANCY OF THE MIND IS IN EVERY WORK...114

CHAPTER LXVII. HOW THE MIND OF MAN MAY BE JOINED WITH THE MIND OF THE STARS, AND INTELLIGENCES OF THE CELESTIALS, AND, TOGETHER WITH THEM, IMPRESS CERTAIN WONDERFUL VIRTUES UPON INFERIOR THINGS. 115

CHAPTER LXVIII. HOW OUR MIND CAN CHANGE AND BIND INFERIOR THINGS TO THE ENDS WHICH WE DESIRE.......................116

CHAPTER LXIX. OF SPEECH, AND THE OCCULT VIRTUE OF WORDS. 117

CHAPTER LXX. OF THE VIRTUE OF PROPER NAMES. 118

CHAPTER LXXI. OF MANY WORDS JOINED TOGETHER, AS IN SENTENCES AND VERSES; AND OF THE VIRTUES AND ASTRICTIONS OF CHARMS...119

CHAPTER LXXII. OF THE WONDERFUL POWER OF ENCHANTMENTS. 120

CHAPTER LXXIII. OF THE VIRTUE OF WRITING, AND OF MAKING IMPRECATIONS, AND INSCRIPTIONS. 122

CHAPTER LXXIV. OF THE PROPORTION, CORRESPONDENCY, AND REDUCTION OF LETTERS TO THE CELESTIAL SIGNS AND PLANETS, ACCORDING TO VARIOUS TONGUES, AND A TABLE THEREOF. 123

HENRY MORLEY'S CRITICISM. 126

AGRIPPA AND THE ROSICRUCIANS. 127

EXPOSITION OF THE CABALA. 132

THE MIRIFIC WORD. 139

REUCHLIN THE MYSTIC. 140

AGRIPPA EXPOUNDS REUCHLIN. 145

THE NOBILITY OF WOMAN. 147

ORDER OF THE EMPYREAN HEAVEN. 156

SYMBOLS OF THE ALCHEMISTS. 160

A MESSAGE FROM THE STARS. 163

THE ETERNAL PRINCIPLE. 163

A MESSAGE TO ALL MYSTICS. 165

THE HINDU MAGIC MIRROR. 165

AGRIPPA.

Mr. Henry Morley, an eminent English scholar, in his Life of Cornelius Agrippa, makes these tributary statements:

He secured the best honors attainable in art and arms; was acquainted with eight languages, being the master of six. His natural bent had been from early youth to a consideration of Divine Mysteries. To learn these and teach them to others had been at all times his chief ambition. He is distinguished among the learned for his cultivation of Occult Philosophy, upon which he has written a complete work.

SUBLIME OCCULT PHILOSOPHY.

JUDICIOUS READER: This is true and sublime Occult Philosophy. To understand the mysterious influences of the intellectual world upon the celestial, and of both upon the terrestrial; and to know how to dispose and fit ourselves so as to be capable of receiving the superior operations of these worlds, whereby we may be enabled to operate wonderful things by a natural power--to discover the secret counsels of men, to increase riches, to overcome enemies, to procure the favor of men, to expel diseases, to preserve health, to prolong life, to renew youth, to foretell future events, to see and know things done many miles off, and such like as these. These things may seem incredible, yet read but the ensuing treatise and thou shalt see the possibility confirmed both by reason and example.

--J. F., the translator of the English edition of 1651.

PREFACE.

In the last half of 1509 and the first months of 1510, Cornelius Agrippa, known in his day as a Magician, gathered together all the Mystic lore he had obtained by the energy and ardor of youth and compiled it into the elaborate system of Magic, in three books, known as Occult Philosophy, the first book of which--Natural Magic--constitutes the present volume. Agrippa published his Occult Philosophy, with additional chapters, in 1533. The only English translation appeared in London in 1651. It is a thoroughly edited and revised edition of this latter work that we produce. Some translating has been done and missing parts supplied. The reader is assured that while we have modified some of the very broad English of the seventeenth century, that he has a thoroughly valid work. Due care has been taken to preserve all the quaintness of the English text as far as consistent with plain reading. We have endeavored to do full justice to our author, the demands of those purely mystical, and the natural conservatism of the antiquary and collector. In this we believe we have fully succeeded.

The life of Agrippa, up to the time of writing his Occult Philosophy, is also given, drawn mostly from Henry Morley's excellent life of Cornelius Agrippa.

That part of the volume credited to Mr. Morley maybe designated as an honest skeptic's contribution to Mysticism, and his chapters are produced entire, as justice to both him and Agrippa cannot be done otherwise, and they are an especially valuable part of Mystic literature.

The table of the Cabala, newly compiled for this volume, will be found to possess superior features over all others.

Following the above we give a chapter on the Empyrean Heaven, which will explain much that our author has written. It is derived mainly from an old occult work on "Physic."

The Symbols of the Alchemists will be found both useful and instructive. The chapter on the Magic Mirror, which ends the work, is believed to be the best contribution on the subject extant.

All the original illustrations and some new and selected ones will be found, as also various etchings of characters. That one on the Empyrean Heaven contains, we have cause to believe, some of the very hidden knowledge relating to the Lost Word. It is a much older plate than the work it was taken from.

Some parts of the volume will interest those who love to work out hidden things.

The editor conveys his warmest thanks to those friends who have encouraged him in the work--on the Cabala table, the illustration of the Grand Solar Man and the translating--outside of which he has not asked or received any help. This being the case our friends will please excuse any particular thing that may not sound pleasantly to the ear.

EARLY LIFE OF CORNELIUS AGRIPPA.

AT Cologne, on the 14th of September, 1486, there was born into the noble house of Nettesheim a son, whom his parents called in baptism Henry Cornelius Agrippa. Some might, at first thought, suppose that the last of the three was a Christian name likely to find especial favor with the people of Cologne, the site of whose town, in days of Roman sovereignty, Marcus Agrippa's camp suggested and the colony of Agrippina fixed. But the existence of any such predilection is disproved by some volumes filed with the names of former natives of Cologne. There were as few Agrippas there as elsewhere, the use of the name being everywhere confined to a few individuals taken from a class that was itself not numerous. A child who came into the world feet-foremost was called an Agrippa by the Romans, and the word itself, so Aulus Gellius explains it, was invented to express the idea, being compounded of the trouble of the woman and the feet of the child. The Agrippas of the sixteenth century were usually sons of scholars, or of persons in the upper ranks, who had been mindful of a classic precedent; and there can be little doubt that a peculiarity attendant on the very first incident in the life here to be told was expressed by the word used as appendix to an already sufficient Christian name.

The son thus christened became a scholar and a subject of discussion among scholars, talking only Latin to the world. His family name, Von Nettesheim, he never latinised, inasmuch as the best taste suggested that--if a Latin designation was most proper of a scholar--he could do, or others could do for him, nothing simpler than to set apart for literary purposes that half of his real style which was already completely Roman. Henry Cornelius Agrippa von Nettesheim became therefore to the world what he is also called in this narrative--Cornelius Agrippa.

He is the only member of the family of Nettesheim concerning whom any records have been left for the instruction of posterity. Nettesheim itself is a place of little note, distant about twenty-five miles to the southwest of Cologne. It lies in a valley, through which flows the stream from one of the small sources of the Roer. The home of the Von Nettesheims, when they were not personally attached to the service of the emperor, was at Cologne. The ancestors of Cornelius Agrippa had been for generations in the service of the royal house of Austria; his father had in this respect walked in the steps of his forefathers, and from a child Cornelius looked for nothing better than to do the same.

It is proper to mention that among the scholars of Germany one, who before the time of Agrippa was known as the most famous of magicians, belonged to the same city of Cologne; for there, in the thirteenth century, Albertus Magnus taught, and it is there that he is buried.

Born in Cologne did not mean in 1486 what it has meant for many generations almost until now--born into the darkness of a mouldering receptacle of relics. Then the town was not priest-ridden, but rode its priests. For nearly a thousand years priestcraft and handicraft have battled for predominance within its walls. Priestcraft expelled the Jews, banished the weavers, and gained thoroughly the mastery at last. But in the time of Cornelius Agrippa handicraft was uppermost, and in sacred Cologne every trader and mechanic did his part in keeping watch on the archbishop. Europe contained then but few cities that were larger, busier, and richer, for the Rhine was a main highway of commerce, and she was enriched, not only by her manufacturers and merchants, but, at the same time also, by a large receipt of toll. Commerce is the most powerful antagonist to despotism, and in whatever place both are brought together one of them must die.

Passing by the earlier times to about the year 1350 there arose a devilish persecution of the Jews in many parts of Europe, and the Jews of Cologne,

3

alarmed by the sufferings to which others of their race had been exposed, withdrew into their houses, with their wives and children, and burnt themselves in the midst of their possessions. The few who had flinched from this self-immolation were banished, and their houses and lands, together with all the land that had belonged to Cologne Jews, remained as spoils in the hands of the Cologne Christians. All having been converted into cash, the gains of the transactions were divided equally between the town and the archbishop. The Jews, twenty years later, were again allowed to reside in the place on payment of a tax for the protection granted them.

In 1369 the city was again in turmoil, caused by a dispute concerning privileges between the authorities of the church and the town council. The weavers, as a democratic body, expressed their views very strong and there was fighting in the streets. The weavers were subdued; they fled to the churches, and were slain at the altars. Eighteen hundred of them, all who survived, were banished, suffering, of course, confiscation of their property, and Cologne being cleared of all its weavers--who had carried on no inconsiderable branch of manufacture--their guild was demolished. This event occurred twenty years after the town had lost, in the Jews, another important part of its industrial population, and the proud city thus was passing into the first stage of its decay.

In 1388 an university was established at Cologne, upon the model of the University of Paris. Theology and scholastic philosophy were the chief studies cultivated in it, and they were taught in such a way as to win many scholars from abroad. Eight years afterwards, churchmen, nobles, and traders were again contesting their respective claims, and blood was again shed in the streets. The nobles, assembled by night at a secret meeting, were surprised, and the final conquest of the trading class was in that way assured. A new constitution was then devised, continuing in force during the lifetime of Cornelius Agrippa.

The Von Nettesheims were likely to be on better terms with the archbishop than with the party who opposed him, and they were in the emperor's service. This must have influenced the early years of Agrippa. In these early years he displayed a rare aptitude for study, and, as Cologne was an university town and printing, discovered shortly before his birth, was carried on there in the production of Latin classics, the writings of ascetics, scholastics, and mystics like Thomas Aquinas and Albertus Magnus, it was only natural he should avail his eager desire for knowledge at these sources. He was remarkably successful in the study of European languages also, becoming proficient in several. Thus his years of home training were passed until he arrived at the age when princes are considered fit to be produced at court. He then left Cologne and became an attendant on the Emperor of Germany, Maximilian the First, whom he served first as secretary, afterwards for seven years as a soldier. At the age of twenty he was

4

employed on secret service by the German court. At this time Spain was in a chaotic political condition. Ferdinand, the widower of Isabella, was excluded from the crown after his wife's death, that inheritance having passed with his daughter Joanna, as a dower, to her husband Philip, who was the son of Maximilian. In September, 1506, Philip died, shortly before having declared war against France. Thus it was that Cornelius went to Paris, ostensibly to attend the university there, but in reality to keep Maximilian advised of the important news regarding the French. In the capacity of secret service, in which he was engaged more than once, he showed himself abundantly able to preserve diplomatic secrets, though concerning his own affairs he was open, frank, and free. Thus he is silent in regard to official duties at this time. In attending the university Agrippa came in contact with several other minds who had a love for the occult-- mystics who found in him a natural leader to guide them into the realms of the unknown. With these he organized a secret band of Theosophists, or possibly Rosicrucians. Among these mystics was one more prominent as the friend of Agrippa, who might be regarded as second in leadership, an Italian by the name of Blasius Caesar Landulphus, who afterwards became noted in medicine, and also a professor in the University of Pavia. Among them were MM. Germain, advocate, and author of a history of Charles V., etc.; Gaigny, theologian, linguist, Latin poet, and successively procurator, rector, and chancellor of the Paris University; Charles Foucard, M. de Molinflor, Charles de Bouelles, canon, professor of theology, and author of works on metaphysics and geometry, among which he treated of the quadrature of the circle and the cubication of the sphere, and other unusual matters; Germain de Brie, canon, linguist, and writer of Greek verse; MM. Fasch, Wigand, and Clairchamps; and Juanetin Bascara de Gerona, a young Catalonian nobleman, temporarily at Paris while on his way to the court of Maximilian.

Disturbances in Spain had spread to Aragon and Catalonia, and in the district of Tarragon the Catalonians had chased one of their local masters, the Senor de Gerona, the last named of the secret band above.

Agrippa and his friends devised a plan whereby Gerona could be restored to his estates. The capture of a fortification known as the Black Fort was necessary to the enterprise, and to effect this a daring stratagem was decided upon. As the whole province of Tarragon could thus be held against the rebellious peasantry it was believed the emperor, Maximilian, would sanction the enterprise in behalf of his kin, and Gerona went to the German court for this purpose. Agrippa also returned to Cologne for a season early in 1507.

It was over a year afterwards when the plans of the conspirators were carried out. The Black Fort was captured, as planned, by a stratagem. After remaining there for a time, Agrippa was sent with some others to garrison the place of Gerona at Villarodona. Landulph had, meanwhile, gone to Barcelona, and it was deemed prudent that Gerona, the peasants of the whole country being now in arms, should join him there. Gerona was, however, captured by the infuriated rustics, who immediately organized themselves in great force to storm his castle and exterminate the garrison there, who-, in Gerona's absence, were under the charge of Agrippa. Timely warning of the attack was conveyed to the garrison. To escape by breaking through the watches of the peasantry was madness, to remain was equally futile. But one way of escape presented itself--an old, half-ruined tower three miles distant, situated in one of the mountain wildernesses which characterize the district of Valls. The tower stood in a craggy, cavernous valley, where the broken mountains make way for a gulf containing stagnant waters, and jagged, inaccessible rocks hem it in. At the gorge by which this place is entered stood the tower, on a hill which was itself surrounded by deep bogs and pools, while it also was within a ring of lofty crags. There was but one way to this tower, except when the ground was frozen, and these events happened in the midsummer of 1508. The way among the pools was by a narrow path of stone, with turf walls as hedges. The site of the tower made it inexpugnable in summer time. It was owned by an abbot, who gave them permission to occupy and fortify it. This they accordingly done, having a poor bailiff, in charge of the place, for company.

The retreat to the tower was safely accomplished under cover of night. Gerona's place was sacked the next day by the peasants, who sought fiercely for the German, as they termed Agrippa. The hiding place of the conspirators becoming known, the flood of wrath poured down towards the tower, but the strength of the position was then felt. With a barricade of overthrown wagons the sole path to the besieged was closed, and behind this barrier they posted themselves with their arquebuses, of which one only sufficed to daunt a crowd of men accustomed to no weapons except slings or bows and arrows. The peasantry, discovering that the tower was not to be stormed, settled down to lay strict siege to the place and thereby starve its little garrison into surrender.

Perilous weeks were passed by the adventurers, but more formidable than actual conflict was the famine consequent on their blockade. Perrot, the keeper, taking counsel with himself as how to help his guests and rid himself of them at the same time, explored every cranny of the wall of rock by which they were surrounded. Clambering among the wastes, with feet accustomed to the difficulties of the mountain, he discovered at last a devious and rugged way, by which the obstacles of crag and chasm were avoided and the mountain top reached. Looking down from there he saw how, on the other side, the mountain rose out of a lake, known as the Black Lake, having an expanse of about four miles, upon the farther shore of which his master's abbey stood. He found a way to the lake through a rocky gorge, but from there to the abbey was a long way, and, to men without a boat, the lake was a more impassable barrier than the mountain. He returned to the tower, where the little garrison heard the result of his explorations. It was seen that a boat was necessary to effect an escape, and to procure that a letter would have to be sent through the ranks of the vigilant besiegers, whose sentries were posted at all points, and who allowed no one to approach the tower; not even the good abbot himself, who had vainly tried to turn the peasants from their purpose.

Under these circumstances the ingenuity of Agrippa was severely tested, and he justified the credit he had won for subtle wit. The keeper had a son, a shepherd-boy, and Agrippa disfigured him with stains of milk-thistle and the juice of other herbs, befouled his skin and painted it with shocking spots to imitate the marks of leprosy, fixed his hair into a filthy bunch, dressed him like a beggar, and gave him a crooked branch for a stick, within which there was scooped a hollow for the letter. Upon the boy so disguised--a fearful picture of the outcast leper--the leper's bell was hung, his father seated him on an ox, and led him by night across the marshes by the ford, where he left him. Stammering, as he went, petitions for alms, the boy walked without difficulty by a very broad road made for him among the peasantry, who regarded his approach with terror and fled from his path. The letter was safely delivered, the boy returning the next day with the desired answer, ringing his bell at the border of the marsh at dark for his father to bring him in. Agrippa and his companions spent the night in preparations for departure. Towards dawn they covered their retreat by a demonstration of their usual state of watchfulness, fired their guns, and gave other indications of their presence. This done, they set forth, in dead silence, carrying their baggage, and were guided by Perrot, the keeper, to the summit. There they lay gladly down among the stones to rest, while their guide descended on the other side and spread a preconcerted signal, a white cloth, upon a rock. When he returned they ate the breakfast they had brought with them, all sitting with their eyes towards the lake. At about nine o'clock two fishermen's barks were discerned, which hoisted a red flag, the good abbot's signal. Rejoicing at the sight of this, the escaped men fired off their guns in triumph from the mountain-top, a hint to the besieging peasantry of their departure, and, at the same time, a signal to the rescuers. Still following Perrot, they next descended, along ways by him discovered, through the rocky gorge, to the meadows that bordered the lake. Entering the boats, before evening they found themselves safe under the abbot's roof. The day of this escape was the 14th of August, 1508. They had been suffering siege, therefore, during almost two months in the mountain fastness.

Cornelius Agrippa being safe could quit the scene, and done so without waiting to see how the difficulty would be solved between the Catalonian peasants and their master. It perplexed him much that he had no tidings of Landulph, his closest friend. The abbot advised him to go to court again, but Agrippa replied that he had no mind to risk being again sent upon hazardous missions. After remaining several days in the abbey he set out, with an old man and his servant Stephen, for Barcelona. Antonius Xanthus, the companion of Agrippa, had seen much of the rough side of the world, was useful as a traveling companion, and became a member of Agrippa's secret league.

Not finding Landulph at Barcelona they traveled to Valentia. From there they sailed for Italy, and by way of the Balearic Islands and Sardinia they went to Naples, where, disheartened by not finding Landulph,

they shipped for Leghorn, and then traveled to Avignon. There they learned, from a traveling merchant, that Landulph was at Lyons. The friends now corresponded, Cornelius writing December 17th--nearly four months after he had left the abbey in search of his friend, the 24th of August. We may imagine many of the things these friends wrote each other. It was the suggestion of Agrippa that all the members of their league be called together that they might be absolved of their oaths regarding the Spanish conspiracy and to resume, once more, their former pleasant relations. He also hoped that Landulph might be able to visit him at Avignon and talk their secrets over, as he was unable to leave for Lyons, his funds being exhausted, until after the lapse of a little time.

The foregoing account, which has been condensed from Mr. Henry Morley's excellent Life of Cornelius Agrippa, is continued in that part of this volume that starts with the heading of "Agrippa and the Rosicrucians." Agrippa's life now becomes so interwoven with mysticism that we give Morley's account in full. The next chapters in his life are replete with the fruition of his mystic nature, its full-blown flower being The Occult Philosophy, or Three Books of Magic, the writing of which completes his early life.

CORNELIUS AGRIPPA TO THE READER.

I do not doubt but the title of our book of Occult Philosophy, or of Magic, may by the rarity of it allure many to read it, amongst which, some of a disordered judgment and some that are perverse will come to hear what I can say, who, by their rash ignorance, may take the name of Magic in the worse sense and, though scarce having seen the title, cry out that I teach forbidden Arts, sow the seed of heresies, offend the pious, and scandalize excellent wits; that I am a sorcerer, and superstitious and devilish, who indeed am a Magician: to whom I answer, that a Magician doth not, amongst learned men, signify a sorcerer or one that is superstitious or devilish; but a wise man, a priest, a prophet; and that the Sybils were Magicianesses, and therefore prophesied most clearly of Christ; and that Magicians, as wise men, by the wonderful secrets of the world, knew Christ, the author of the world, to be born, and came first of all to worship him; and that the name of Magic was received by philosophers, commended by divines, and is not unacceptable to the Gospel. I believe that the supercilious censors will object against the Sybils, holy Magicians and the Gospel itself sooner than receive the name of Magic into favor. So conscientious are they that neither Apollo nor all the Muses, nor an angel from heaven can redeem me from their curse. Whom therefore I advise that they read not our writings, nor understand them, nor remember them. For they are pernicious and full of poison; the gate of Acheron is in this book; it speaks stones--let them take heed that it beat not out their brains. But you that come without prejudice to read it, if you have so much discretion of prudence as bees have in gathering honey, read securely, and believe that you shall receive no little profit, and much pleasure; but if you shall find any things that may not please you, let them alone and make no use of them, for I do not approve of them, but declare them to you. But do not refuse other things, for they that look into the books of physicians do, together with antidotes and medicines, read also of poisons. I confess that Magic teacheth many superfluous things, and curious prodigies for ostentation; leave them as empty things, yet be not ignorant of their causes. But those things which are for the profit of men--for the turning away of evil events, for the destroying of sorceries, for the curing of diseases, for the exterminating of phantasms, for the preserving of life, honor, or fortune-- may be done without offense to God or injury to religion, because they are, as profitable, so necessary. But I have admonished you that I have writ many things rather narratively than affirmatively; for so it seemed needful that we should pass over fewer things, following the judgments of Platonists and other Gentile Philosophers when they did suggest an argument of writing to our purpose. Therefore if any error have been committed, or anything hath been spoken more freely, pardon my youth, for I wrote this being scarce a young man, that I may excuse myself, and say, whilst I was a child I spake as a child, and I understood as a child, but being become a man, I retracted those things which I did being a boy, and in my book of the vanity and uncertainty of Sciences I did, for the most part, retract this book. But here, haply, you may blame me again, saying, "Behold, thou, being a youth, didst write, and now, being old, hast retracted it; what, therefore, hast thou set forth?" I confess, whilst I was very young, I set upon the writing of these books, but, hoping that I should set them forth with corrections, and enlargements--and for that cause I gave them to Trithemius, a Neapolitanian Abbot, formerly a Spanhemensian, a man very industrious after secret things. But it happened afterwards that, the work being intercepted, before I finished it, it was carried about imperfect and impolished, and did fly aboard in Italy, in France, in Germany, through many men's hands; and some men, whether more impatiently or imprudently I know not, would have put it thus imperfect to the press, with which mischief, I, being affected, determined to set it forth myself, thinking that there might be less danger if these books came out of my hands with some amendments than to come forth, torn and in fragments, out of other men's hands. Moreover, I thought it no crime if I should not suffer the testimony of my youth to perish. Also, we have added some chapters and inserted many things which did seem unfit to pass by, which the curious reader shall be able to understand by the inequality of the very phrase, for we were unwilling to begin the work anew and to unravel all that we had done, but to correct it and put some flourish upon it. Wherefore, I pray thee, courteous reader, weigh not these things according to the present time of setting them forth, but pardon my curious youth if thou find any thing in them that may displease thee.

When Agrippa first wrote his Occult Philosophy he sent it to his friend Trithemius, an Abbot of Wurtzburg, with the ensuing letter. Trithemius detained the messenger until he had read the manuscript and then answered Agrippa's letter with such sound advice as mystics would do well to follow for all time to come. Trithemius is known as a mystic author and scholar.

AGRIPPA TO TRITHEMIUS.

TO R. P. D. JOHN TRITHEMIUS, AN ABBOT OF SAINT JAMES, IN THE SUBURBS OF HERBIPOLIS, HENRY CORNELIUS AGRIPPA OF NETTESHEIM SENDETH GREETING:

WHEN I was of late, most reverend father, for a while conversant with you in your Monastery of Herbipolis, we conferred together of divers things concerning Chemistry, Magic, and Cabala, and of other things, which as yet lie hid in Secret Sciences and Arts; and then there was one great question amongst the rest--Why Magic, whereas it was accounted by all ancient philosophers to be the chiefest science, and by the ancient wise men and priests was always held in great veneration, came at last, after the beginning of the Catholic Church, to be always odious to and suspected by the holy Fathers, and then exploded by Divines, and condemned by sacred Canons, and, moreover, by all laws and ordinances forbidden? Now, the cause, as I conceive, is no other than this, viz.: Because, by a certain fatal depravation of times and men, many false philosophers crept in, and these, under the name of Magicians, heaping together, through various sorts of errors and factions of false religions, many cursed superstitions and dangerous rites, and many wicked sacrileges, even to the perfection of Nature; and the same set forth in many wicked and unlawful books, to which they have by stealth prefixed the most honest name and title of Magic; hoping, by this sacred title, to gain credit to their cursed and detestable fooleries. Hence it is that this name of Magic, formerly so honorable, is now become most odious to good and honest men, and accounted a capital crime if any one dare profess himself to be a Magician, either in doctrine or works, unless haply some certain old doting woman, dwelling in the country, would be believed to be skillful and have a divine power, that she (as saith Apuleis the satirist) "can throw down the heaven, lift up the earth, harden fountains, wash away mountains, raise up ghosts, cast down the Gods, extinguish the stars, illuminate hell," or, as Virgil sings:

She'll promise by her charms to cast great cares,
Or ease the minds of men, and make the Stars
For to go back, and rivers to stand still,
And raise the nightly ghosts even at her will;
To make the earth to groan, and trees to fall
From the mountains--

Hence those things which Lucan relates of Thessala the Magicianess, and Homer of the omnipotency of Circe. Whereof many others, I confess, are as well of a fallacious opinion as a superstitious diligence and pernicious labor; for when they cannot come under a wicked art yet they presume they may be able to cloak themselves under that venerable title of Magic.

These things being so, I wondered much and was not less indignant that, as yet, there had been no man who had either vindicated this sublime and sacred discipline from the charge of impiety or had delivered it purely and sincerely to us. What I have seen of our modern writers--Roger Bacon, Robert of York, an Englishman, Peter Apponus, Albertus [Magnus] the Teutonich, Arnoldas de villa Nova, Anselme the Parmensian. Picatrix the Spaniard, Cicclus Asculus of Florence, and many other writers of an obscure name--when they promise to treat of Magic do nothing but relate irrational tales and superstitions unworthy of honest men. Hence my spirit was moved, and, by reason partly of admiration, and partly of indignation, I was willing to play the philosopher, supposing that I should do no discommendable work--seeing I have been always from my youth a curious and undaunted searcher for wonderful effects and operations full of mysteries--if I should recover that ancient Magic (the discipline of all wise men) from the errors of impiety, purify and adorn it with its proper lustre, and vindicate it from the injuries of calumniators; which thing, though I long deliberated of it in my mind, I never durst undertake; but after some conference betwixt us of these things, at Herbipolis, your transcending knowledge and learning, and your ardent adhortation, put courage and boldness into me. There selecting the opinions of philosophers of known credit, and purging the introduction of the wicked (who, dissemblingly, and with a counterfeited knowledge, did teach that traditions of Magicians must be learned from very reprobate books of darkness or from institutions of wonderful operations), and, removing all darkness, I have at last composed three compendious books of Magic, and titled them Of Occult Philosophy, being a title less offensive, which books I submit (you excelling in the knowledge of these things) to your correction and censure, that if I have wrote anything which may tend either to the contumely of Nature, offending God, or injury of religion, you may condemn the error; but if the scandal of impiety be dissolved and purged, you may defend the Tradition of Truth; and that you would do so with these books, and Magic itself, that nothing may be concealed which may be profitable, and nothing approved of which cannot but do hurt; by which means these three books, having passed your examination with approbation, may at length be thought worthy to come forth with good success in public, and may not be afraid to come under the censure of posterity.

Farewell, and pardon these my bold undertakings.

TRITHEMIUS TO AGRIPPA.

JOHN TRITHEMIUS, ABBOT OF SAINT JAMES OF HERBIPOLIS, FORMERLY OF SPANHEMIA, TO HIS HENRY CORNELIUS AGRIPPA OF NETTESHEIM, HEALTH AND LOVE:

YOUR work, most renowned Agrippa, entitled Of Occult Philosophy, which you have sent by this bearer to me, has been examined. With how much pleasure I received it no mortal tongue can express nor the pen of any write. I wondered at your more than vulgar learning--that you, being so young, should penetrate into such secrets as have been hid from most learned men; and not only clearly and truly but also properly and elegantly set them forth. Whence first I give you thanks for your good will to me, and, if I shall ever be able, I shall return you thanks to the utmost of my power. Your work, which no learned man can sufficiently commend, I approve of. Now that you may proceed toward higher things, as you have begun, and not suffer such excellent parts of wit to be idle, I do, with as much earnestness as I can, advise, intreat and beseech you that you would exercise yourself in laboring after better things, and demonstrate the light of true wisdom to the ignorant, according as you yourself are divinely enlightened. Neither let the consideration of idle, vain fellows withdraw you from your purpose; I say of them, of whom it is said, "The wearied ox treads hard," whereas no man, to the judgment of the wise, can be truly learned who is sworn to the rudiments of one only faculty. But you have been by God gifted with a large and sublime wit, and it is not that you should imitate oxen but rather birds; neither think it sufficient that you study about particulars, but bend your mind confidently to universals; for by so much the more learned any one is thought, by how much fewer things he is ignorant of. Moreover, your wit is fully apt to all things, and to be rationally employed, not in a few or low things, but many and sublimer. Yet this one rule I advise you to observe--that you communicate vulgar secrets to vulgar friends, but higher and secret to higher and secret friends only: Give hay to an ox, sugar to a parrot only. Understand my meaning, lest you be trod under the oxen's feet, as oftentimes it falls out. Farewell, my happy friend, and if it lie in my power to serve you, command me, and according to your pleasure it shall without delay be done; also, let our friendship increase daily; write often to me, and send me some of your labors I earnestly pray you. Again farewell.

From our Monastery of Peapolis, the 8th day of April, A. D. MDX.

In January, 1531, Agrippa wrote from Mechlin to Hermann of Wied, Archbishop of Cologne, to whom he dedicated his Occult Philosophy. In this letter he says: "Behold! amongst such things as were closely laid up--the books Of Occult Philosophy, or of Magic," "a new work of most ancient and abstruse learning;" "a doctrine of antiquity, by none, I dare say, hitherto attempted to be restored." "I shall be devotedly yours if these studies of my youth shall by the authority of your greatness come into knowledge," "seeing many things in them seemed to me, being older, as most profitable, so most necessary to be known. You have therefore the work, not only of my youth but of my present age," "having added many things."

CHAPTER I. HOW MAGICIANS COLLECT VIRTUES FROM THE THREE-FOLD WORLD IS DECLARED IN THESE THREE BOOKS.

SEEING there is a Three-fold World--Elementary, Celestial and Intellectual--and every inferior is governed by its superior, and receiveth the influence of the virtues thereof, so that the very Original and Chief Worker of all doth by angels, the heavens, stars, elements, animals, plants, metals and stones convey from Himself the virtues of His Omnipotency upon us, for whose service He made and created all these things: Wise men conceive it no way irrational that it should be possible for us to ascend by the same degrees through each World, to the same very original World itself, the Maker of all things and

First cause, from whence all things are and proceed; and also to enjoy not only these virtues, which are already in the more excellent kind of things, but also besides these, to draw new virtues from above. Hence it is that they seek after the virtues of the Elementary World, through the help of physic, and natural philosophy in the various mixtions of natural things; then of the Celestial World in the rays, and influences thereof, according to the rules of Astrologers, and the doctrines of mathematicians, joining the Celestial virtues to the former. Moreover, they ratify and confirm all these with the powers of divers Intelligence, through the sacred ceremonies of religions. The order and process of all these I shall endeavor to deliver in these three books: Whereof the first contains Natural Magic, the second Celestial, and the third Ceremonial. But I know not whether it be an unpardonable presumption in me, that I, a man of so little judgment and learning, should in my very youth- so confidently set upon a business so difficult, so hard and intricate as this is. Wherefore, whatsoever things have here already, and shall afterward be said by me, I would not have anyone assent to them, nor shall I myself, any further than they shall be approved of by the universal church and the congregation of the faithful.

CHAPTER II. WHAT MAGIC IS, WHAT ARE THE PARTS THEREOF, AND HOW THE PROFESSORS THEREOF MUST BE QUALIFIED.

MAGIC is a faculty of wonderful virtue, full of most high mysteries, containing the most profound contemplation of most secret things, together with the nature, power, quality, substance and virtues thereof, as also the knowledge of whole Nature, and it doth instruct us concerning the differing and agreement of things amongst themselves, whence it produceth its wonderful effects, by uniting the virtues of things through the application of them one to the other, and to their inferior suitable subjects, joining and knitting them together thoroughly by the powers and virtues of the superior Bodies. This is the most perfect and chief Science, that sacred and sublimer kind of Philosophy, and lastly the most absolute perfection of all most excellent Philosophy. For seeing that all regulative Philosophy is divided into Natural, Mathematical and Theological: (Natural Philosophy teacheth the nature of those things which are in the world, searching and inquiring into their causes, effects, times, places, fashions, events, their whole and parts, also

The Number and the Nature of those things,
Called Elements--what Fire, Earth, Aire forth brings;
From whence the Heavens their beginnings had;
Whence Tide, whence Rainbow, in gay colors clad.
What makes the Clouds that gathered are, and black,
To send forth Lightnings, and a Thund'ring crack;
What doth the Nightly Flames, and Comets make;
What makes the Earth to swell, and then to quake;
What is the Seed of Metals, and of Gold;
What Virtues, Wealth, Both Nature's Coffer hold.

All these things doth Natural Philosophy, the viewer of Nature, contain, teaching us, according to Virgil's Muse:
Whence all things flow--
Whence Mankind, Beast; whence Fire, whence Rain and Snow;
Whence Earthquakes are; why the whole Ocean beats
Over its banks and then again retreats;
Whence strength of Herbs, whence Courage, rage of Brutes
All kinds of Stone, of creeping Things, and Fruits.

But Mathematical Philosophy teacheth us to know the quantity of natural bodies, as extended into three dimensions, as also to conceive of the motion and course of celestial bodies.
As in great haste,
What makes the golden Stars to march so fast?
What makes the Moon sometimes to mask her face,
The Sun also, as if in some disgrace?
And, as Virgil sings:
How th' Sun doth rule with twelve Zodiac Signs,
The Orb that's measur'd round about with Lines--
It doth the Heavens' Starry Way make known,
And strange Eclipses of the Sun and Moon;
also, and the Stars of Rain,
The Seven Stars likewise, and Charles, his wain;
Why Winter Suns make tow'rds the West so fast;
What makes the Nights so long ere they be past?

All which are understood by Mathematical Philosophy.
Hence, by the Heavens we may foreknow
The Seasons all; times for to reap and sow,
And when 'tis fit to launch into the deep,
And when to war, and when in peace to sleep;
And when to dig up trees, and them again
To set, that they may bring forth amain.

Now Theological Philosophy, or Divinity, teacheth what God is, what the Mind, what an Intelligence, what an Angel, what a Devil, what the Soul, what Religion, what sacred Institutions, Rites, Temples, Observations, and sacred Mysteries are. It instructs us also concerning Faith, Miracles, the virtues of Words and Figures, the secret operations and mysteries of Seals; and, as Apuleius saith, it teacheth us rightly to understand and to be skilled in the Ceremonial Laws, the equity of Holy things and rule of Religions. But to recollect myself.)

These three principal faculties Magic comprehends, unites and actuates; deservedly, therefore, was it by the Ancients esteemed as the highest and most sacred Philosophy. It was, as we find, brought to light by most sage authors and most famous writers, amongst which principally Zamolxis and Zoroaster were so famous that many believed they were the inventors of this Science. Their track Abbaris the Hyperborean, Charmondas, Danigeron, Eudoxus, Hermippus followed. There were also other eminent, choice men, as Mercurius Tresmegistus, Porphyrius, Iamblicus, Plotinus, Proclus, Dardanus, Orpheus the Thracian, Gog the Grecian, Germa the Babylonian, Apollonius of Tyana. Osthanes also wrote excellently of this Art, whose books being as it were lost, Democritus of Abdera recovered, and set them forth with his own Commentaries. Besides, Pythagoras, Empedocles, Democritus, Plato, and many other renowned Philosophers travelled far by sea to learn this Art; and being returned, published it with wonderful devoutness, esteeming of it as a great secret. Also it is well known that Pythagoras and Plato went to the Prophets of Memphis to learn it, and travelled through almost all Syria, Egypt, Judea, and the Schools of the Chaldeans that they might not be ignorant of the most sacred Memorials and Records of Magic, as also that they might be furnished with Divine things. Whosoever, therefore, is desirous to study in this Faculty, if he be not skilled in Natural Philosophy, wherein are discovered the qualities of things, and in which are found the occult properties of every Being, and if he be not skillful in the Mathematics, and in the Aspects, and Figures of the Stars, upon which depend the sublime virtue and property of everything; and if he be not learned in Theology, wherein are manifested those immaterial substances, which dispense and minister all things, he cannot be possibly able to understand the rationality of Magic. For there is no work that is done by mere Magic, nor any work that is merely Magical, that doth not comprehend these three Faculties.

CHAPTER III. OF THE FOUR ELEMENTS, THEIR QUALITIES, AND MUTUAL MIXTIONS.

THERE are four Elements, and original grounds of all corporeal things--Fire, Earth, Water, Air--of which all elemented inferior bodies are compounded; not by way of heaping them up together; but by transmutation and union; and when they are destroyed they are resolved into Elements. For there is none of the sensible Elements that is pure, but they are more or less mixed, and apt to be changed one into the other: Even as Earth becoming dirty, and being dissolved, becomes Water, and the same being made thick and hard, becometh Earth again; but being evaporated through heat, passeth into Air, and that being kindled, passeth into Fire; and this being extinguished, returns back again into Air; but being cooled again after its burning, becomes Earth, or Stone, or Sulphur, and this is manifested by Lightning. Plato also was of that opinion, that Earth was wholly changeable, and that the rest of the Elements are changed, as into this, so into one another successively. But it is the opinion of the subtler sort of Philosophers, that Earth is not changed, but relented and mixed with other Elements, which do dissolve it, and that it returns back into itself again. Now, every one of the Elements hath two specifical qualities--the former whereof it retains as proper to itself; in the other, as a mean, it agrees with that which comes next after it. For Fire is hot and dry, the Earth dry and cold, the Water cold and moist, the Air moist and hot. And so after this manner the Elements, according to two contrary qualities, are contrary one to the other, as Fire to Water, and Earth to Air. Moreover, the Elements are upon another account opposite one to the other: For some are heavy, as Earth and Water, and others are light, as Air and Fire. Wherefore the Stoics called the former passives, but the latter actives. And yet once again, Plato distinguisheth them after another manner, and assigns to every one of them three qualities, viz., to the Fire brightness, thinness and motion, but to the Earth darkness, thickness and quietness. And according to these qualities the Elements of Fire and Earth are contrary. But the other Elements borrow their qualities from these, so that the Air receives two qualities of the Fire, thinness and motion, and one of the Earth, viz., darkness. In like manner Water receives two qualities of the Earth, darkness and thickness, and one of Fire, viz., motion. But Fire is twice more thin than Air, thrice more movable, and four times more bright; and the Air is twice more bright, thrice more thin, and four times more movable than Water. Wherefore Water is twice more bright than Earth, thrice more thin, and four times more movable. As therefore the Fire is to the Air, so Air is to the Water, and Water to the Earth; and again, as the Earth is to the Water, so is the Water to the Air, and the Air to the Fire. And this is the root and foundation of all bodies, natures, virtues and wonderful works; and he which shall know these qualities of the Elements, and their mixtions, shall easily bring to pass such things that are wonderful, and astonishing, and shall be perfect in Magic.

CHAPTER IV. OF A THREE-FOLD CONSIDERATION OF THE ELEMENTS.

THERE are, then, as we have said, four Elements, without the perfect knowledge whereof we can effect nothing in Magic. Now each of them is three-fold, that so the number of four may make up the number of twelve; and by passing by the number of seven into the number of ten, there may be a progress to the supreme Unity, upon which all virtue and wonderful operation depends. Of the first Order are the pure Elements, which are neither compounded nor changed, nor admit of mixtion, but are incorruptible, and not of which, but through which the virtues of all natural things are brought forth into act. No man is able to declare their virtues, because they can do all things upon all things. He which is ignorant of these, shall never be able to bring to pass any wonderful matter. Of the second Order are Elements that are compounded, changeable and inpure, yet such as may by art be reduced to their pure simplicity, whose virtue, when they are thus reduced to their simplicity, doth above all things perfect all occult and common operations of Nature; and these are the foundation of the whole Natural Magic. Of the third Order are those Elements, which originally and of themselves are not Elements, but are twice compounded, various and changeable one into the other. They are the infallible Mediums, and therefore are called the middle nature, or Soul of the middle nature. Very few there are that understand the deep mysteries thereof. In them is, by means of certain numbers, degrees and orders, the perfection of every effect in anything soever, whether Natural, Celestial or Supercelestial; they are full of wonders and mysteries, and are operative, as in Magic Natural, so in Divine: For from these, through them, proceed the bindings, loosings and transmutations of all things, the knowing and foretelling of all things to come, also the driving forth of evil and the gaining of good spirits. Let no man, therefore, without these three sorts of Elements, and the knowledge thereof, be confident that he is able to work any thing in the occult Sciences of Magic and Nature. But whosoever shall know how to reduce those of one Order into those of another, impure into pure, compounded into simple, and shall know how to understand distinctly the nature, virtue and power of them in number, degrees and order, without dividing the substance, he shall easily attain to the knowledge and perfect operation of all Natural things and Celestial secrets.

CHAPTER V. OF THE WONDERFUL NATURES OF FIRE AND EARTH.

THERE are two things, saith Hermes, viz., Fire and Earth, which are sufficient for the operation of all wonderful things: the former is active, the latter passive. Fire, as saith Dionysius, in all things, and through all things, comes and goes away bright; it is in all things bright, and at the same time occult and unknown. When it is by itself (no other matter coming to it, in which it should manifest its proper action) it is boundless and invisible, of itself sufficient for every action that is proper to it, movable, yielding itself after a manner to all things that come next to it, renewing, guarding Nature, enlightening, not comprehended by lights that are veiled over, clear, parted, leaping back, bending upwards, quick in motion, high, always raising motions, comprehending another, not comprehended itself, not standing in need of another, secretly increasing of itself, and manifesting its greatness to things that receive it; Active, Powerful, Invisibly present in all things at once; it will not be affronted or opposed, but as it were in a way of revenge, it will reduce, on a sudden, things into obedience to itself; incomprehensible, impalpable, not lessened, most rich in all dispensations of itself. Fire, as saith Pliny, is the boundless and mischievous part of the nature of things, it being a question whether it destroys or produceth most things. Fire itself is one, and penetrates through all things, as say the Pythagoreans, also spread abroad in the Heavens, and shining: but in the infernal place straitened, dark and tormenting; in the mid way it partakes of both. Fire, therefore, in itself is one, but in that which receives it, manifold; and in differing subjects it is distributed in a different manner, as Cleanthes witnesseth in Cicero. That fire, then, which we use is fetched out of other things. It is in stones, and is fetched out by the stroke of the steel; it is in Earth, and makes that, after digging up, to smoke; it is in Water, and heats springs and wells; it is in the depth of the Sea, and makes that, being tossed with winds, warm; it is in the Air, and makes it (as we oftentimes see) to burn. And all animals and living things whatsoever, as also all vegetables, are preserved by heat; and everything that lives, lives by reason of the inclosed heat. The properties of the Fire that is above, are heat, making all things fruitful, and light, giving life to all things. The properties of the infernal Fire are a parching heat, consuming all things, and darkness, making all things barren. The Celestial and bright Fire drives away spirits of darkness; also this, our Fire made with wood, drives away the same in as much as it hath an analogy with and is the vehiculum of that Superior light; as also of him who saith, "I am the Light of the World," which is true Fire, the Father of Lights, from whom every good thing, that is given, comes; sending forth the light of His Fire, and communicating it first to the Sun and the rest of the Celestial bodies, and by these, as by mediating instruments, conveying that light into our Fire. As, therefore, the spirits of darkness are stronger in the dark, so good spirits, which are Angels of Light, are augmented, not only by that light, which is Divine, of the Sun, and Celestial, but also by the light of our common Fire. Hence it was that the first and most wise institutors of religions and ceremonies ordained that prayers, singings and all manner of divine worships whatsoever should not be performed without lighted candles or torches (hence, also, was that significant saying of Pythagoras, "Do not speak of God without a Light"), and they commanded that for the driving away of wicked spirits, Lights and Fires should be kindled by the corpses of the dead, and that they should not be removed until the expiations were after a holy manner performed and they buried. And the great Jehovah himself in the old law commanded that all his sacrifices should be offered with Fire, and that Fire should always be burning upon the altar, which custom the priests of the altar did always observe and keep amongst the Romans.

Now the basis and foundation of all the Elements is the Earth, for that is the object, subject, and receptacle of all Celestial rays and influences; in it are contained the seeds and seminal virtues of all things; and therefore it is said to be Animal, Vegetable and Mineral. It being made fruitful by the other Elements and the Heavens, it brings forth all things of itself. It receives the abundance of all things and is, as it were, the first fountain from whence all things spring. It is the center, foundation and mother of all things. Take as much of it as you please, separated, washed, depurated, subtilized, if you let it lie in the open air a little while, it will, being full and abounding with heavenly virtues, of itself bring forth plants, worms and other living things, also stones, and bright sparks of metals. In it are great secrets, if at any time it shall be purified by the help of Fire, and reduced unto its simplicity by a convenient washing. It is the first matter of our creation, and the truest medicine that can restore and preserve us.

CHAPTER VI. OF THE WONDERFUL NATURES OF WATER, AIR AND WINDS.

THE other two Elements, viz., Water and Air, are not less efficacious than the former; neither is Nature wanting to work wonderful things in them. There is so great a necessity of Water, that without it no living thing can live. No herb nor plant whatsoever, without the moistening of Water can branch forth. In it is the seminary virtue of all things, especially of animals. The seeds also of trees and plants, although they are earthy, must notwithstanding of necessity be rotted in Water before they can be fruitful;

whether they be imbibed with the moisture of the Earth, or with dew or rain or any other Water that is on purpose put to them. For Moses writes, that only Earth and Water bring forth a living soul. But he ascribes a twofold production of things to Water, viz., of things swimming in the Waters, and of things flying in the Air above the Earth. And that those productions that are made in and upon the Earth are partly attributes to the very Water, the same Scripture testifies, where it saith that the plants and the herbs did not grow, because God had not caused it to rain upon the Earth. Such is the efficacy of this Element of Water that spiritual regeneration cannot be done without it, as Christ himself testified to Nicodemus. Very great, also, is the virtue of it in the religious worship of God, in expiations and purifications; yea, the necessity of it is no less than that of Fire. Infinite are the benefits, and divers are the uses thereof, as being that by virtue of which all things subsist, are generated, nourished and increased. Thence it was that Thales, of Miletus, and Hesiod concluded that Water was the beginning of all things, and said it was the first of all the Elements, and the most potent, and that because it hath the mastery over all the rest. For, as Pliny saith, Waters swallow up the Earth, extinguish flames, ascend on high, and by the stretching forth of the clouds, challenge the Heaven for their own; the same falling become the cause of all things that grow in the Earth. Very many are the wonders that are done by Waters, according to the writings of Pliny, Solinus, and many other historians of the wonderful virtue whereof. Ovid also makes mention in these verses:

Horn'd Hammon's Waters at high noon
　Are cold; hot at Sun-rise and setting Sun.
Wood, put in bub'ling Athemas is Fir'd,
The Moon then farthest from the Sun retir'd;
Ciconian streams congeal his guts to Stone
That thereof drinks, and what therein is thrown
Crathis and Sybaris (from the Mountains rol'd)
Color the hair like Amber or pure Gold.
Some fountains, of a more prodigious kinde,
Not only change the body but the minde.
Who hath not heard of obscene Salmacis?
Of th' Aethiopian lake? for, who of this
But only taste, their wits no longer keep,
Or forthwith fall into a deadly sleep.
Who at Clitorius fountain thirst remove
Loath Wine and, abstinent, meer Water love.
With streams oppos'd to these Lincestus flowes--
They reel, as drunk, who drink too much of those.
A Lake in fair Arcadia stands, of old
Call'd Pheneus, suspected as twofold--

21

Fear and forbear to drink thereof by night--

By night unwholesome, wholesome by day-light.

Josephus also makes relation of the wonderful nature of a certain river betwixt Arcea and Raphanea, cities of Syria, which runs with a full channel all the Sabbath day and then on a sudden ceaseth, as if the springs were stopped, and all the six days you may pass over it dry shod; but again, on the seventh day (no man knowing the reason of it), the Waters return again in abundance as before. Wherefore the inhabitants thereabout called it the Sabbath-day river, because of the Seventh day, which was holy to the Jews. The Gospel also testifies to a sheep-pool, into which whosoever stepped first, after the Water was troubled by the Angel, was made whole of whatsoever disease he had. The same virtue and efficacy we read was in a spring of the Jonian Nymphs, which was in the territories belonging to the town of Elis, at a village called Heraclea, near the river Citheron which whosoever stepped into, being diseased, came forth whole and cured of all his diseases. Pausanias also reports that in Lyceus, a mountain of Arcadia, there was a spring called Agria, to which, as often as the dryness of the region threatened the destruction of fruits, Jupiter's priest of Lyceus went, and after the offering of sacrifices, devoutly praying to the Waters of the Spring, holding a Bough of an Oak in his hand, put it down to the bottom of the hallowed Spring. Then the Waters, being troubled, Vapor ascending from thence into the Air was blown into clouds with which, being joined together, the whole Heaven was overspread; which being a little after dissolved into rain, watered all the country most wholesomely. Moreover, Ruffus, a physician of Ephesus, besides many other authors, wrote strange things concerning the wonders of Waters, which for ought I know, are found in no other author.

It remains that I speak of the Air. This is a vital spirit, passing through all beings, giving life and subsistence to all things, binding, moving and filling all things. Hence it is that the Hebrew doctors reckon it not amongst the Elements, but count it as a Medium or glue, joining things together, and as the resounding spirit of the World's instrument. It immediately receives into itself the influences of all celestial bodies and then communicates them to the other Elements, as also to all mixed bodies. Also it receives into itself, as it were a divine looking-glass, the species of all things, as well natural as artificial, as also of all manner of speeches, and retains them; and carrying them with it, and entering into the bodies of men, and other animals, through their pores, makes an impression upon them, as well when they sleep as when they be awake, and affords matter for divers strange Dreams and Divinations. Hence they say it is, that a man passing by a place where a man was slain, or the carcass newly hid, is moved with fear and dread; because the Air in that place, being full of the dreadful species of manslaughter, doth being breathed in, move and trouble the spirit of the man with the like species, whence it is that he comes to be afraid. For everything that makes a sudden impression, astonisheth nature. Whence it is, that many philosophers were of opinion that Air is the cause of dreams, and of many other impressions of the mind, through the prolonging of Images, or similitudes, or species (which are fallen from things and speeches, multiplied in the very Air) until they come to the senses, and then to the phantasy, and soul of him that receives them, which being freed from cares and no way hindered, expecting to meet such kind of species, is informed by them. For the species of things, although of their own proper nature they are carried to the senses of men, and other animals in general, may notwithstanding get some impression from the Heaven whilst they be in the Air, by reason of which, together with the aptness and disposition of him that receives them, they may be carried to the sense of one rather than of another. And hence it is possible naturally, and far from all manner of superstition, no other spirit coming between, that a man should be able in a very little time to signify his mind unto another man abiding at a very long and unknown distance from him; although he cannot precisely give an estimate of the time when it is, yet of necessity it must be within twenty-four hours; and I myself know how to do it, and have often done it. The same also in time past did the Abbot Trithemius both know and do. Also, when certain appearances, not only spiritual but also natural, do flow forth from things (that is to say, by a certain kind of flowing forth of bodies from bodies and do gather strength in the Air), they offer and show themselves to us as well through light as motion, as well to the sight as to other senses, and sometimes work wonderful things upon us, as Plotinus proves and teacheth. And we see how by the south wind the Air is condensed into thin clouds, in which, as in a looking-glass, are reflected representations at a great distance of castles, mountains, horses and men and other things which, when the clouds are gone, presently vanish. And Aristotle, in his Meteors, shows that a rainbow is conceived in a cloud of the Air, as in a looking-glass. And Albertus saith that the effigies of bodies may, by the strength of nature, in a moist Air be easily represented, in the same manner as the representations of things are in things. And Aristotle tells of a man to whom it happened, by reason of the weakness of his sight, that the Air that was near to him became, as it were, a looking-glass to him, and the optic beam did reflect back upon himself, and could not penetrate the Air, so that whithersoever he went he thought he saw his own image, with his face towards him, go before him. In like manner, by the artificialness of some certain looking-glasses, may be produced at a distance in the Air, beside the looking-glasses, what images we please; which when ignorant men see, they think they see the appearances of spirits, or souls; when, indeed, they are nothing else but semblances kin to themselves, and without life. And it is well known, if in a dark place where there is no light but by the coming in of a beam of the sun somewhere through a little hole, a white paper or plain looking-glass be set up against that light, that there may be seen upon them whatsoever things are done without, being shined upon by the sun. And there is another sleight or trick yet more wonderful: If any one shall take images artificially painted, or written letters, and in a clear night set them against the beams of the full moon, whose resemblances, being multiplied in the Air, and caught upward, and reflected back together with the beams of the moon, any other man that is privy to the thing, at a long distance sees, reads and knows them in the very compass and circle of the moon; which Art of declaring secrets is indeed very profitable for towns and cities that are besieged, being a thing which Pythagoras long since did often do, and which is not unknown to some in these days; I will not except myself. And all these and many more, and greater than these, are grounded in the very nature of the Air, and have their reasons and causes declared in mathematics and optics. And as these resemblances are reflected back to the sight, so also sometimes to the hearing, as is manifest in the Echo. But there are more secret arts than these, and such whereby any one may at a very remote distance hear and understand what another speaks or whispers softly.

There are also, from the airy element, Winds; for they are nothing else but Air moved and stirred up. Of these there are four that are principal, blowing from the four corners of the Heaven, viz.: Notus from the South, Boreas from the North, Zephyrus from the West, Eurus from the East, which Pontanus comprehending in these verses, saith:

Cold Boreas from the top of 'lympus blows,
And from the bottom cloudy Notus flows.
From setting Phoebus fruitful Zeph'rus flies,
And barren Eurus from the Sun's up-rise.

Notus is the Southern Wind, cloudy, moist, warm and sickly, which Hieronymus calls the butler of the rains. Ovid describes it thus:

Out flies South-wind with dropping wings, who shrouds
His fearful aspect in the pitchie clouds,
His white Haire streams, his Beard big-swol'n with showers;
Mists binde his Brows, rain from his Bosome powres.

But Boreas is contrary to Notus, and is the Northern Wind, fierce and roaring, and discussing clouds; makes the Air serene, and binds the Water with frost. Him doth Ovid thus bring in speaking of himself:

Force me befits: with this thick clouds I drive;
Toss the blew Billows, knotty Okes up-rive;
Congeal soft snow, and beat the Earth with hallo:
When I my brethren in the Aire assaile,
(For that's our Field) we meet with such a shock,
That thundering Skies with our encounters rock

And cloud-struck lightning flashes from on high,
When through the Crannies of the Earth I flie
And force her in her hollow Caves; I make
The Ghosts to tremble, and the ground to quake.

And Zephyrus, which is the Western Wind, is most soft, blowing from the West with a pleasant gale; it is cold and moist, removing the effects of Winter, bringing forth branches and flowers. To this Eurus is contrary, which is the Eastern Wind, and is called Apeliotes; it is waterish, cloudy and ravenous. Of these two Ovid sings thus:

To Persis and Sabea, Eurus flies;
Whose gums perfume the blushing Morne's up-rise:
Next to the Evening, and the Coast that glows
With setting Phoebus, flow'ry Zeph'rus blows;
In Scythia horrid Boreas holds his rain,
Beneath Boites, and the frozen Wain;
The land to this oppos'd doth Auster steep
With fruitful showres and clouds which ever weep.

CHAPTER VII. OF THE KINDS OF COMPOUNDS, WHAT RELATION THEY STAND IN TO THE ELEMENTS, AND WHAT RELATION THERE IS BETWIXT THE ELEMENTS THEMSELVES AND THE SOUL, SENSES AND DISPOSITIONS OF MEN.

NEXT after the four simple Elements follow the four kinds of perfect Bodies compounded of them, and they are Stones, Metals, Plants and Animals: and although unto the generation of each of these all the Elements meet together in the composition, yet every one of them follows, and resembles one of the Elements, which is most predominant. For all Stones are earthy for they are naturally heavy and descend, and so hardened with dryness that they cannot be melted. But Metals are waterish and may be melted, which naturalists confess, and chemists find to be true, viz., that they are generated of a viscous Water or waterish argent vive. Plants have such an affinity with the Air, that unless they be abroad in the open air, they do neither bud nor increase. So also all Animals

Have in their Natures a most fiery force,
And also spring from a Celestial source.

And Fire is so natural to them, that that being extinguished they presently die. And, again, every one of those kinds is distinguished within itself by reason of degrees of the Elements. For amongst the Stones they especially are called earthy that are dark and more heavy; and those waterish which are transparent and are compacted of water, as crystal, beryl and pearls in the shells of fishes; and they are called airy which swim upon the water, and are spongeous, as the stones of a sponge, the pumice stone and the stone sophus; and they are called fiery out of which fire is extracted, or which are produced of fire, as thunder-bolts, fire-stones and the stone asbestos. Also amongst Metals, lead and silver are earthy; quicksilver is waterish; copper and tin are airy; and gold and iron are fiery. In Plants also, the roots resemble the earth by reason of their thickness; and the leaves water, because of their juice; flowers the air, because of their subtility, and the seeds the fire, by reason of their multiplying spirit. Besides, they are called some hot, some cold, some moist, some dry, borrowing their names from the qualities of the Elements. Amongst Animals also, some are in comparison of others earthy, and dwell in the bowels of the earth, as worms and moles, and many other small creeping vermin; others are watery, as fishes; others airy, which cannot live out of the air; others also are fiery, living in the fire, as salamanders, and crickets, such as are of a fiery heat, as pigeons, ostriches, lions, and such as the wise men call beasts breathing fire. Besides, in animals the bones resemble the earth, flesh the air, the vital spirit the fire, and the humors the water. And these humors also partake of the Elements, for yellow choler is instead of fire, blood instead of air, phlegm instead of water, and black choler, or melancholy,instead of earth. And lastly, in the Soul itself, according to Austin, the understanding resembles fire, reason the air, imagination the water, and the senses the earth. And these senses also are divided amongst themselves by reason of the Elements, for the sight is fiery, neither can it perceive without fire and light; the hearing is airy, for a sound is made by the striking of the air; the smell and taste resemble the water, without the moisture of which there is neither smell nor taste; and lastly, the feeling is wholly earthy, and taketh gross bodies for its object. The actions, also, and the operations of man are governed by the Elements. The earth signifies a slow and firm motion; the water signifies fearfulness and sluggishness, and remissness in working; air signifies cheerfulness and an amiable disposition; but fire a fierce, quick and angry disposition. The Elements, therefore, are the first of all things, and all things, are of and according to them, and they are in all things, and diffuse their virtues through all things.

CHAPTER VIII. HOW THE ELEMENTS ARE IN THE HEAVENS, IN STARS, IN DEVILS, IN ANGELS, AND LASTLY IN GOD HIMSELF.

IT IS the unanimous consent of all Platonists, that as in the original and exemplary World, all things are in all; so also in this corporeal world, all things are in all; so also the Elements are not only in these inferior bodies, but also in the Heavens, in Stars in Devils, in Angels, and lastly in God, the maker and original example of all things. Now in these inferior bodies the

Elements are accompanied with much gross matter; but in the Heavens the Elements are with their natures and virtues, viz., after a celestial and more excellent manner than in sublunary things. For the firmness of the Celestial Earth is there without the grossness of water; and the agility of the Air without running over its bounds; the heat of Fire without burning, only shining and giving life to all things by its heat. Amongst the Stars, also, some are fiery, as Mars and Sol; airy, as Jupiter and Venus; watery, as Saturn and Mercury; and earthy, such as inhabit the eighth Orb and the Moon (which, notwithstanding, by many is accounted watery), seeing, as if it were Earth, it attracts to itself the celestial waters, with which, being imbibed, it doth, by reason of its nearness to us, pour out and communicate to us. There are, also, amongst the Signs, some fiery, some earthy, some airy, some watery; the Elements rule them also in the Heavens, distributing to them these four threefold considerations of every Element, viz., the beginning, middle and end: So Aires possesseth the beginning of fire, Leo the progress and increase, and Sagittarius the end. Taurus the beginning of the earth, Virgo the progress, Capricorn the end. Gemini the beginning of the air, Libra the progress, Aquarius the end. Cancer the beginning of water, Scorpius the middle, and Pisces the end. Of the mixtions, therefore, of these Planets and Signs, together with the Elements, are all bodies made. Moreover, Devils also are upon this account distinguished the one from the other, so that some are called fiery, some earthy, some airy, and some watery. Hence, also, those four Infernal Rivers--fiery Phlegethon, airy Cocytus, watery Styx, earthy Acheron. Also in the Gospel we read of hell fire, and eternal fire, into which the cursed shall be commanded to go; and in the Revelation we read of a lake of fire, and Isaiah speaks of the damned that the Lord will smite them with corrupt air. And in Job, they shall skip from the waters of the snow to extremity of heat; and in the same we read, that the Earth is dark, and covered with the darkness of death and miserable darkness. Moreover, also, these Elements are placed in the Angels in Heaven and the blessed Intelligences. There is in them a stability of their essence, which is an earthly virtue, in which is the steadfast seat of God; also their mercy and piety is a watery cleansing virtue. Hence by the Psalmist they are called Waters, where he, speaking of the Heavens, saith, Who rulest the Waters that are higher than the Heavens. Also in them their subtile breath is Air, and their love is shining Fire. Hence they are called in Scripture the Wings of the Wind; and in another place the Psalmist speaks of them, Who makest Angels thy Spirits and thy Ministers a flaming fire. Also according to orders of Angels, some are fiery, as Seraphim, and Authorities and Powers; earthy, as Cherubim; watery, as Thrones and Archangels; airy, as Dominions and Principalities. Do we not also read of the original maker of all things, that the earth shall be opened and bring forth a Savior? It is not spoken of the same that he shall be a fountain of living Water, cleansing and regenerating? Is not the same Spirit breathing the breath of life; and the same, according to Moses' and Paul's testimony, a consuming Fire? That Elements, therefore, are to be found everywhere, and in all things after their manner, no man can deny: First in these inferior bodies seculent and gross, and in celestials more pure and clear; but in supercelestials living, and in all respects blessed. Elements, therefore, in the exemplary world are Ideas of things to be produced, in Intelligences are distributed powers, in Heavens are virtues, and in inferior bodies gross forms.

CHAPTER IX. OF THE VIRTUES OF THINGS NATURAL, DEPENDING IMMEDIATELY UPON ELEMENTS.

OF the natural virtues of things, some are Elementary, as to heat, to cool, to moisten, to dry; and they are called operations, or first qualities; and the second act: for these qualities only do wholly change the whole substance, which none of the other qualities can do. And some are in things compounded of Elements, and these are more than first qualities, and such are those that are maturating, digesting, resolving, mollifying, hardening, restringing, absterging, corroding, burning, opening, evaporating, strengthening, mitigating, conglutinating, obstructing, expelling, retaining, attracting, repercussing, stupefying, bestowing, lubrifying and many more. Elementary qualities do many things in a mixed body which they cannot do in the Elements themselves. And these operations are called secondary qualities, because they follow the nature and proportion of the mixtion of the first virtues, as largely it is treated of in physic books. As maturation, which is the operation of natural heat, according to a certain proportion in the substance of the matter, so induration is the operation of cold; so also is congelation, and so of the rest. And these operations sometimes act upon a certain member, as such which provoke water, milk, the flow, and they are called third qualities, which follow the second, as the second do the first. According, therefore, to these first, second, and third qualities many diseases are both cured and caused. Many things also there are artificially made, which men much wonder at; as is Fire which burns Water, which they call the Greek Fire, of which Aristotle teacheth many compositions in his particular treatise of this subject. In like manner there is made a Fire that is extinguished with oil, and is kindled with cold water, when it is sprinkled upon it; and a Fire which is kindled either with Rain, Wind or the Sun; and there is made a Fire which is called burning Water, the confection whereof is well known, and it consumes nothing but itself. And also there are made Fires that cannot be quenched, and incombustible Oils and perpetual Lamps, which can be extinguished neither with wind, nor water, nor any other way; which seems utterly incredible, but that there had been such a most famous Lamp, which once did shine in the Temple of Venus, in which the stone Asbestos did burn, which being once fired can never be extinguished. Also, on the contrary, Wood, or any other combustible matter may be so ordered, that it can receive no harm from the Fire; and there are made certain confections, with which the hands being anointed, we may carry red-hot iron in them, or put them into melted metal; or go with our whole bodies, being first anointed therewith, into the Fire without any manner of harm; and such like things as these may be done. There is also a kind of flax, which Pliny calls Asbestum, the Greeks call Asbeson, which is not consumed by Fire, of which Anaxilaus saith, that a tree compassed about with it may be cut down with insensible blows, that cannot be heard.

CHAPTER X. OF THE OCCULT VIRTUES OF THINGS.

THERE are also other virtues in things, which are not from any Element, as to expel poison, to drive away the noxious vapors of minerals, to attract iron or anything else; and these virtues are a sequel of the species and form of this or that thing; whence also they being a little in quantity, are of great efficacy; which is not granted to any Elementary quality. For these virtues, having much form and little matter, can do very much; but an Elementary virtue, because it hath more materiality, requires much matter for its acting. And they are called Occult Qualities, because their causes lie hid, and man's intellect cannot in any way reach and find them out. Wherefore philosophers have attained to the greatest part of them by long experience, rather than by the search of reason: for as in the stomach the meat is digested by heat, which we know, so it is changed by a certain hidden virtue which we know not: for truly it is not changed by heat, because then it should rather be changed by the fire-side than in the stomach. So there are in things, besides the Elementary qualities which we know, other certain imbred virtues created by Nature, which we admire and are amazed at, being such as we know not, and indeed seldom or never have seen. As we read in Ovid of the Phoenix, one only bird, which renews herself:

All Birds from others do derive their birth,
But yet one Fowle there is in all the Earth,
Call'd by th' Assyrians Phoenix, who the wain
Of age repairs, and sows her self again.
And in another place--
Aegyptus came to see this wondrous sight;
And this rare Bird is welcom'd with delight.
Long since Matreas brought a very great wonderment upon the Greeks and Romans concerning himself. He said that he nourished and bred a beast that did devour itself. Hence many to this day are solicitous what this

beast of Matreas should be. Who would not wonder that fishes should be digged out of the Earth, of which Aristotle, Theophrastus, and Polybius the historian, makes mention? And those things which Pausanius wrote concerning the Singing Stones? All these are effects of Occult Virtues. So the ostrich concocts cold and most hard iron, and digests it into nourishment for his body; whose stomach, they also report, cannot be hurt with red-hot iron. So that little fish, call echeneis, doth so curb the violence of the winds, and appease the rage of the sea, that, let the tempests be never so imperious and raging, the sails also bearing a full gale, it doth notwithstanding by its mere touch stay the ships and makes them stand still, that by no means they can be moved. So salamanders and crickets live in the fire; although they seem sometimes to burn, yet they are not hurt. The like is said of a kind of bitumen, with which the weapons of the Amazons were said to be smeared over, by which means they could be spoiled neither with sword nor fire; with which also the gates of Caspia, made of brass, are reported to be smeared over by Alexander the Great. We read also that Noah's Ark -vas joined together with this bitumen, and that it endured some thousands of years upon the Mountains of Armenia. There are many such kind of wonderful things, scarce credible, which notwithstanding are known by experience. Amongst which Antiquity makes mention of Satyrs, which were animals, in shape half men and half brutes, yet capable of speech and reason; one whereof St. Hierome reporteth, spake once unto holy Antonius the Hermit, and condemned the error of the Gentiles in worshiping such poor creatures as they were, and desired him that he would pray unto the true God for him; also he affirms that there was one of these Satyrs shewed openly alive, and afterwards sent to Constantine the Emperor.

CHAPTER XI.HOW OCCULT VIRTUES ARE INFUSED INTO THE SEVERAL KINDS OF THINGS BY IDEAS THROUGH THE HELP OF THE SOUL OF THE WORLD, AND RAYS OF THE STARS; AND WHAT THINGS ABOUND MOST WITH THIS VIRTUE.

PLATONISTS say that all inferior bodies are exemplified by the superior Ideas. Now they define an Idea to be a form, above bodies, souls, minds, and to be one, simple, pure, immutable, indivisible, incorporeal and eternal; and that the nature of all Ideas in the first place is in very Goodness itself (i. e.), God, by way of cause; and that they are distinguished amongst themselves by some relative considerations only, lest whatsoever is in the world should be but one thing without any variety, and that they agree in essence, lest God should be a compound substance. In the second place, they place them in the very Intelligible Itself (i. e.), in the Soul of the World, differing the one from the other by absolute forms, so that all the Ideas in God indeed are but one form, but in the Soul of the World they are many. They are placed in the minds of all other things, whether they be joined to the body or separated from the body, by a certain participation, and now by degrees are distinguished more and more. They place them in Nature, as certain small Seed of Forms infused by the Ideas, and lastly they place them in matter, as Shadows. Hereunto may be added, that in the Soul of the World there be as many Seminal Forms of things as Ideas in the mind of God, by which forms she did in the Heavens above the Stars frame to herself shapes also, and stamped upon all these some properties. On these Stars therefore, shapes and properties, all virtues of inferior species, as also their properties do depend; so that every species hath its Celestial Shape, or figure that is suitable to it, from which also proceeds a wonderful power of operating, which proper gift it receives from its own Idea, through the Seminal Forms of the Soul of the World. For Ideas are not only essential causes of every species, but are also the causes of every virtue, which is in the species; and this is that which many philosophers say, that the properties which are in the nature of things (which virtues, indeed, are the operations of the Ideas) are moved by certain virtues, viz., such as have a certain and sure foundation; not fortuitous, nor casual, but efficacious, powerful and sufficient--doing nothing in vain. Now these Virtues do not err in their actings, but by accident, viz., by reason of the impurity or inequality of the matter: For upon this account there are found things of the same species more or less powerful, according to the purity or indisposition of the matter; for all Celestial Influences may be hindered by the indisposition and insufficiency of the matter. Whence it was a proverb amongst the Platonists, that Celestial Virtues were infused according to the desert or merit of the matter: Which also Virgil makes mention of when he sings:

Their natures fiery are, and from above,
And from gross bodies freed, divinely move.

Wherefore those things in which there is less of the Idea of the matter (i. e.), such things which have a greater resemblance of things separated, have more powerful virtues in operation, being like to the operation of a separated Idea. We see then that the situation and figure of Celestials is the cause of all those excellent Virtues that are in inferior species.

CHAPTER XII. HOW IT IS THAT PARTICULAR VIRTUES ARE INFUSED INTO PARTICULAR INDIVIDUALS, EVEN OF THE SAME SPECIES.

THERE are also in many individuals, or particular things, peculiar gifts, as wonderful as in the species and these also are from the figure and situation of Celestial Stars. For every Individual, when it begins to be under a determined Horoscope, and Celestial Constellation, contracts together with its essence a certain wonderful virtue both of doing and suffering something that is remarkable, even besides that which it receives from its species; and this it doth partly by the influence of the Heaven and partly through that obedientialness, of the matter of things to be generated, to the Soul of the World, which obedientialness indeed is such as that of our bodies to our souls. For we perceive that there is this in us, that according to our conceptions of things our bodies are moved, and that cheerfully, as when we are afraid of or fly from any thing. So, many times when the celestial souls conceive several things, then the matter is moved obediently to it. Also in Nature there appear divers prodigies, by reason of the imagination of superior motions. So also they conceive and imagine divers virtues, not only things natural but also sometimes things artificial, and this especially if the Soul of the operator be inclined towards the same. Whence Avicen saith, that whatsoever things are done here, must have been before in the motions and conceptions of the Stars and Orbs. So in things various effects, inclinations and dispositions are occasioned not only from the matter variously disposed, as many suppose, but from a various influence and diverse form; not truly with a specifical difference, but peculiar and proper.

And the degrees of these are variously distributed by the first cause of all things. God himself, who being unchangeable, distributes to every one as he pleaseth, with whom, notwithstanding, second causes, Angelical and Celestial, co-operate, disposing of the corporeal matter and other things that are committed to them. All virtues, therefore, are infused by God, through the Soul of the World, yet by a particular power of resemblances and intelligences over-ruling them, and concourse of the rays, and aspects of the Stars in a certain peculiar harmonious consent.

CHAPTER XIII. WHENCE THE OCCULT VIRTUES OF THINGS PROCEED.

IT is well known to all that there is a certain virtue in the Loadstone by which it attracts iron, and that the Diamond doth by its presence take away that virtue of the Loadstone. So also, Amber and Jet, rubbed and warmed, draw a straw to them; and the stone Asbestos, being once fired, is never or scarce extinguished. A Carbuncle shines in the dark; the stone Aetites put above the young fruit of women or plants strengthens them, but being put under, weakeneth. The Jasper stauncheth blood; the little fish Echeneis stops the ships; Rhubarb expels choler; the liver of the Chameleon, burnt, raiseth showers and thunders. The stone Heliotrope dazzles the sight, and makes him that wears it to be invisible; the stone Lyucurius takes away delusions from before the eyes, the perfume of the stone Lypparis calls forth all the beasts, the stone Synochitis brings up infernal ghosts, the stone Anachitis makes the images of the Gods appear. The Ennectis, put under them that dream, causeth oracles. There is an herb in Aethiopia with which, they report, ponds and lakes are dried up, and all things that are shut to be opened; and we read of an herb, called Latace, which the Persian kings give to their embassadors, that whithersoever they shall come they shall abound with plenty of all things. There is also a Scythian herb with which, being tasted or at least held in the mouth, they report the Scythians will endure twelve days' hunger and thirst; and Apuleius saith that he was taught by an Oracle that there were many kinds of herbs and stones with which men might prolong their lives forever, but that it was not lawful for men to understand the knowledge of those things because, whereas they have but a short time to live, they study mischief with all their might and attempt all manner of wickedness; if they should be sure of a very long time, they would not spare the Gods themselves. But from whence these virtues are none of all these have shewed who have set forth huge volumes of the properties of things, not Hermes, not Bochus, not Aaron, not Orpheus, not Theophrastus, not Thebith, not Zenothemis, not Zoroaster, not Evax, not Dioscorides, not Isaaick the Jew, not Zacharias the Babylonian, not Albertus, not Arnoldus; and yet all these have confessed the same, that Zacharias writes to Mithridites, the great power and human destinies are couched in the virtues of Stones and Herbs. But to know from whence these come, a higher speculation is required. Alexander the peripatetic, not going any further than his senses and qualities, is of the opinion that these proceed from Elements, and their qualities, which haply might be supposed to be true, if those were of the same species; but many of the operations of the Stones agree neither in genere nor specie. Therefore Plato and his scholars attribute these virtues to Ideas, the formers of things. But Avicen reduceth these kinds of operations to Intelligence, Hermes to the Stars, Albertus to the specifical forms of things. And although these authors seem to thwart one the other, yet none of them, if they be rightly understood, goes beside the truth; since all their sayings are the same in effect in most things. For God, in the first place, is the end and beginning of all Virtues; he gives the seal of the Ideas to his servants, the Intelligences; who, as faithful officers, sign all things intrusted to them with an Ideal Virtue; the Heavens and Stars, as instruments, disposing the matter in the mean while for the receiving of those forms which reside in Divine Majesty (as saith Plato in Timeus) and to be conveyed by Stars; and the Giver of Forms distributes them by the Ministry of his Intelligences, which he hath set as Rulers and Controllers over his Works, to whom such a power is intrusted in things committed to them that so all Virtues of Stones, Herbs, Metals, and all other things may come from the Intelligences, the Governors. The Form, therefore, and Virtue of things comes first from the Ideas, then from the ruling and governing Intelligences, then from the aspects of the Heavens disposing, and lastly from the tempers of the Elements disposed, answering the influences of the Heavens, by which the Elements themselves are ordered, or disposed. These kinds of operations, therefore, are performed in these inferior things by express forms, and in the Heavens by disposing virtues, in Intelligences by mediating rules, in the Original Cause by Ideas and exemplary forms, all of which must of necessity agree in the execution of the effect and virtue of everything.

There is, therefore, a wonderful virtue and operation in every Herb and Stone, but greater in a Star, beyond which, even from the governing Intelligences every thing receiveth and obtains many things for itself, especially from the Supreme Cause, with whom all things do mutually and exactly correspond, agreeing in an harmonious consent, as it were in hymns, always praising the highest Maker of all things, as by the three children in the fiery furnace were all things called upon to praise God with singings. Bless ye the Lord all things that grow upon the Earth, and all things which move in the Waters, all fowls of the Heavens, beasts and cattle, together with the sons of men. There is, therefore, no other cause of the necessity of effects than the connection of all things with the First Cause, and their correspondency with those Divine patterns and eternal Ideas whence every thing hath its determinate and particular place in the exemplary world, from whence it lives and receives its original being: And every virtue of herbs, stones, metals, animals, words and speeches and all things that are of God, is placed there. Now the First Cause, which is God, although he doth by Intelligences and the Heavens work upon these inferior things, Both sometimes (these mediums being laid aside, or their officiating being suspended) works those things immediately by himself, which works then are called Miracles. But whereas secondary causes, which Plato and others call handmaids, do by the command and appointment of the First Cause, necessarily act, and are necessitated to produce their effects, if God shall notwithstanding, according to his pleasure, so discharge and suspend them, that they shall wholly desist from the necessity of that command and appointment; then they are called the greatest Miracles of God. So the fire in the Chaldeans' furnace did not burn the Children. So also the Sun at the command of Joshua went back from its course the space of a whole day; so also at the prayer of Hezekiah it went back ten degrees or hours. So when Christ was crucified the Sun was darkened, though at full Moon. And the reason of these operations can be by no rational discourse, no Magic, or occult or profound Science whatsoever be found out or understood, but are to be learned and inquired into by Divine Oracles only.

CHAPTER XIV. OF THE SPIRIT OF THE WORLD, WHAT IT IS, AND HOW BY WAY OF MEDIUM IT UNITES OCCULT VIRTUES TO THEIR SUBJECTS.

DEMOCRITUS and Orpheus, and many Pythagoreans, having most diligently searched into the virtues of celestial things and natures of inferior things, said: That all things are full of God and not without cause. For there is nothing of such transcending virtues, which being destitute of Divine assistance, is content with the nature of itself. Also they called those Divine Powers which are diffused in things, Gods; which Zoroaster called Divine Allurements; Synesius, Symbolical Inticements; others called them Lives, and some also Souls, saying that the virtues of things did depend upon these because it is the property of the Soul to be from one matter extended into divers things about which it operates: So is a man who extends his intellect unto intelligible things, and his imagination unto imaginable things; and this is that which they understood when they said, viz.: That the Soul of one thing went out and went into another thing, altering it, and hindering the operations of it: as the diamond hinders the operation of the loadstone, that it cannot attract iron. Now seeing the Soul is the first thing that is movable and, as they say, is moved of itself; but the body, or the matter, is of itself unable and unfit for motion, and doth much degenerate from the Soul, therefore they say there is need of a more excellent medium, viz., such a one that may be, as it were, no body, but, as it were, a Soul; or, as it were, no Soul, but, as it were, a body, viz., by which the soul may be joined to the body. Now they conceive such a medium to be the Spirit of the World, viz., that which we call the quintessence, because it is not from the four Elements, but a certain first thing, having its being above and besides them. There is, therefore, such a kind of spirit required to be, as it were the medium, whereby Celestial Souls are joined to gross bodies, and bestow upon them wonderful gifts. This Spirit is after the same manner in the body of the world, as ours is in the body of man. For as the powers of our soul are communicated to the members of the body by the spirit, so also the Virtue of the Soul of the World is diffused through all things by the quintessence: For there is nothing found in the whole world that hath not a spark of the virtue thereof. Yet it is more, nay, most of all, infused into those things which have received or taken in most of this Spirit. Now this Spirit is received or taken in by the rays of the Stars, so far forth as things render themselves conformable to them. By this Spirit, therefore, every occult property is conveyed into herbs, stones, metals, and animals through the Sun, Moon, Planets, and through Stars higher than the Planets.

Now this Spirit may be more advantageous to us if any one knew how to separate it from the Elements; or at least to use those things chiefly which do most abound with this Spirit. For these things, in which this Spirit is less drowned in a body and less checked by matter, do more powerfully and perfectly act, and also more readily generate their like; for in it are all generative and seminary virtues. For which cause the Alchemists endeavored to separate this Spirit from Gold and Silver; which being rightly separated and extracted, if thou shalt afterward project it upon any matter of the same kind (i. e.), any metal, presently will turn it into Gold or Silver. And we know how to do that, and have seen it done; but we could make no more Gold than the weight of that was out of which we extracted the Spirit; for seeing that [gold] is an extense form, and not intense, it cannot beyond its own bounds change an imperfect body into a perfect; which I deny not, but may be done by another way.

CHAPTER XV. HOW WE MUST FIND OUT AND EXAMINE THE VIRTUES OF THINGS BY WAY OF SIMILITUDE.

IT is now manifest that the occult properties in things are not from the nature of the Elements, but infused from above, hid from our senses, and scarce at last known by our reason, which indeed come from the Life and the Spirit of the World, through the rays of the Stars; and can no otherwise but by experience and conjecture be inquired into by us. Wherefore, he that desires to enter upon this study must consider that every thing moves and turns itself to its like, and inclines that to itself with all its might, as well in property, viz., Occult Virtue, as in quality, viz., Elementary Virtue. Sometimes also in substance itself, as we see in salt, for whatsoever hath long stood with salt becomes salt; for every agent, when it hath begun to act, doth not attempt to make a thing inferior to itself, but, as much as may be, like and suitable to itself. Which also we manifestly see in sensible animals, in which the nutritive virtue doth not change the meat into an herb or a plant, but turns it into sensible flesh. In what things, therefore, there is an excess of any quality or property, as heat, cold, boldness, fear, sadness, anger, love, hatred, or any other passion or virtue (whether it be in them by nature or, sometimes also, by art or chance, as boldness in a wanton), these things do very much move and provoke to such a quality, passion or virtue. So fire moves to fire, and water moves to water, and he that is bold moves to boldness. And it is well known amongst physicians that brain helps the brain, and lungs the lungs. So also it is said that the right eye of a frog helps the soreness of a man's right eye, and the left eye thereof helps the soreness of his left eye, if they be hanged about his neck in a cloth of its natural color. The like is reported of the eyes of a crab. So the feet of a tortoise helps them that have the gout in their being applied thus--as foot to foot, hand to hand, right to right, left to left.

After this manner they say that any animal that is barren causeth another to be barren, and of the animal especially the generative parts. So they report that a female shall be barren if, betimes, drink be made of a certain sterile animal, or anything steeped therewith. If, however, we would obtain any property or virtue, let us seek such animals, or such other things whatsoever, in which such a property is in a more eminent manner than in any other thing, and in these let us take that part in which such a property or virtue is most vigorous; as if at any time we would promote love, let us seek some animal which is most loving, of which kind are pigeons, turtles, sparrows, swallows, wagtails, and in these take those members or parts in which the vital virtue is most vigorous, such as the heart, breast, and also like parts. And it must be done at that time when these animals have this affection most intense, for then they do provoke and draw love. In like manner, to increase boldness, let us look for a lion, or a cock, and of these let us take the heart, eyes or forehead. And so we must understand that which Psellus the Platonist saith, viz., that dogs, crows, and cocks conduce much to watchfulness, also the nightingale and bat and horned owl, and in these the heart, head and eyes especially. Therefore, it is said, if any shall carry the heart of a crow or a bat about him, he shall not sleep till he cast it away from him. The same doth the head of a bat, dried and bound to the right arm of him that is awake, for if it be put upon him when he is asleep, it is said that he shall not be awaked till it be taken off from him. After the same manner doth a frog and an owl make one talkative, and of these specially the tongue and heart. So the tongue also of a water-frog, laid under the head, makes a man speak in his sleep; and the heart of a screech-owl, laid upon the left breast of a woman that is asleep, is said to make her utter all her secrets. The same also the heart of the horned owl is said to do, also the suet of a hare, laid upon the breast of one that is asleep. Upon the same account do animals that are long lived conduce to long life; and whatsoever things have a power in themselves to renew themselves conduce to the renovation of our body and restoring of youth, which physicians have often professed they know to be true; as is manifest of the viper and snake. And it is known that harts renew their old age by the eating of snakes. After the same manner the phoenix is renewed by a fire which she makes for herself; and the like virtue there is in a pelican, whose right foot being put under warm dung, after three months there is of that generated a pelican. Therefore some physicians by some certain confections made of vipers, and hellebore, and the flesh of some such kind of animals, do restore youth, and indeed do sometimes restore it so, as Medea restored old Pileas. It is also believed that the blood of a bear, if it be sucked out of her wound, doth increase strength of body, because that animal is the strongest creature.

CHAPTER XVI. HOW THE OPERATIONS OF SEVERAL VIRTUES PASS FROM ONE THING INTO ANOTHER, AND ARE COMMUNICATED ONE TO THE OTHER.

THOU must know that so great is the power of natural things that they not only work upon all things that are near them, by their virtue, but also besides this, they infuse into them a like power, through which, by the same virtue, they also work upon other things, as we see in the loadstone, which stone indeed doth not only draw iron rings, but infuseth a virtue into the rings themselves, whereby they can do the same, which Austin and Albertus say they saw. After this manner it is, as they say, that a wanton, grounded in boldness and impudence, is like to infect all that are near her, by this property, whereby they are made like herself. So Paul saith to the Corinthians, Evil communications doth corrupt good manners. Therefore they say if any one shall put on the inward garment of a wanton, or shall have about him that looking-glass which she daily looks into, he shall thereby become bold, confident, impudent and wanton. In like manner, they say, that a cloth that was about a corpse hath received from thence the property of sadness and melancholy; and that the halter wherewith a man was hanged hath certain wonderful properties. The like story tells Pliny: If any shall put a green lizard, made blind, together with iron or gold rings, into a glass vessel, putting under them some earth, and then shutting the vessel, and when it appears that the lizard hath received his sight, shall put him out of the glass, that those rings shall help sore eyes. The same may be done with rings and a weasel, whose eyes after they are, with any kind of prick, put out, it is certain are restored to sight again. Upon the same account rings are put for a certain time in the nest of sparrows or swallows, which afterwards are used to procure love and favor.

CHAPTER XVII. HOW BY ENMITY AND FRIENDSHIP THE VIRTUES OF THINGS ARE TO BE TRIED AND FOUND OUT.

IN the next place it is requisite that we consider that all things have a friendliness and enmity amongst themselves, and every thing hath something that it fears and dreads, that is an enemy and destructive to it; and, on the contrary, something that it rejoiceth and delighteth in and is strengthened by. So in the Elements, Fire is an enemy to Water, and Air to Earth, but yet they agree amongst themselves. And, again, in Celestial bodies, Mercury, Jupiter, the Sun and Moon are friends to Saturn; Mars and Venus enemies to him. All the planets besides Mars are friends to Jupiter, also all besides Venus hate Mars; Jupiter and Venus love the Sun, Mars, Mercury and the Moon are enemies to him. All besides Saturn love Venus.

Jupiter, Venus and Saturn are friends to Mercury; the Sun, Moon and Mars his enemies. Jupiter, Venus and Saturn are friends to the Moon; Mars and Mercury her enemies. There is another kind of enmity amongst the stars, viz., when they have opposite houses, as Saturn to the Sun and Moon, Jupiter to Mercury, and Mars to Venus. And their enmity is stronger whose exaltations are opposite, as of Saturn and the Sun, of Jupiter and Mars, and of Venus and Mercury. But their friendship is the strongest who agree in nature, quality, substance and power, as Mars with the Sun, as Venus with the Moon, and as Jupiter with Venus; as also their friendship whose exaltation is in the house of another, as that of Saturn with Venus, of Jupiter with the Moon, of Mars with Saturn, of the Sun with Mars, of Venus with Jupiter, and of the Moon with Venus. And of what sort the friendships and enmities of the superiors be, such are the inclinations of things subjected to them in those inferior. These dispositions, therefore, of friendship and enmity are nothing else but certain inclinations of things of the one to another, desiring such-and-such a thing if it be absent, and to move towards it unless it be hindered; and to acquiesce in it when it is obtained, shunning the contrary and dreading the approach of it, and not resting in or being contented with it. Heraclitus, therefore, being guided by this opinion, professed that all things were made by enmity and friendship.

Now the inclinations of Friendship are such in all Vegetables and Minerals, as is that attractive virtue or inclination which the loadstone hath upon iron, and the emerald upon riches and favor, the jasper upon the birth of any thing, and the stone achates upon eloquence. In like manner there is a kind of bituminous clay that draws fire, and leaps into it, wheresoever it sees it. Even so doth the root of the herb aproxis draw fire from afar off. Also the same inclination there is betwixt the male palm-tree and female; whereof, when the bough of one shall touch the bough of the other, they fold themselves into mutual embraces; neither doth the female palm-tree bring forth fruit without the male. And the almond tree, when she is alone is less fruitful. The vines love the elm, and the olive-tree and myrtle love one the other; also the olive-tree and fig-tree.

Now, in Birds and Animals, there is amity betwixt the blackbird and thrush, betwixt the crow and heron, betwixt peacocks and pigeons, turtles and parrots. When Sappho writes to Phaon:

To Birds unlike oftimes joyned are white Doves;
Also the Bird that's green, black Turtle loves.

Again, the whale and the little fish, his guide, are friendly. Neither is this amity in Animals amongst themselves, but also with other things, as with Metals, Stones and Vegetables: So the cat delights in the herb catnip and rubbeth herself upon it, and there be mares in Cappadocia that expose themselves to the blast of the wind. So frog, toads, snakes, and all manner of creeping poisonous things, delight in the plant called pas-flower, of whom, as the physicians say, if any one eat he shall die with laughing. The tortoise, also, when he is hunted by the adder, eats origanum, and is thereby strengthened; and the stork, when he hath eat snakes, seeks for a remedy in origanum; and the weasel, when he goes to fight with the basilisk, eats rue-- whence we come to know that origanum and rue are effectual against poison. So in some Animals there is an imbred skill and medicinal art; for when the toad is wounded with a bite or poison of another animal, he is wont to go to rue or sage and rub the place wounded, and so escape the danger of the poison. So men have learned many excellent remedies of diseases and virtues of things, from brutes; so swallows have shewed us that sallendine is very medicinable for the sight, with which they cure the eyes of their young; and the pyet, when she is sick puts a bay-leaf into her nest, and is recovered. In like manner, cranes, jackdaws, partridges, and black-birds purge their nauseous stomachs with the same, with which also crows allay the poison of the chameleon; and the lion, if he be feverish, is recovered by eating of an ape. The lapwing, being surfeited with eating of grapes, cures himself with southernwood; so the harts have taught us that the herb ditany is very good to draw out darts; for they, being wounded with an arrow, cast it out by eating of this herb; the same do goats in Candy. So hinds, a little before they bring forth, purge themselves with a certain herb called mountain osier. Also they that are hurt with spiders seek a remedy by eating of crabs. Swine also being hurt by snakes cure themselves by eating of them; and cows, when they perceive they are poisoned with a kind of French poison, seek for cure in the oak. Elephants, when they have swallowed a chameleon, help themselves with the wild olive. Bears, being hurt with mandrakes, escape the danger by eating of ants. Geese, ducks, and such like watery fowls, cure themselves with the herb called wall-sage. Pigeons, turtles, and hens, with the herb called pellitory of the wall. Cranes, with bulrushes. Leopards cure themselves, being hurt, with the herb called wolf's-bane; boars, with ivy; hinds, with the herb called cinnara.

CHAPTER XVIII. OF THE INCLINATIONS OF ENMITIES.

ON the contrary, there are Inclinations of Enmities, and they are, as it were, the odium, and anger, indignation, and a certain kind of obstinate contrariety of nature, so that any thing shuns its contrary and drives it away out of its presence. Such kinds of inclinations hath rhubarb against choler, treacle against poison, the sapphire stone against hot boils and feverish heats and diseases of the eyes; the amethyst against drunkenness, the jasper against flux of blood and offensive imaginations, the emerald and angus castus against lust, achates against poison, piony against the falling sickness, coral against the ebullition of black choler and pains in the stomach. The topaz against spiritual heats, such as are covetousness, lust, and all manner of excesses of love. The like inclinations is there also of ants against the herb origanum; and the wing of a bat and the heart of a lapwing, from the presence of which they fly. Also origanum is contrary to a certain poisonous fly, which cannot endure the Sun, and resists salamanders, and loathes cabbage with such a deadly hatred that they destroy one the other. So cucumbers hate oil, and will run themselves into a ring lest they should touch it. And it is said that the gall of a crow makes men afraid and drives them away from where it is, as also certain other things. So a diamond doth disagree with the loadstone, that being set by it, it will not suffer iron to be drawn to it; and sheep fly from frog-parsley as from some deadly thing, and that, which is more wonderful, Nature hath pictured the sign of this death in the livers of sheep, in which the very figure of frog-parsley, being described, doth naturally appear. So goats do so hate garden basil as if there were nothing more pernicious. And again, amongst animals, mice and weasels do disagree; whence it is said that mice will not touch cheese if the brains of a weasel be put in the rennet, and besides that the cheese will not be corrupt with age. So a lizard is so contrary to scorpions that it makes them afraid with its very sight, as also it puts them into a cold sweat; therefore they are killed with the oil of lizards, which oil also cures the wounds made by scorpions. There is also an enmity betwixt scorpions and mice; wherefore if a mouse be applied to a prick or wound made by a scorpion, it cures it, as it is reported. There is also an enmity betwixt scorpions and stalabors, asps and wasps. It is reported, also that no thing is so much an enemy to snakes as crabs, and that if swine be hurt therewith they eat them and are cured. The sun, also being in Cancer, serpents are tormented. Also scorpion and crocodile kill one the other; and if the bird ibis doth but touch a crocodile with one of his feathers, he makes him immovable. The bird called bustard flies away at the sight of a horse, and a hart runs away at the sight of a ram, as also a viper. An elephant trembles at the hearing of the grunting of a hog, so doth a lion at the sight of a cock; and panthers will not touch them that are anointed all over with the broth of a hen, especially if garlic hath been boiled in it. There is also enmity betwixt foxes and swans, bulls and jackdaws. Amongst birds, also, some are at perpetual strife one with another, as also with other animals, as jackdaws and owls, the kite and crows, the turtle and ring-tail, egepis and eagles, harts and dragons. Also amongst water animals there is enmity, as betwixt dolphins and whirlpools, mullets and pikes, lampreys and congers. Also the fish called pourcontrel makes the lobster so much afraid that the lobster seeing the other but near him, is struck dead. The lobster and conger tear one the other. The civet cat is said to stand so in awe of the panther that he hath no power to resist him or touch his skin; and they say that if the skins of both of them be hanged up one against the other, the hairs of the panther's skin fall off. And Orus Apollo saith in his hicroglyphics, if any

41

one be girt about with the skin of the civet cat that he may pass safely through the middle of his enemies and not at all be afraid. Also the lamb is very much afraid of the wolf and flies from him. And they say that if the tail or skin or head of a wolf be hanged upon the sheep-coate the sheep are much troubled and cannot eat their meat for fear. And Pliny makes mention of a bird, called marlin, that breaks crows' eggs, whose young are so annoyed by the fox that she also will pinch and pull the fox's whelps, and the fox herself also; which when the crows see, they help the fox against her, as against a common enemy. The little bird called a linnet, living in thistles, hates asses, because they eat the flowers of thistles. Also there is such a bitter enmity betwixt the little bird called easlon and the ass that their blood will not mix together, and that at the braying of the ass both the eggs and young of the easlon perish. There is also such a disagreement betwixt the olive-tree and a wanton, that if she plant it, it will either be always unfruitful or altogether wither. A lion fears nothing so much as fired torches, and will be tamed by nothing so much as by these; and the wolf fears neither sword nor spear, but a stone--by the throwing of which, a wound being made, worms breed in the wolf. A horse fears a camel so that he cannot endure to see so much as his picture. An elephant, when he rageth, is quieted by seeing a cock. A snake is afraid of a man that is naked, but pursues a man that is clothed. A mad bull is tamed by being tied to a fig-tree. Amber draws all things to it besides garden basil and those things which are smeared with oil, betwixt which there is a kind of a natural antipathy.

CHAPTER XIX. HOW THE VIRTUES OF THINGS ARE TO BE TRIED AND FOUND OUT, WHICH ARE IN THEM SPECIALLY, OR IN ANY ONE INDIVIDUAL BY WAY OF SPECIAL GIFT.

MOREOVER, thou must consider that the Virtues of things are in some things according to the Species, as boldness and courage in a lion and cock, fearfulness in a hare or lamb, ravenousness in a wolf, treachery and deceitfulness in a fox, flattery in a dog, covetousness in a crow and jackdaw, pride in a horse, anger in a tiger and boar, sadness and melancholy in a cat, lust in a sparrow, and so of the rest. For the greatest part of Natural Virtues doth follow the Species. Yet some are in things Individually; as there be some men which do so wonderfully abhor the sight of a cat that they cannot look upon her without quaking; which fear, it is manifest, is not in them, as they are men. And Avicen tells of a man that lived in his time, whom all poisonous things did shun, all of them dying which did by chance bite him, he himself not being hurt; and Albertus reports that in a city of the Ubians he saw a wench who would catch spiders to eat them, and being much pleased with such a kind of meat, was wonderfully nourished therewith. So is boldness in a wanton, and fearfulness in a thief. And upon this account it is that philosophers say that any particular thing that never was sick is good against any manner of sickness; therefore they say that a bone of a dead man, who never had a fever, being laid upon the patient, frees him of his quartan. There are also many singular virtues infused into particular things by Celestial bodies, as we have shewed before.

CHAPTER XX. THE NATURAL VIRTUES ARE IN SOME THINGS THROUGHOUT THEIR WHOLE SUBSTANCE, AND IN OTHER THINGS IN CERTAIN PARTS AND MEMBERS.

AGAIN thou must consider that the Virtues of things are in some things in the whole (i. e.), the whole substance of them, or in all their parts, as that little fish echeneis, which is said to stop a ship by its mere touch; this it doth not do according to any particular part, but according to the whole substance. So the civet cat hath this in its whole substance, that dogs, by the very touch of his shadow, hold their peace. So salendine is good for the sight, not according to any one but all its parts; not more in the root than in the leaves and seeds, and so of the rest. But some Virtues are in things according to some parts of it, viz., only in the tongue, or eyes, or some other members and parts; so in the eyes of a basilisk is a most violent power to kill men as soon as they see them. The like power is there in the eyes of the civet cat, which makes any animal that it hath looked upon to stand still, to be amazed, and not able to move itself. The like virtue is there in the eyes of some wolves, who, if they see a man first, make him amazed and so hoarse, that if he would cry out, he hath not the use of his voice. Of this Virgil makes mention when he sings:
Moeris is dumb, hath lost his voice, and why?
The Wolf on Moeris first hath cast his eye.
So also there were some certain women in Scythia, and amongst the Illyrians and Triballians, who as often as they looked angrily upon any man, were said to slay him. Also we read of a certain people of Rhodes, called Telchines, who corrupted all things with their sight, wherefore Jupiter drowned them. Therefore witches, when they would after this manner work by witchcraft, use the eyes of such kind of animals in their waters for the eyes, for the like effects. In like manner do ants fly from the heart of a lapwing and not from the head, foot or eyes. So the gall of lizards, being bruised in water, is said to gather weasels together; not the tail or the head of it. The gall of goats, put into the earth in a brazen vessel, gathers frogs together; and a goat's liver is an enemy to butterflies and all maggots. Dogs

shun them that have the heart of a dog about them; and foxes will not touch those poultry that have eaten the liver of a fox. So divers things have divers virtues dispersed variously through several parts, as they are from above infused into them according to the diversity of things to be received; as in a man's body the bones receive nothing but life, the eyes sight, and the ears hearing. And there is in man's body a certain little bone, which the Hebrews call LVZ, of the bigness of a pulse that is husked, which is subject to no corruption, neither is it overcome with fire, but is always preserved unhurt, out of which, as they say, as a plant out of the seed, our animal bodies shall in the resurrection of the dead spring up. And these Virtues are not cleared by reason, but by experience.

CHAPTER XXI. OF THE VIRTUES OF THINGS WHICH ARE IN THEM ONLY IN THEIR LIFE TIME, AND SUCH AS REMAIN IN THEM EVEN AFTER THEIR DEATH.

MOREOVER, we must know that there are some properties in things only whilst they live, and some that remain after their death. So the little fish echeneis stops the ships, and the basilisk and catablepa kill with their sight when they are alive; but when they are dead do no such thing. So they say that in the colic, if a live duck be applied to the abdomen it takes away the pain and herself dies. Like to this is that which Archytas says: If you take a heart, newly taken out of an animal, and, whilst it is yet warm, hang it upon one that hath a quartan fever, it drives it away. So if any one swallow the heart of a lapwing, or a swallow, or a weasel, or a mole, whilst it is yet warm with natural heat it shall be helpful to him for remembering, understanding, and for foretelling. Hence is this general rule, viz.: That whatsoever things are taken out of animals, whether they be any member, the hair, nails, or such like, they must be taken from those animals whilst they be yet living; and, if it be possible, that so they may be alive afterwards. Whence they say, when you take the tongue of a frog, you must put the frog into the water again; and if you take the tooth of a wolf, you must not kill the wolf; and so of the rest. So writes Democritus, if any one take out the tongue of a water-frog, yet living, no other part of the body sticking to it, and she be let go into the water again, and lay it upon the place where the heart beats of a woman, she shall answer truly whatsoever you ask her. Also they say, that if the eyes of a frog be before sunrising bound to the sick party, and the frog be let go again, blind, into the water, they will drive away tertian ague; as also that they will, being bound with the flesh of a nightingale in the skin of a hart, keep one always watchful without sleep. Also the ray of the fork-fish, being bound to the navel, is said to make a woman have an easy travail, if the ray be taken from the fish alive and it put into the sea again. So they say the right eye of a serpent, being applied, doth help the watering of the eyes if the serpent be let go alive. And there is a certain fish or great serpent, called Myrus, whose eye, if it be pulled out, and bound to the forehead of the patient, is said to cure the inflammation of the eyes; and that the eye of the fish grows again; and that he is taken blind who will not let the fish go. Also the teeth of all serpents, being taken out whilst they are alive, and hanged about the patient, are said to cure the quartan. So doth the tooth of a mole, taken out whilst she is alive, being afterwards let go, cure the toothache; and dogs will not bark at those that have the tail of a weasel that is escaped. And Democritus relates that the tongue of a chameleon, if it be taken from her alive, doth conduce to a good success in trials, and is profitable for women that are in travail, if it be about the outside of the house, for you must take heed that it be not brought into the house, because that would be most dangerous.

Moreover, there be some properties that remain after death, and of these the Platonists say, that they are things in which the Idea of the matter is less swallowed up. In these, even after death, that which is immortal in them doth not cease to work wonderful things. So in the herbs and plants, pulled asunder and dried, that Virtue is quick and operative which was infused at first into them by the Idea. Thence it is that as the eagle all her life time doth overcome all other birds, so also her feathers, after her death, destroy and consume the feathers of all other birds. Upon the same account doth a lion's skin destroy all other skins; and the skin of the civet cat destroys the skin of the panther; and the skin of a wolf corrodes the skin of a lamb. And some of these do not do it by way of a corporeal contact, but also sometimes by their very sound. So a drum made of the skin of a wolf makes a drum made of a lamb-skin not so sound. Also a drum made of the skin of the fish called rochet drives away all creeping things, at what distance soever the sound of it is heard; and the strings of an instrument made of the intestines of a wolf, and being strung upon a harp or lute with strings made of the intestines of a sheep, will make no harmony.

CHAPTER XXII. HOW INFERIOR THINGS ARE SUBJECTED TO SUPERIOR BODIES, AND HOW THE BODIES, THE ACTIONS, AND DISPOSITIONS OF MEN ARE ASCRIBED TO STARS AND SIGNS.

IT IS manifest that all things inferior are subject to the superior, and after a manner (as saith Proclus) they are one in the other, viz., in inferiors are superior and in superiors are inferior: So in the Heaven are things terrestrial, but as in their cause, and in a celestial manner; and in the Earth are things celestial, but after a terrestrial manner, as in an effect. So we say that there be here certain things which are Solary and certain which are Lunary, in which the Sun and Moon make a strong impression of their virtues. Whence it is that these kind of things receive more operations and properties, like to those of the Stars and Signs which they are under. So we know that Solary things respect the heart and head by reason that Leo is the house of the Sun, and Aries the exaltation of the Sun. So things under Mars are good for the head and secrets by reason of Aries and Scorpio. Hence they whose senses fail and heads ache by reason of drunkenness, find cold water and vinegar good to bathe the head and secrets. But in reference to these it is necessary to know how man's body is distributed to Planets and Signs. Know, therefore, that according to the doctrine of the Arabians, the Sun rules over the brain, heart, the thigh, the marrow, the right eye, and the spirit; also the tongue, the mouth, and the rest of the organs of the senses, as well internal as external; also the hands, feet, legs, nerves, and the power of imagination. That Mercury rules over the spleen, stomach, bladder, womb, and right ear, as also the faculty of the common sense. That Saturn rules over the liver and fleshy part of the stomach. That Jupiter rules over the abdomen and navel, whence it is written by the Ancients, that the effigy of a navel was laid up in the temple of Jupiter Hammon. Also some attribute to him the ribs, breasts, bowels, blood, arms, and the right hand and left ear, and the powers natural. And some set Mars over the blood, the veins, the kidneys, the bag of the gall, the buttocks, the back, motion of the sperm, and the irascible power. Again they set Venus over the kidneys, the secrets, the womb, the seed, and concupiscible power; as also the flesh, fat, belly, breast, navel, and the venereal parts and such as serve thereto; as also the os sacrum, the back-bone, and loins; as also the head, and the mouth, with which they give a kiss as a token of love. Now the Moon, although she may challenge the whole body, and every member thereof according to the variety of the Signs, yet more particularly they ascribe to her the brain, lungs, marrow of the backbone, the stomach, the menstrual and excretory parts, and the left eye, as also the power of increasing. But Hermes saith: That there are seven holes in the head of an animal, distributed to the seven Planets, viz.: The right ear to Saturn, the left to Jupiter, the right nostril to Mars, the left to Venus, the right eye to the Sun, the left to the Moon, and the mouth to Mercury.

The several Signs, also, of the Zodiac take care of their members: So Aries governs the head and face; Taurus, the neck; Gemini, the arms and shoulders; Cancer, the breast, lungs, stomach and arms; Leo, the heart, stomach, liver and back; Virgo, the bowels and bottom of the stomach; Libra, the kidneys, thighs and buttocks; Scorpius, the secrets; Sagittarius, the thighs and groins; Capricornus, the knees; Aquarius, the legs and shins; Pisces, the feet. And as the triplicities of these Signs answer one the other, and agree in celestials, so also they agree in the members; which is sufficiently manifest by experience, because with the coldness of the feet the belly and breast are affected, which members answer the same triplicity;

whence it is, if a medicine be applied to the one it helps the other, as by the warming of the feet the pain of the belly ceaseth. Remember, therefore, this order, and know that things which are under any one of the Planets have a certain particular aspect or inclination to those members that are attributed to that planet, and especially to the Houses and exaltation's thereof. For the rest of the dignities, as those triplicities and marks and face, are of little account in this. Upon this account, therefore, peony, balm, clove-gilly-flowers, citron-peel, sweet-marjoram, cinnamon, saffron, lignum aloes, frankincense, amber, musk, and myrrh help the head and heart, by reason of the Sun and Aries and Leo. So doth ribwort, the herb of Mars, help the head and secrets by reason of Aries and Scorpio; and so of the rest. Also all things under Saturn conduce to sadness and melancholy; those under Jupiter to mirth and honor; those under Mars to boldness, contention and anger; those under the Sun to glory, victory and courage; those under Venus to love, lust and concupiscence; those under Mercury to eloquence; those under the Moon to a common life. Also all the actions and dispositions of men are distributed according to the Planets; for Saturn governs old men, monks, melancholy men, and hidden treasures and those things which are obtained with long journeys and difficulty; but Jupiter governs those that are religious, prelates, kings and dukes, and such kind of gains that are got lawfully; Mars rules over barbers, chirurgeons, physicians, sergeants, butchers executioners, all that make fires, bakers, and soldiers, who are every where called martial men. Also do the other Stars signify their office, as they are described in the books of Astrologers.

CHAPTER XXIII. HOW WE SHALL KNOW WHAT STARS NATURAL THINGS ARE UNDER, AND WHAT THINGS ARE UNDER THE SUN, WHICH ARE CALLED SOLARY.

NOW it is very hard to know what Star or Sign every thing is under; yet it is known through the imitation of their rays, or motion, or figure of the superiors. Also some of them are known by their colors and odors; also some by the effects of their operations, answering to some Stars. So, then, Solary things, or things under the power of the Sun, are amongst Elements, the lucid flame; in the humors, the purer blood and spirit of life; amongst tastes, that which is quick, mixed with sweetness; amongst metals, gold, by reason of its splendor, and its receiving that from the Sun which makes it cordial; and amongst stones, they which resemble the rays of the Sun by their golden sparklings, as doth the glittering stone aetites, which hath power against the falling sickness and poisons. So also the stone which is called the Eye of the Sun, being of a figure like to the apple of the eye, from the middle whereof shines forth a ray; it comforts the brain and strengthens the sight. So the carbuncle, which shines by night, hath a virtue against all airy and vaporous poison. So the chrysolite stone, which is of a light green color, in which, when it is held against the Sun, there shines forth a golden star; and this comforts those parts that serve for breathing, and helps those that be asthmatical; and if it be bored through, and the hole filled with the mane of an ass, and bound to the left arm, it drives away idle imaginations and melancholy fears, and puts away foolishness. So the stone called iris, which is like crystal in color, being often found with six corners; when, under some roof, part of it is held against the rays of the Sun and the other part is held in the shadow, it gathers the rays of the Sun into itself, which, whilst it sends them forth, by way of reflection, makes a rainbow appear on the opposite wall. Also the stone heliotrope, green like the jasper or emerald, beset with red specks, makes a man constant, renowned and famous; also it conduceth to long life; and the virtue of it, indeed, is most wonderful upon the beams of the Sun, which it is said to turn into blood (i. e.), to appear of the color of blood, as if the Sun were eclipsed, viz., when it is joined to the juice of a herb of the same name, and be put into a vessel of water. There is also another virtue of it more wonderful, and that is upon the eyes of men, whose sight it doth so dim and dazzle that it doth not suffer him that carries it to see it, and this it doth not do without the help of the herb of the same name, which also is called heliotrope (i. e.), following the Sun. These virtues doth Albertus Magnus and William of Paris confirm in their writings. The stone hyacinth also hath a virtue from the Sun against poisons and pestiferous vapors; it makes him that carries it to be safe and acceptable; it conduceth also to riches and wit; it strengthens the heart; being held in the mouth it doth wonderfully cheer up the mind. Also there is the stone pyrophylus, of a red mixture, which Albertus Magnus saith Aesculapius makes mention of in one of his Epistles unto Octavius Augustus, saying that there is a certain poison so wonderfully cold, which preserves the heart of man (being taken out) from burning, so that if for any time it be put into the fire it is turned into a stone, and this is that stone which is called pyrophylus, from the fire. It hath a wonderful virtue against poison, and it makes him that carries it to be renowned and dreadful to his enemies. But, above all, that stone is most Solary which Apollonius is reported to have found, and which is called pantaura, which draws other stones to it, as the loadstone doth iron, and is most powerful against all poisons. It is called by some pantherus, because it is spotted like the beast called the panther. It is therefore also called pantochras, because it contains all colors, and Aaron calls it evanthum. There are also other Solary stones, as the topazius, chrysopassus, the rubine, and balagius. So also is auripigmentum, and things of a golden color and very lucid.

Amongst plants, also, and trees, those are Solary which turn towards the Sun, as the marigold, and those which fold in their leaves when the Sun is near upon setting, but when it riseth unfold their leaves by little and little.

The lote-tree also is Solary, as is manifest by the figure of the fruit and leaves. So is peony, sallendine, balm, ginger, gentian, and dittany; and vervain, which is of use in prophesying and expiations, as also driving away evil-spirits. The bay-tree also is consecrated to Phoebus, so is the cedar, the palm-tree, the ash, the ivy and vine, and whatsoever repel poisons and lightnings, and those things which never fear for the extremities of the winter. Solary also are mint, mastic, zedoary, saffron, balsam, amber, musk, yellow honey, lignum aloes, cloves, cinnamon, calamus, aromaticus, pepper, frankincense, sweet-marjoram, also libanotis, which Orpheus calls the sweet perfume of the Sun.

Also amongst animals those are called Solary which are magnanimous, courageous, ambitious of victory and renown--as the lion, king of beasts; the crocodile, the spotted wolf, the ram, the boar; the bull, king of the herd, which was by the Egyptians at Heliopolis dedicated to the Sun, which they called Verites; and an ox was consecrated to Apis in Memphis, and in Herminthus a bull by the name of Pathis. The wolf, also, was consecrated to Apollo and Latona. Also the beast called baboon is Solary, which twelve times in a day (viz., every hour) barks and in time of Aequinoctium micturateth twelve times every hour; the same also it doth in the night, whence the Egyptians did engrave him upon their fountains.

Also, amongst birds, these are Solary: The phoenix, being but one of that kind; and the eagle, the queen of birds; also the vulture, the swan, and those which sing at the rising Sun and, as it were, call upon it to rise, as the cock and crow; also the hawk, which because it, in the divinity of the Egyptians, is an emblem of the spirit and light, is by Porphyrius reckoned amongst the Solary birds. Moreover, all such things as have some resemblance of the works of the Sun, as worms shining in the night, and the beetle. Also, according to Appious' interpretation, such things whose eyes are changed according to the course of the Sun are accounted Solary; and things which come of them.

And amongst fish, the sea-calf is chiefly Solary, who doth resist lightning; also shell-fish and the fish called Pulmo, both of which shine in the night; and the fish called stella, for his parching heat; and the fish called strombi that follow their king; and margari, which also have a king, and, being dried, are hardened into a stone of a golden color.

CHAPTER XXIV. WHAT THINGS ARE LUNARY, OR UNDER THE POWER OF THE MOON.

THESE things are Lunary, amongst the Elements, viz.: The earth, then the water, as well that of the sea as of the rivers; and all moist things, as the moisture of trees and animals, especially they which are white, as the whites of , fat, sweat, phlegm, and the superfluities of bodies. Amongst tastes, salt and insipid; amongst metals, silver; amongst stones, crystal, the silver marcasite, and all those stones that are white and green. Also the stone selenite (i. e., the Moon, Lunary), shining from a white body, with a yellow brightness; imitating the motion of the Moon, by having in it the figure of the Moon, which daily increaseth or decreaseth as doth the Moon. Also pearls, which are generated in shells of fishes, and stalactites, formed from the droppings of water; also the beryl, or aqua-marine, greenish and six-sided.

Amongst plants and trees, these are Lunary, as the selenotropion, which turns towards the Moon as doth the heliotropion towards the Sun; and the palm-tree, which sends forth a bough at every rising of the new Moon. Hyssop, also, and rosemary, agnus castus, and the olive-tree, are Lunary. Also the herb chinosta, which increaseth and decreaseth with the Moon, viz., in substance and number of leaves, not only in sap but in virtue-- which, indeed, is in some sort common to all plants, except onions, which last are under the influence of Mars, and have contrary properties.

As amongst flying things the Saturnine bird called a quail is a great enemy of the Moon and Sun, Lu-nary animals are such as delight to be in man's company, and such as do naturally excel in love or hatred, as all kinds of dogs. The chameleon also is Lunary, which always assumes a color according to the variety of the color of the object--as the Moon changeth her nature according to the variety of the Sign which it is found in. Lunary also are swine, hinds, goats, and all those animals, whatsoever, that observe and imitate the motion of the Moon, as the baboon, and the panther, which is said to have a spot upon her shoulder like the Moon, increasing into a roundness and having horns that bend inwards. Cats also are Lunary, whose eyes become greater or less according to the course of the Moon; and those things (which are of like nature, as catamenial blood, of which are made wonderful and strange things by magicians. The civet cat, also, changing her sex with the Moon, being obnoxious to divers sorceries; and all animals that live in water as well as on land, as otters, and such as prey upon fish. Also all monstrous beasts, such as without any manifest seed are equivocally generated, as mice, which sometimes seem to be generated of the putrefaction of the earth. Amongst fowl, geese, ducks, didappers, and all kinds of watery fowl as prey upon fish, as the heron, and those that are equivocally produced, as wasps of the carcasses of horses, bees of the putrefaction of cows, small flies of putrefied wine, and beetles of the flesh of asses. But most Lunary of all is the two-horned beetle, horned after the manner of a bull, which digs under cow-dung and there remains for the space of twenty-eight days (in which time the Moon measures the whole Zodiac), and in the twenty-ninth day, when it thinks there will be a conjunction of their brightness, it opens the dung and casts it into water, from whence then come beetles.

Amongst fish, these are Lunary: Aelurus, whose eyes are changed according to the course of the Moon, and whatsoever observes the motion of the Moon, as the tortoise, the echeneis, crabs, oysters, cockles and frogs.

CHAPTER XXV. WHAT THINGS ARE SATURNINE, OR UNDER THE POWER OF SATURN.

SATURNINE things, amongst Elements, are earth and also water; amongst humors, black choler that is moist, as well natural as adventitious (adust choler excepted). Amongst tastes, sour, tart, and dead-like. Amongst metals, lead, and gold, by reason of its weight, and the golden marcasite. Amongst stones, the onyx, the ziazza, the camonious, the sapphire, the brown jasper, the chalcedon, the loadstone, and all dark, weighty, earthy things. Amongst plants and trees, the daffodil, dragon's-wort, rue, cummin, hellebore, the tree from whence benzoin comes, mandrake, opium, and those things which are never sown, and never bear fruit, and those which bring forth berries of a dark color and black fruit, as the black fig-tree, the pine-tree, the cypress-tree, and a certain tree used at burials, which never springs afresh with berries, rough, of a bitter taste, of a strong smell, of a black shadow, yielding a most sharp pitch, bearing a most unprofitable fruit, never dies with age, deadly, and dedicated to Pluto. As is the herb pas-flower, with which they were wont, anciently, to strow the graves before they put the dead bodies into them; wherefore it was lawful to make their garlands at feasts with all herbs and flowers besides pas-flowers, because it was mournful and not conducing to mirth. Also all creeping animals, living apart, and solitary, nightly, sad, contemplative, dull, covetous, fearful, melancholy, that take much pains, slow, that feed grossly, and such as eat their young. Of these kinds, therefore, are the mole, the wolf, the ass, the toad, the cat, the hog, the bear, the camel, the basilisk, the hare, the ape, the dragon, the mule, all serpents and creeping things, scorpions, ants, and such things as proceed from putrefaction in the earth, in water, or in the ruins of houses, as mice and many sorts of vermin. 'Amongst birds, those are Saturnine which have long necks and harsh voices, as cranes, ostriches, and peacocks, which are dedicated to Saturn and Juno. Also the screech-owl, the horned-owl, the bat, the lapwing, the crow, the quail, which is the most envious bird of all. Amongst fishes, the eel, living apart from all other fish; the lamprey, the dog-fish, which devours her young; also the tortoise, oysters, cockles, to which may be added sea-sponges and all such things as come of them.

CHAPTER XXVI. WHAT THINGS ARE UNDER THE POWER OF JUPITER, AND ARE CALLED JOVIAL.

THINGS under Jupiter, amongst Elements, are the air; amongst humors, blood and the Spirit of Life; also all things which respect the increase, nourishment, and vegetation of the life. Amongst tastes, such as are sweet and pleasant. Amongst metals, tin, silver and gold, by reason of their temperateness. Amongst stones, the hyacinth, beryl, sapphire, emerald, green jasper, and those of airy colors. Amongst plants and trees, sea-green, garden basil, bugloss, mace, spike, mint, mastic, elecampane, the violet, darnel, henbane, the poplar-tree, and those which are called lucky trees, as the oak, the aesculus, or horse-chestnut, which is like an oak but much larger; the holm or holly-tree, the beech-tree, the hazel-tree, the service-tree, the white fig-tree, the pear-tree, the apple-tree, the vine, the plum-tree, the ash, the dogwood tree, and the olive-tree, and also oil-tree. Also all manner of corn, as barley and wheat; also raisins, licorice, sugar, and all such things whose sweetness is manifest and subtile, partaking somewhat of an astringent and sharp taste, as are nuts, almonds, pine-apples, filberts, pistachio-nuts, roots of peony, myrobalan, rhubarb, and manna; Orpheus adds storax. Amongst animals, such as have some stateliness and wisdom in them, and those which are mild, well trained up, and of good dispositions, as the hart and elephant; and those which are gentle, as sheep and lambs. Amongst birds, those that are of a temperate complexion, as hens, together with the yolk of their eggs. Also the partridge, the pheasant, the swallow, the cuckoo, and the stork and pelican, birds given to a kind of devotion, which are emblems of gratitude. The eagle is dedicated to Jupiter--she is the ensign of emperors, and an emblem of Justice and Clemency. Amongst fish, the dolphin, the fish, called anchia or anchovy; and the sheath or sheat-fish, by reason of his devoutness.

CHAPTER XXVII. WHAT THINGS ARE UNDER THE POWER OF MARS, AND ARE CALLED MARTIAL.

THESE things are Martial: Amongst Elements, fire, together with all adust and sharp things. Amongst humors, choler; also bitter tastes, tart and burning the tongue, and causing tears. Amongst metals, iron and red brass; and all fiery, red, and sulphureous things. Amongst stones, the diamond, loadstone, the bloodstone, the jasper, the stone that consists of divers kinds, and the amethyst. Amongst plants and trees, hellebore, garlic, euphorbium, castanea, ammoniac, radish, the laurel or sweet-bay, wolf's-bane, scammony; and all such as are poisonous, by reason of too much heat, and those which are beset, round about with prickles, or, by touching the skin, burn it, prick it, or make it swell, as cardis, the nettle, crow-foot and such as, being eaten, cause tears, as onions, ascolonia, leeks, mustard-seed, and all thorny trees; and the dogwood-tree, which is dedicated to Mars. And all such animals as are warlike, ravenous, bold, and of clear fancy, as the horse, mule, goat, kid, wolf, leopard, and wild ass. Serpents, also, and dragons, full of displeasure and poison. Also all such as are offensive to men, as gnats, flies, and the baboon, by reason of his anger. All birds that are ravenous, devour flesh, and break bones, as the eagle, the falcon, the hawk, and the vulture; and those which are called the fatal birds, as the horn-owl, the screech-owl, castrels, and kites; and such as are hungry and ravenous, and such as make a noise in their swallowing, as crows, daws, and the pie, which, above all the rest, is dedicated to Mars. And amongst fishes, the pike, the barbel, the fork-fish, the fish that hath horns like a ram, the sturgeon, and the glacus, all which are great devourers and ravenous.

CHAPTER XXVIII. WHAT THINGS ARE UNDER THE POWER OF VENUS, AND ARE CALLED VENEREAL.

THESE things are under Venus: Amongst Elements, air and water. Amongst humors, phlegm, with blood, spirit, and seed. Amongst tastes, those which are sweet, unctuous, and delectable. Amongst metals, silver, and brass, both yellow and red. Amongst stones, the beryl, chrysolite, emerald, sapphire, green jasper, carnelian, the stone aetites, the lazuli stone, coral, and all of a fair, various, white, and green color. Amongst plants and trees, the vervain, violet, maiden-hair; valerian, which by the Arabians is called phu! and tithymal, for its fragrant and sweet smell; also thyme, the gum ladanum, amber-gris, sanders or red sandal-wood, coriander, and all sweet perfumes; and delightful and sweet fruits,as sweet pears, figs, pomegranates, which, the poets say, were, in Cyprus, first sown by Venus. Also the Rose of Lucifer was dedicated to her; also the Myrtle-tree of Hesperus. Moreover, all luxurious, delicious animals, and of a strong love, as dogs, conies, odorous sheep and goats, both female and male, which generate sooner than any other animal; also the bull, for his disdain, and the calf, for his wantonness. Amongst birds, the swan, the wagtail, the swallow, the pelican, the bergander, which are very loving to their young. Also the crow, and the pigeon, which is dedicated to Venus; and the turtle-dove, one whereof was commanded to be offered at the purification, after bringing forth. The sparrow also was dedicated to Venus, which was commanded in the law to be used in the purification, after the leprosy, a martial disease, than which nothing was of more force to resist it. Also, the Egyptians called the Eagle by the name of Venus, because she never fails to answer the call of her mate. Amongst fishes, these are venereal: The lustful pilchard, the lecherous gilt-head, the whiting, for her love to her young, and the crab, fighting for his mate.

CHAPTER XXIX. WHAT THINGS ARE UNDER THE POWER OF MERCURY, AND ARE CALLED MERCURIAL.

THINGS under Mercury are these: Amongst Elements, water, though it moves all things indistinctly. Amongst humors, those especially which are mixed, as also the animal spirit. Amongst tastes, those that are various, strange, and mixed. Amongst metals, quick-silver, tin, and the silver marcasite. Amongst stones, the emerald, achate or agate, red marble, and topaz, and those which are of divers colors and various figures naturally; and those that are artificial, as glass; and those which have a color mixed with green and yellow. Amongst plants and trees, the hazel, five-leaved grass, the herb mercury, fumitory, pimpernel, marjoram, parsley, and such as have shorter and less leaves, being compounded of mixed natures and divers colors. Animals, also, that are of quick sense, ingenious, strong, inconstant, and swift; and such as become easily acquainted with men, as dogs, weasels, apes, foxes, the hart and mule; and all animals that are of both sexes, and those which can change their sex, as the hare, civet cat, and such like. Amongst birds, those which are naturally witty, melodious and inconstant, as the linnet, nightingale, blackbird, lark, thrush, the gnat-snapper, the bird calandra, the parrot, the pie, the bird ibis, the bird porphyrio, the black beetle with one horn, and the sea-bird trochilus, which goes into the crocodile's mouth for its food. Amongst fishes, the fish called pour-contrel, for deceitfulness and changeableness; the fork-fish for its industry, and the mullet, also, that shakes off the bait on the hook with his tail.

CHAPTER XXX. THAT THE WHOLE SUBLUNARY WORLD, AND THOSE THINGS WHICH ARE IN IT, ARE DISTRIBUTED TO PLANETS.

MOREOVER, whatsoever is found in the whole world is made according to the governments of the Planets, and accordingly receives its virtue. So in fire, the enlivening light thereof is under the government of the Sun; the heat of it under Mars, in the Earth; the various superficies thereof under the Moon and Mercury, and the starry heaven; the whole mass of it under Saturn. But in the middle Elements, air is under Jupiter, and water under the Moon; but being mixed, are under Mercury and Venus. In like manner natural active causes observe the Sun, the matter the Moon, the fruitfulness of active causes, Jupiter; the fruitfulness of the matter, Venus; the sudden effecting of any thing, Mars; and Mercury, that for his vehemency, this for his dexterity and manifold virtue. But the permanent continuation of all things is ascribed to Saturn. Also, amongst vegetables, every thing that bears fruit is from Jupiter, and every thing that bears flowers is from Venus; all seed and bark is from Mercury, and all roots from Saturn, and all wood from Mars, and leaves from the Moon. Wherefore, all that bring forth fruit, and not flowers, are of Saturn and Jupiter; but they that bring forth flowers and seed, and not fruit, are of Venus and Mercury; those which are brought forth of their own accord, without seed, are of the Moon and Saturn. All beauty is from Venus, all strength from Mars, and every planet rules and disposeth that which is like to it. Also in stones, their weight, clamminess and slipticness is of Saturn, their use and temperament of Jupiter, their hardness from Mars, their life from the Sun, their beauty and fairness from Venus, their occult virtue from Mercury, and their common use from the Moon.

CHAPTER XXXI. HOW PROVINCES AND KINGDOMS ARE DISTRIBUTED TO PLANETS.

MOREOVER, the whole orb of the earth is distributed by kingdoms and provinces to the Planets and Signs: For Macedonia, Thracia, Illyria, Arriana, Gordiana, India, many of which countries are in the lesser Asia, are under Saturn with Capricornus; but with Aquarius under him are the Sauromatian Country, Oxiana, Sogdiana, Arabia, Phazania, Media and , which countries, for the most part, belong to the more inward Asia. Under Jupiter, with Sagittarius, are Tuscana, Celtica, Spaine, and happy Arabia; and under him, with Pisces, are Lycia, Lydia, Cilicia, Pamphylia, Paphlagonia, Nasamonia, and Lybia. Mars, with Aries, governs Britany, France, Germany, Bastarnia, the lower parts of Syria, Idumea, and Judea; with Scorpio, he rules Syria, Comagena, Cappadocia, Metagonium, Mauritania, and Getulia. The Sun, with Leo, governs Italy, Apulia, Sicilia, Phenicia, Chaldea, and the Orchenians. Venus, with Taurus, governs the Isles Cyclades, the seas of little Asia, Cyprus, Parthia, Media, Persia; but, with Libra, she commands the people of the Island Bractia, of Caspia, of Seres, of Thebais, of Oasis, and of Troglodys. Mercury, with Gemini, rules Hircania, Armenia, Mantiana, Cyrenaica, Marmarica, and the lower Egypt; but, with Virgo, he rules Greece, Achaia, Creta, Babylon, Mesopotamia, Assyria, and Ela, whence they of that place are in Scripture called Elamites. The Moon, with Cancer, governs Bithivia, Phrygia, Colchica, Numidia, Africa, Carthage, and all Carchedonia.

These we have, in this manner, gathered from Ptolemy's opinion, to which, according to the writings of other astrologers, many more may be added. But he who knows how to compare these divisions of provinces according to the Divisions of the Stars, with the Ministry of the Ruling

Intelligences, and Blessings of the Tribes of Israel, the Lots of the Apostles, and Typical Seals of the Sacred Scripture, shall be able to obtain great and prophetical oracles, concerning every region, of things to come.

CHAPTER XXXII. WHAT THINGS ARE UNDER THE SIGNS, THE FIXED STARS, AND THEIR IMAGES.

THE like consideration is to be had in all things concerning the Figures of the Fixed Stars: Therefore they will have the terrestrial ram to be under the rule of the celestial Aries, and the terrestrial bull and ox to be under the celestial Taurus. So also that Cancer should rule over crabs, and Leo over lions; Virgo over virgins, and Scorpio over scorpions; Capricornus over goats, Sagittarius over horses, and Pisces over fishes. Also the celestial Ursa over bears, the Hydra over serpents, and the Dog Star over dogs, and so of the rest. Now, Apuleius distributes certain and peculiar herbs to the Signs and Planets, viz: To Aries, the herb sage; to Taurus, the vervain that grows straight; to Gemini, the vervain that grows bending; to Cancer, comfrey; to Leo, sow-bread; to Virgo, calamint; to Libra, mug-wort; to Scorpio, scorpion-grass; to Sagittarius, pimpernel; to Capricornus, the dock; to Aquarius, dragon's wort; to Pisces, hart-wort. And to the Planets these, viz.: To Saturn, sengreen; to Jupiter, agrimony; to Mars, sulphur-wort; to the Sun, mari-gold; to Venus, wound-wort; to Mercury, mullein; to the Moon, peony. But Hermes, whom Albertus follows, distributes to the Planets these, viz.: To Saturn, the daffodil; to Jupiter, henbane; to Mars, rib-wort; to the Sun, knot-grass; to Venus, vervain; to Mercury, cinque-foil; to the Moon, goose-foot. We also know by experience that asparagus is under Aries, and garden basil under Scorpio; for of the shavings of ram's-horn, sowed, comes forth asparagus; and garden basil, rubbed betwixt two stones, produceth scorpions. Moreover, I will, according to the doctrine of Hermes, and of Thebit, reckon up some of the more eminent Stars, whereof the first is called the Head of Algol, and, amongst stones, rules over the diamond; amongst plants, black hellebore and mug-wort. The second are the Pleiades, or Seven Stars, which, amongst stones, rule over crystal and the stone diodocus; amongst plants, the herb diacedon, and frankincense and fennel; and amongst metals, quicksilver. The third is the star Aldeboran, which hath under it, amongst stones, the carbuncle and ruby; amongst plants, the milky thistle and matry-silva. The fourth is called the Goat Star, which rules, amongst stones, the sapphire; amongst plants, horehound, mint, mug-wort and mandrake. The fifth is called the great Dog Star, which, amongst stones, rules over the beryl; amongst plants, savin, mug-wort and dragon's-wort; and, amongst animals, the forked tongue of a snake. The sixth is called the lesser Dog Star, and, amongst stones, rules over achate or agate; amongst plants, the flowers of marigold and pennyroyal. The seventh is called the Heart of the Lyon, which, amongst stones, rules over the granate or garnet; amongst plants, sallendine, mugwort and mastic. The eighth is the Taile of the lesser Bear, which, amongst stones, rules over the loadstone; amongst herbs, over succory or chicory, whose leaves and flowers turn towards the north; also mug-wort and the flowers of periwinkle; and, amongst animals, the tooth of a wolf. The ninth is called the Wing of the Crow, under which, amongst stones, are such stones as are of the color of the black onyx stone; amongst plants, the bur, quadraginus, henbane and comfrey; and, amongst animals, the tongue of a frog. The tenth is called Spica, which hath under it, amongst stones, the emerald; amongst plants, sage, trifoil, periwinkle, mug-wort and mandrake. The eleventh is called Alchamech, which, amongst stones, rules over the jasper; amongst plants, the plantain. The twelfth is called Elpheia; under this, amongst stones, is the topaz; amongst plants, rosemary, trifoil and ivy. The thirteenth is called the Heart of the Scorpion, under which, amongst stones, is the sardonius and amethyst; amongst plants, long aristolochy and saffron. The fourteenth is the Falling Vultur, under which, amongst stones, is the chrysolite; amongst plants, succory and fumitory. The fifteenth is the Taile of Capricorn, under which, amongst stones, is chalcedony; amongst plants, marjoram, mug-wort, and catnip, and the root of mandrake.

Moreover, this we must know, that every stone or plant or animal, or any other thing, is not governed by one star alone, but many of them receive influence, not separated, but conjoined, from many stars. So amongst stones, the chalcedon is under Saturn and Mercury, together with the Taile of Scorpion, and Capricorn. The sapphire, under Jupiter, Saturn and the star Alhajoth; tutia is under Jupiter and the Sun and Moon; the emerald, under Jupiter, Venus and Mercury and the star Spica. The amethyst, as saith Hermes, is under Mars, Jupiter and the Heart of the Scorpion. The jasper, which is of divers kinds, is under Mars, Jupiter and the star Alchamech. The chrysolite is under the Sun, Venus and Mercury, as also under the star which is called the Falling Vultur. The topaz, under the Sun and the star Elpheia; the diamond, under Mars and the Head of Algol. In like manner, amongst vegetables, the herb dragon is under Saturn and the celestial Dragon; mastic and mint are under Jupiter and the Sun, but mastic is also under the Heart of the Lyon, and mint, under the Goat Star. Hellebore is dedicated to Mars and the Head of Algol; moss and sanders to the Sun and Venus; coriander to Venus and Saturn. Amongst animals, the sea calf is under the Sun and Jupiter; the fox and ape, under Saturn and Mercury; and domestical dogs under Mercury and the Moon. And thus we have shewed more things in these inferiors by their superiors.

CHAPTER XXXIII. OF THE SEALS
AND CHARACTERS OF NATURAL THINGS.

ALL Stars have their peculiar natures, properties, and conditions, the Seals and Characters whereof they produce, through their rays, even in these inferior things, viz., in elements, in stones, in plants, in animals, and their members; whence every natural thing receives, from a harmonious disposition and from its star shining upon it, some particular Seal, or character, stamped upon it; which Seal of character is the significator of that star, or harmonious disposition, containing in it a peculiar Virtue, differing from other virtues of the same matter, both generically, specifically, and numerically. Every thing, therefore, hath its character pressed upon it by its star for some particular effect, especially by that star which doth principally govern it. And these Characters contain and retain in them the peculiar Natures, Virtues, and Roots of their Stars, and produce the like operations upon other things, on which they are reflected, and stir up and help the influences of their Stars, whether they be Planets, or fixed Stars, or Figures, or celestial Signs, viz., as oft as they shall be made in a fit matter, and in their due and accustomed times. Which ancient Wise Men considering-- such as labored much in the finding out of the occult properties of things-- did set down in writing the Images of the Stars, their Figures, Seals, Marks, Characters, such as Nature herself did describe, by the rays of the Stars, in these inferior bodies--some in stones, some in plants, and joints and knots of boughs, and some in divers members of animals. For the bay-tree, the lote-tree, and the marigold are Solary Plants, and in their roots and knots, being cut off, shew the Characters of the Sun. So also in the bones and shoulder-blades in animals; whence there arose a spatulary kind of divining (i. e.) by the shoulder-blades; and in the stones and stony things the Characters and Images of celestial things are often found. But seeing that in so great a diversity of things there is not a traditional knowledge, only in a few things, which human understanding is able to reach: Therefore, leaving those things which are to be found out in plants and stones, and other things, as also in the members of divers animals, we shall limit ourselves to man's nature only, which, seeing it is the most complete Image of the whole Universe, containing in itself the whole heavenly harmony, will, without all doubt, abundantly afford us the Seals and Characters of all the Stars and Celestial Influences, and those, as the more efficacious, which are less differing from the celestial nature. But as the number. of the Stars is known to God alone, so also their effects and Seals upon these inferior things, wherefore no human intellect is able to attain to the knowledge of them. Whence very few of those things became known to us which the ancient philosophers and chiromancers attained to, partly by reason and partly by experience; and there be many things yet lying hid in the treasury of Nature. We shall here, in this place, note some few Seals and Characters of the Planets, such as the ancient chiromancers knew of, in the hands of men. These doth Julian call Sacred and Divine Letters, seeing that by them, according to the holy Scripture, is the life of men writ in their hands. And there are in all nations of all languages always the same and like to them, and permanent; to which were added and found out afterwards many more; as by the ancient, so by latter chiromancers. And they that would know them must have recourse to their volumes. It is sufficient here to shew from

HERE FOLLOW THE FIGURES OF DIVINE LETTERS:

The Letters or Characters of Saturn.

The Letters or Characters of Jupiter.

The Letters or Characters of Mars.

The Letters or Characters of the Sun.

The Letters or Characters of Venus.

The Letters or Characters of Mercury.

The Letters or Characters of the Moon.

whence the Characters of Nature have their original source, and in what things they are to be enquired after.

CHAPTER XXXIV. HOW, BY NATURAL THINGS AND THEIR VIRTUES, WE MAY DRAW FORTH AND ATTRACT THE INFLUENCES AND VIRTUES OF CELESTIAL BODIES.

NOW, if thou desirest to receive virtue from any part of the World, or from any Star, thou shalt (those things being used which belong to this Star) come under its peculiar influence, as wood is fit to receive flame by reason of sulphur, pitch and oil. Nevertheless, when thou dost do any one species of things, or individual, rightly apply many things (which are things of the same subject, scattered, amongst themselves, conformable to the same Idea and Star), presently, by this matter so opportunely fitted, a singular gift is infused by the Idea, by means of the Soul of the World. I say "opportunely fitted," viz., under a harmony, like to the harmony which did infuse a certain virtue into the matter. For although things have some virtues, such as we speak of, yet those virtues do so lie hid that there is seldom any effect produced by them. But, as in a grain of mustard-seed, bruised, the sharpness which lay hid is stirred up; and as the heat of the fire doth make letters apparent to the sight which before could not be read, being writ with the juice of an onion, or with milk; and as letters wrote upon a stone with the fat of a goat, and altogether unperceived, when the stone is put into vinegar appear and shew themselves; and as a blow with a stick stirs up the madness of a dog which before lay asleep--so doth the Celestial Harmony disclose virtues lying in the water; stirs them up, strengtheneth them, and makes them manifest; and as I may so say, produceth that into Act which before was only in Power, when things are rightly exposed to it in a Celestial Season. As for example: If thou dost desire to attract virtue from the Sun, and to seek those things that are Solary, amongst vegetables, plants, metals, stones, and animals, those things are to be used and taken chiefly which in a Solary order are higher. For these are more available. So thou shalt draw a singular gift from the Sun, through the beams thereof, being seasonably received together, and through the Spirit of the World.

CHAPTER XXXV. OF THE MIXTIONS OF NATURAL THINGS, ONE WITH ANOTHER, AND THEIR BENEFIT.

IT is most evident that in the inferior nature all the powers of superior bodies are not found comprehended in any one thing, but are dispersed through many kinds of things amongst us; as there are many Solary things, whereof every one doth not contain all the virtues of the Sun; but some have some properties from the Sun, and others other-some. Wherefore, it is sometimes necessary that there be mixtions in operations, that if a hundred or a thousand virtues of the Sun were dispersed through so many plants, animals, and the like, we may gather all these together, and bring them into one form, in which we shall see all the said virtues, being united, contained. Now, there is a twofold virtue in commixtion; one, viz., which was first planted in its parts, and is celestial; the other is obtained by a certain and artificial mixtion of things, mixt amongst themselves, and of the mixtions of them according to certain proportions, such as agree with the heaven, under a certain constellation. And this virtue descends by a certain likeness and aptness that is in things, amongst themselves, towards their superiors, and just as much as the following things do by degrees correspond with them that go before, where the patient is fitly applied to its superior agent. So from a certain composition of herbs, vapors, and such like, made according to the principles of natural philosophy and astronomy, there results a certain common form, endowed with many gifts of the Stars, as, in the honey of bees, that which is gathered out of the juice of innumerable flowers and brought into one form, contains the virtue of all, by a kind of divine and admirable art of the bees. Yet this is not to be less wondered at, which Eudoxus Giudius reports, of an artificial kind of honey which a certain Nation of Giants in Lybia knew how to make out of flowers, and that very good and not far inferior to that of the bees. For every mixtion, which consists of many several things, is then most perfect when it is so firmly compacted in all parts that it becomes one, is every where firm to itself, and can hardly be dissipated--as we sometimes see stones and divers bodies to be, by a certain natural power, so conglutinated and united that they seem to be wholly one thing; as we see two trees, by grafting, to become one; also oysters with stones, by a certain occult virtue of Nature; and there have been seen some animals which have been turned into stones, and so united with the substance of the stone that they seem to make one body, and that also homogeneous; so the tree ebony is one while wood and another while stone. When, therefore, any one makes a mixtion of many matters under the celestial influences, then the variety of celestial actions on the one hand, and of natural powers on the other hand, being joined together, doth indeed cause wonderful things--by ointments, by collyries, by fumes, and such like--which are read of in the books of Chiramis, Archyta, Democritus, and Hermes, who is named Alchorat, and many others.

CHAPTER XXXVI. OF THE UNION OF MIXED THINGS, AND THE INTRODUCTION OF A MORE NOBLE FORM AND THE SENSES OF LIFE.

MOREOVER, we must know, that by how much the more noble the form of anything is, by so much the more prone and apt it is to receive, and powerful to act. Then the virtues of things do then become wonderful, viz., when they are put to matters that are mixed, and prepared in fit seasons, to make them alive, by procuring life for them from the Stars, as also a sensible Soul as a more noble form. For there is so great a power in prepared matters, which, we see, do then receive life when a perfect mixtion of qualities seems to break the former contrariety. For so much the more perfect life things receive, shews by how much their temper is more remote from contrariety.

Now, the Heaven, as a prevalent cause, doth (from the beginning of every thing to be generated by the due concoction and perfect digestion of the matter), together with life, bestow celestial influences and wonderful gifts, according to the Capacity that is in that Life and sensible Soul to receive more noble and sublime virtues. For the Celestial Virtue doth otherwise lie asleep, as sulphur kept from the flame, but in Living Bodies it doth always burn, as kindled sulphur; and then by its vapor, like the lighted sulphur, it fills all the places that are next to it.

So certain wonderful works are wrought, such as are read of in the book of Nemith, which is titled a Book of the Laws of Pluto, because such kind of monstrous generations are not produced according to the Laws of Nature. For we know that of worms are generated gnats; of a horse, wasps; of a calf or ox, bees; of a crab, his legs being taken off and he buried in the ground, a scorpion; of a duck, dried into powder and put into hot water, are generated frogs; but if the duck be baked in a pie, and cut into pieces, and then put into a moist place under the ground, toads are generated of it. Of the herb garden basil, bruised betwixt two stones, are generated scorpions; and of the hairs of a catameniel person, buried under compost, are bred serpents; and the hair of a horse's tail, put into water, receiveth life and is turned into a pernicious worm. And there is an art wherewith, by a hen sitting upon eggs, may be generated a form like to a man (which I have seen and know how to make), which magicians say hath in it wonderful virtues; and this they call the true mandrake. You must, therefore, know which and what kind of matters are either of Nature or Art, begun or perfected, or compounded of more things, and what celestial influences they are able to receive. For a congruity of natural things is sufficient for the receiving of influence from those celestial; because when nothing doth hinder the Celestials to send forth their lights upon Inferiors, they suffer no matter to be destitute of their virtue. Wherefore, as much matter as is perfect and pure, is not unfit to receive the celestial influence. For that is the binding and continuity of the matter to the Soul of the World, which doth so daily flow in upon things natural, and all things which Nature hath prepared, that it is impossible that a prepared matter should not receive life, or a more noble form.

CHAPTER XXXVII. HOW, BY SOME CERTAIN NATURAL AND ARTIFICIAL PREPARATIONS, WE MAY ATTRACT CERTAIN CELESTIAL AND VITAL GIFTS.

PLATONISTS, together with Hermes, say, and Jarchus Brachmanus and the Mecubals of the Hebrews confess, that all sublunary things are subject to generation and corruption, and that also there are the same things in the Celestial World, but after a celestial manner, as also in the Intellectual World, but in a far more perfect and better fashion and manner, and in the most perfect manner of all in the Exemplary. And, after this course, that every inferior thing should, in its kind, answer its superior thing, and through this the Supreme Itself, and receive from heaven that celestial power they call the quintessence, or the Spirit of the World, or the Middle Nature; and from the Intellectual World a spiritual and enlivening virtue, transcending all qualities whatsoever; and, lastly, from the Exemplary, or original, World, through the mediation of the other, according to their degree receive the original power of the whole perfection. Hence, every thing may be aptly reduced from these Inferiors to the Stars, from the Stars to their Intelligences, and from thence to the First Cause itself--from the series and order whereof all Magic and all Occult Philosophy flows: For every day some natural thing is drawn by art, and some divine thing is drawn by Nature, which, the Egyptians, seeing, called Nature a Magicianess (i. e.), the very Magical power itself, in the attracting of like by like, and of suitable things by suitable.

Now, such kind of attraction, by the mutual correspondency of things amongst themselves, of superiors with inferiors, the Grecians called sympathies. So the earth agrees with cold water, the water with moist air, the air with fire, the fire with the heaven in water; neither is fire mixed with water, but by air; nor the air with the earth, but by water. So neither is the soul united to the body, but by the spirit; nor the understanding to the spirit, but by the soul. So we see that when Nature hath framed the body of an infant, by this very preparative she presently fetcheth its spirit from the Universe. This spirit is its instrument to obtain of God its understanding and mind in its soul and body, as in wood the dryness is fitted to receive oil, and the oil, being imbibed, is food for the fire, the fire is the vehicle of light. By these examples you see how by some certain natural and artificial preparations we are in a capacity to receive certain celestial gifts from above. For stones and metals have a correspondency with herbs, herbs with animals, animals with the heavens, the heavens with Intelligences, and they with divine properties and attributes and with God himself, after whose image and likeness all things are created.

Now, the first image of God is the world; of the world, man; of man, beasts; of beasts, the zeophyton or zoophyte (i. e.), half animal and half plant; of the zeophyton, plants; of plants, metals; and of metals, stones. And, again, in things spiritual, the plant agrees with a brute in vegetation, a brute with a man in sense, man with an angel in understanding, and an angel with God in immortality. Divinity is annexed to the mind, the mind to the intellect, the intellect to the intention, the intention to the imagination, the imagination to the senses, and the senses, at last, to things. For this is the band and continuity of Nature, that all superior virtue doth flow through every inferior with a long and continued series, dispersing its rays even to the very last things; and inferiors, through their superiors, come to the very Supreme of all. For so inferiors are successively joined to their superiors, that there proceeds an influence from their head, the First Cause, as a certain string stretched out to the lowermost things of all; of which string, if one end be touched the whole doth presently shake, and such a touch doth sound to the other end; and at the motion of an inferior the superior also is moved, to which the other doth answer, as strings in a lute well tuned.

CHAPTER XXXVIII. HOW WE MAY DRAW NOT ONLY CELESTIAL AND VITAL, BUT ALSO CERTAIN INTELLECTUAL AND DIVINE GIFTS FROM ABOVE.

MAGICIANS teach that celestial gifts may, through inferiors being conformable to superiors, be drawn down by opportune influences of the heaven; and so, also, by these celestial gifts, the celestial angels (as they are servants of the stars) may be procured and conveyed to us. Iamblichus, Proclus and Synesius, with the whole school of Platonists, confirm that not only celestial and vital but also certain intellectual, angelical and divine gifts may, be received from above by some certain matters having a natural power of divinity (i. e.), which have a natural correspondency with the superiors, being rightly received and opportunely gathered together according to the rules of natural philosophy and astronomy. And Mercurius Trismegistus writes, that an Image, rightly made of certain proper things, appropriated to any one certain angel will presently be animated by that angel. Of the same, also, Austin (St. Augustine) makes mention in his eighth book, De Civitate Dei (the City of God). For this is the harmony of the world, that things supercelestial be drawn down by the celestial, and the supernatural by those natural, because there is One Operative Virtue that is diffused through all kinds of things; by which virtue, indeed, as manifest things are produced out of occult causes, so a magician doth make use of things manifest to draw forth things that are occult, viz., through the rays of the Stars, through fumes, lights, sounds, and natural things which are agreeable to those celestial, in which, aside from their corporeal qualities, there is, also, a kind of reason, sense and harmony, and incorporeal and divine measures and orders.

So we read that the ancients were wont often to receive some divine and wonderful thing by certain natural things: So the stone that is bred in the apple of the eye of a civet eat, held under the tongue of a man, is said to make him to divine or prophesy; the same is selenite, the moon-stone, reported to do. So they say that the Images of Gods may be called up by the stone called anchitis; and that the ghosts of the dead may be, being called up, kept up by the stone synochitis. The like doth the herb aglauphotis do, which is also called marmorites, growing upon the marbles of Arabia, as saith Pliny, and the which magicians use. Also there is an herb called rheangelida with which magicians drinking of can prophesy. Moreover, there are some herbs by which the dead are raised to life; whence Xanthus the historian tells that with a certain herb called balus, a young dragon being killed, was made alive again; also, that by the same herb a certain man of Tillum, whom a dragon killed, was restored to life; and Juba reports, that in Arabia a certain man was by a certain herb restored to life. But whether or no any such things can be done, indeed, upon man by the virtue of herbs or any other natural thing, we shall discourse in the following chapter. Now, it is certain and manifest, that such things can be done upon other animals. So if flies, that are drowned, be put into warm ashes they revive. And bees, being drowned, do in like matter recover life in the juice of the herb catnip; and eels, being dead for want of water, if with their whole bodies they be put under mud in vinegar and the blood of a vulture being put to them, will all of them, in a few days, recover life. They say that if the fish echeneis be cut into pieces and cast into the sea, the parts will within a little time come together and live. Also we know that the pelican doth restore her young to life, being killed, with her own blood.

CHAPTER XXXIX. THAT WE MAY, BY SOME CERTAIN MATTERS OF THE WORLD, STIR UP THE GODS OF THE WORLD AND THEIR MINISTERING SPIRITS.

NO MAN is ignorant that evil spirits, by evil and profane arts, may be raised up as Psellus saith sorcerers are wont to do, whom most detestable and abominable filthiness did follow and accompany, such as were in times past in the sacrifices of Priapus, and in the worship of the idol which was called Panor, to whom they did sacrifice with shameful nakedness. Neither to these is that unlike (if it be true and not a fable) which is read concerning the detestable heresy of old churchmen, and like to these are manifest in witches and mischievous women, which wickednesses the foolish dotage of women is subject to fall into. By these, and such as these, evil spirits are raised. As a wicked spirit spake once to John of one Cynops, a sorcerer: "All the power," saith he, "of Satan dwells there; and he is entered into a confederacy with all the principalities together, and likewise we with him; and Cynops obeys us and we, again, obey him." Again, on the contrary side, no man is ignorant that super-celestial angels or spirits may be gained by us through good works, a pure mind, secret prayers, devout humiliation, and the like. Let no man, therefore, doubt that in like manner by some certain matters of the world, the gods of the world may be raised by us, or, at least, the ministering spirits, or servants of these gods, and, as Mercurius saith, the airy spirits (not supercelestial, but less higher). So we read that the ancient priests made statues and images, -foretelling things to come, and infused into them the Spirits of the Stars, which were not kept there by constraint in some certain matters, but rejoiced in them, viz., as acknowledging such kinds of matter to be suitable to them, they do always and willingly abide in them, and speak and do wonderful things by them; no otherwise than evil spirits are wont to do when they possess men's bodies.

CHAPTER XL. OF BINDINGS; WHAT SORT THEY ARE OF, AND IN WHAT WAYS THEY ARE WONT TO BE DONE.

WE have spoken concerning the virtues and wonderful efficacy of natural things. It remains now that we understand a thing of great wonderment--and it is a binding of men into love or hatred, sickness or health, or such like. Also the binding of thieves and robbers, that they cannot steal in any place; the binding of merchants, that they cannot buy or sell in any place; the binding of an army, that they cannot pass over any bound; the binding of ships, that no winds, though never so strong, shall be able to carry them out of the haven. Also the binding of a mill, that it can by no force whatsoever be turned round; the binding of a cistern or fountain, that the water cannot be drawn up out of them; the binding of the ground, that it cannot bring forth fruit; the binding of any place, that nothing can be built upon it; the binding of fire, that though it be never so strong, can burn no combustible thing that is put to it. Also the bindings of lightnings and tempests, that they shall do no hurt; the binding of dogs, that they cannot bark; the binding of birds and wild beasts, that they shall not be able to fly or run away. And such like as these, which are scarce credible, yet often known by experience. Now, there are such kind of bindings as these made by sorceries, collyries, unguents, and love potions; by binding to or hanging up of things; by rings, by charms, by strong imaginations and passions, by images and characters, by enchantments and imprecations, by lights, by numbers, by, sounds, by words, and names, invocations, and sacrifices; by swearing, conjuring, consecrations, devotions, and by divers superstitions, and observations, and such like.

CHAPTER XLI. OF SORCERIES, AND THEIR POWER.

THE force of sorceries is reported to be so great that they are believed to be able to subvert, consume and change all inferior things, according to Virgil's muse:

Moeris for me these herbs in Pontus chose,
 And curious drugs, for there great plenty grows;
 I, many times, with these have Moeris
 spied Chang'd to a wolfe, and in the woods to hide;
 From Sepulchres would souls departed charm,
 And Corn bear standing from another's Farm.
Also, in another place, concerning the companions of Ulysses, whom
The cruel Goddess, Circe, there invests
 With fierce aspects, and chang'd to savage beasts.
And, a little after,
When love from Picus, Cerce could not gaine,
 Him, with her charming-wand, and hellish bane,
 Chang'd to a bird, and spots his speckled wings
 With sundry colors
Now, there are some kinds of these sorceries mentioned by Lucan concerning that sorceress, Thessala, calling up ghosts, where he saith:

Here all Nature's products unfortunate:
 Foam of mad Dogs, which waters fear and hate;
 Guts of the Lynx; Hyena's, knot imbred;
 The marrow of a Hart with Serpents fed
 Were not wanting; no, nor the sea Lamprey,
 Which stops the ships; nor yet the Dragon's eye.
And such as Apuleius tells of concerning Pamphila, that sorceress, endeavoring to procure love; to whom Fotis, a certain maid, brought the hairs of a goat (cut off from a bag or bottle made with the skin thereof) instead of Baeotius' (a young man) hair. Now she, saith Apuleius, being out of her wits for the young man, goeth up to the tiled roof and, in the upper part thereof, makes a great hole open to all the oriental and other aspects, and most fit for these her arts, and there privately worships; having before furnished her mournful house with suitable furniture, with all kinds of spices, with plates of iron with strange words engraven upon them, with parts of sterns of ships that were cast away and much lamented, and with divers members of buried carcasses cast abroad--here noses and fingers, there the fleshy nails of those that were hanged, and, in another place, the blood of them that were murdered, and their skulls, mangled with the teeth

of wild beasts. Then she offers sacrifices (their enchanted entrails lying panting), and sprinkles them with divers kinds of liquors; sometimes with fountain water, sometimes with cow's milk, sometimes with mountain honey, and mead. Then she ties those hairs into knots, and lays them on the fire, with divers odors, to be burnt. Then presently, with an irresistible power of magic, and blind force of the gods, the bodies of those whose hairs did smoke, and crash, did assume the spirit of a man, and feel, and hear, and walk, and come whither the stink of their hair led them, and, instead of Baeotius, the young man, come skipping and leaping with joy and love into the house. Austin also reports that he heard of some women sorceresses, that were so well versed in these kind of arts, that, by giving cheese to men, they would presently turn them into working cattle and, the work being done, restored them into men again.

CHAPTER XLII. OF THE WONDERFUL VIRTUES OF SOME KINDS OF SORCERIES.

NOW I will shew you what some of the Sorceries are, that by the example of these there may be a way opened for the consideration of the whole subject of them. Of these, therefore, the first is the catamenia, which, how much power it hath in sorcery, we will now consider; for, as they say, if it comes over new wine it makes it sour, and if it doth but touch the vine, it spoils it forever; and, by its very touch, it makes all plants and trees barren, and they that be newly set to die; it burns up all the herbs in the garden and makes fruit fall off from the trees; it darkens the brightness of a looking-glass, dulls the edges of knives and razors, and dims the beauty of ivory. It makes iron presently rusty; it makes brass rust and smell very strong; it makes dogs mad if they do but taste of it, and if they, being thus mad, shall bite any one, that wound is incurable. It kills whole hives of bees, and drives them from the hives that are but touched with it. It makes linen black that is boiled with it; it makes mares cast their foal if they do but touch it, and makes asses barren as long as they eat of the corn that hath been touched with it. The ashes of catamenious clothes, if they be cast upon purple garments that are to be washed, change the color of them, and takes away colors from flowers. They say that it drives away tertian and quartan agues if it be put into the wool of a black ram, and tied up in a silver bracelet; as, also, if the soles of the patient's feet be anointed therewith, and especially if it be done by the woman herself, the patient not knowing of it. Moreover, it cures the fits of the falling sickness; but most especially it cures them that are afraid of water, or drink after they are bitten with a mad dog, if only a catamenious cloth be put under the cup. Besides, they report, that if catamenious persons shall walk, being nude, about the standing corn, they make all cankers, worms, beetles, flies, and all hurtful things, to fall off from the corn; but they must take heed that they do it before sun-rising, or else they will make the corn to wither. Also, they say, they are able to expel hail, tempests, and lightnings, more of which Pliny makes mention of. Know this, that they are a greater poison if they happen in the decrease of the Moon, and yet much greater if they happen betwixt the decrease and change of the Moon; but if they happen in the eclipse of the Moon or the Sun, they are an incurable poison. But they are of the greatest force of all when they happen in the first early years, even in the years of virginity, for if they do but touch the posts of the house there can no mischief take effect in it. Also, they say, that the threads of any garment touched therewith cannot be burnt, and if they be cast into the fire it will spread no further. Also, it is said, that the root of peony, being given with castor oil smeared over, using the catamenious cloth, cureth the falling sickness. Moreover, if the stomach of a hart be burnt or roasted, and to it be put a perfuming made with a catamenious cloth, it will make cross-bows useless for the killing of any game. The hairs of a catamenious person, put under compost, breed serpents; and, if they be burnt, will drive away serpents with their smell. So great a poisonous force is in them that they are poison to poisonous creatures.

There is, also, hippomanes, which amongst sorceries is not the least taken notice of, and it is a little venemous piece of flesh as big as a fig, and black, which is in the forehead of a colt newly foaled, which unless the mare herself presently eat, she will never after love her foal or let it suckle. And for this cause, they say, there is a most wonderful power in it to procure love, if it be powdered and drank in a cup with the blood of him that is in love. There is another sorcery of the same name, hippo-manes, a venemous humor of the mare in her mating season, of which Virgil makes mention when he sings:

Hence comes that poison which the Shepherds call
 Hippomanes, and from the Mares doth fall,
 The woeful bane which cruel stepdames use,
 And with a charme 'mongst pow'rful drugs infuse.
Of this doth Juvenal, the satirist, make mention:
Hippomanes, poysons that boyled are, and charmes
Are given to Sons in law, with such like harmes.

Apollonius, also, in his Argonautica, makes mention of the herb of Prometheus, which he saith groweth from corrupt blood dropping upon the earth, whilst the vulture was gnawing upon the liver of Prometheus upon the hill Caucasus. The flower of this herb, he saith, is like saffron, having a double stalk hanging out, one further than the other the length of a cubit; the root under the earth, as flesh newly cut, sends forth a blackish juice as it were of a beech, with which, saith he, if any one shall, after he hath performed his devotion to Proserpina, smear over his body, he cannot be hurt either with sword or fire. Also Saxo Gramaticus writes, that there was a certain man, called Froton, who had a garment which, when he had put on, was such he could not be hurt with the point or edge of any weapon. The civet cat also abounds with sorceries, for, as Pliny reports, the posts of a door being touched with her blood, the arts of jugglers and sorcerers are so invalid that the gods cannot be called up, and will by no means be persuaded to talk with them. Also, that they are anointed with the ashes of the ankle-bone of her left foot, being decocted with the blood of a weasel, shall become odious to all. The same, also, is done with the eye, being, decocted. Also, it is said, that the straight-gut is administered against the injustice and corruption of princes and great men in power, and for success of petitions, and to conduce to the ending of suits and controversies, if any one hath never so little of it about him; and that if it be bound unto the left arm, it is such a perfect charm that if any man do but look upon a woman, it will make her follow him presently; and that the skin of the civet cat's forehead doth withstand bewitchings. They say, also, that the blood of a basilisk, which they call the blood of Saturn, hath such great force in sorcery that it procures for him that carries it about him good success of his petitions from great men in power, and of his prayers from God, and also remedies of diseases, and grant of any privilege. They say, also, that a tyke, if it be pulled out of the left ear of a dog, and if be it is altogether black, hath great virtue in the prognosticating of life, for if the sick party shall answer him that brought it in, and who, standing at his feet, shall ask of him concerning his disease, there is certain hope of life; and that he shall die if he make no answer.

They say, also, that a stone that is bit with a mad dog hath power to cause discord, if it be put in drink, and that lie shall not be barked at by dogs that puts the tongue of a dog in his shoe under his great toe, especially if the herb of the same name, viz., hound's-tongue, be joined with it. And that a membrane of the secondines of a dog doth the same; and that dogs will shun him that hath a dog's heart. And Pliny reports that there is a red toad that lives in briers and brambles, and is full of sorceries and doth wonderful things, for the little bone which is in his left side, being cast into cold water, makes it presently very hot; by which also the rage of dogs is restrained, and their love is procured if it be put in their drink; and, if it be bound to any one, it stirreth up desire. On the contrary, the little bone which is on the right side makes hot water cold, and that it can never be hot again unless that be taken out; also it is said to cure quartans if it be bound to the sick in a snake's skin, as also all other fevers, and to restrain love and desire. And that the spleen and heart is an effectual remedy against the poisons of the said toad. Thus much Pliny writes. Also, it is said, that the sword with which a man is slain hath wonderful power in sorceries. For if the snaffle of the bridle, or spurs, be made of it, they say that with these any horse, though never so wild, may be tamed and gentled; and that if a horse should be shod with shoes made of it, he would be most swift and fleet, and never, though never so hard rode, tire. But yet they will that some certain characters and names should be written upon it. They say, also, if any man shall dip a sword, wherewith men were beheaded, in wine, and the sick drink thereof, he shall be cured of his quartan. They say, also, that a cup of liquor being made with the brains of a bear, and drank out of the skull, shall make him that drinks it be as fierce and as raging as a bear, and think himself to be changed into a bear, and judge all things he sees to be bears, and so to continue in that madness until the force of that draught shall be dissolved, no other distemper being all this while perceived in him.

CHAPTER XLIII. OF PERFUMES OR SUFFUMIGATIONS; THEIR MANNER AND POWER.

SOME suffumigations, also, or perfumings, that are proper to the Stars, are of great force for the opportune receiving of celestial gifts under the rays of the Stars, in as much as they do strongly work upon the air and breath. For our breath is very much changed by such kind of vapors, if both vapors be of another like. The air, also, being through the said vapors easily moved, or affected with the qualities of inferiors or those celestial, daily; and, quickly penetrating our breast and vitals, doth wonderfully reduce us to the like qualities. Wherefore, suffumigations are wont to be used by them that are about to soothsay or predict for to affect their fancy or conception; which suffumigations, indeed, being duly appropriated to any certain deities, do fit us to receive divine inspiration. So they say that fumes made with linseed, flea-bane seed, roots of violets, and parsley, doth make one to foresee things to come and doth conduce to prophesying. Let no man wonder how great things suffumigations can do in the air, especially when he shall with Porphyrius consider that by certain vapors, exhaling from proper suffumigations, airy spirits are presently raised, as also thunderings and lightnings, and such like things. As the liver of a chameleon, being burnt on top of the house, doth, as is manifest, raise showers and lightnings. In like manner the head and throat of the chameleon, if they be burnt with oaken wood, cause storms and lightnings. There are also suffumigations under opportune influences of the Stars that make the images of spirits forthwith appear in the air or elsewhere. So, they say, that if of coriander, smallage, henbane, and hemlock, be made a fume, that spirits will presently come together; hence they are called spirit's herbs. Also, it is said, that fume made of the root of the reedy herb sagapen, with the juice of hemlock and henbane, and the herb tapsus barbatus, red sanders, and black poppy, makes spirits and strange shapes appear; and if smallage be added to them, the fume chaseth away spirits from any place and destroys their visions. In like manner, a fume made of calamint, peony, mints, and palma christi, drives away all evil spirits and vain imaginations.

Moreover, it is said, that by certain fumes certain animals are gathered together and also put to flight, as Pliny mentions concerning the stone liparis, that with the fume thereof all beasts are called out. So the bones in the upper part of the throat of a hart, being burnt, gather all the serpents together; but the horn of the hart, being burnt, doth with its fume chase them all away. The same doth a fume of the feathers of peacocks. Also, the lungs of an ass, being burnt, puts all poisonous things to flight; the fume of the burnt hoof of a horse drives away mice; the same doth the hoof of a mule; with which, also, if it be the hoof of the left foot, flies are driven away. And, they say, if a house or any place be smoked with the gall of a cuttle-fish, made into a confection with red storax, roses, and lignum-aloes, or lignaloes, and if then there be some sea-water, or blood, cast into that place, the whole house will seem to be full of water or blood; and if some earth of plowed ground be cast there, the earth will seem to quake. Now, such kinds of vapors, we must conceive, do infect any body and infuse virtue into it, which Both continue long, even as any contagious or poisonous vapor of the pestilence, being kept for two years in the wall of a house infects the inhabitants, and as the contagion of pestilence, or leprosy, lying hid in a garment, doth long after infect him that wears it. Therefore, were certain suffumigations used to affect images, rings, and such like instruments of magic and hidden treasures, and, as Porphyrius saith, very effectually. So, they say, if any one shall hide gold or silver, or any other precious thing, the Moon being in conjunction with the Sun, and shall fume the hiding place with coriander, saffron, henbane, smallage, and black poppy, of each alike quantity, bruised together, and tempered with the juice of hemlock, that which is so hid shall never be found or taken away; and that spirits shall continually keep it, and if any one shall endeavor to take it away he shall be hurt by them and shall fall into a frenzy.

And Hermes saith that there is nothing like the fume of spermaceti for the raising of spirits. Wherefore, if a fume be made of that and lignum-aloes, red storax, pepper-wort, musk, and saffron, all tempered together, with the blood of a lapwing, it will quickly gather airy spirits together, and if it be used about the graves of the dead, it gathers together spirits and the ghosts of the dead.

So, as often as we direct any work to the Sun, we must make suffumigations with Solary things, and if to the Moon, with Lunary things, and so of the rest. And we must know that as there is a contrariety and enmity in stars and spirits, so also in suffumigations unto the same. So there is also a contrariety betwixt lignum aloes and sulphur, frankincense, and quicksilver; therefore, spirits that are raised by the fume of lignum aloes are allayed by the burning of sulphur. As Proclus gives an example of a spirit, which was wont to appear in the form of a lion, but, by the setting of a cock before it, vanished away because there is a contrariety betwixt a cock and a lion, and so the like consideration and practice is to be observed concerning such like things.

CHAPTER XLIV. THE COMPOSITION OF SOME FUMES APPROPRIATED TO THE PLANETS.

WE make a suffumigation for the Sun in this manner, viz., of saffron, ambergris, musk, lignum aloes, lignum balsam, the fruit of the laurel, cloves, myrrh, and frankincense; all which being bruised and mixt in such a proportion as may make a sweet odor, must be incorporated with the brain of an eagle, or the blood of a white cock, after the manner of pills or troches.

For the Moon we make a suffumigation of the head of a dried frog, the eyes of a bull, the seed of white poppy, frankincense, and camphor; which must be incorporated with catamenia, or the blood of a goose.

For Saturn, take black poppy seed, henbane, root of mandrake, the loadstone, and myrrh, and make them up with the brain of a cat or the blood of a bat.

For Jupiter, take the seed of ash, lignum aloes, storax, the gum benjamin or benzoin, the lazuli stone, and the tops of the feathers of a peacock; and incorporate them with the blood of a stork, or a swallow, or the brain of a hart.

For Mars, take euphorbium, bedellium, gum ammoniac, the roots of both hellebores, the loadstones, and a little sulphur; and incorporate them all with the brain of a hart, the blood of a man and the blood of a black cat.

For Venus, take musk, ambergris, lignum aloes, red roses and red coral, and make them up with the brain of sparrows and the blood of pigeons.

For Mercury, take mastic, frankincense, cloves, and the herb cinque-foil, and the stone achate, and incorporate them all with the brain of a fox or weasel, and the blood of a magpie.

Besides, to Saturn are appropriated for fumes all odoriferous roots, as pepper-wort root, etc., and the frankincense tree; to Jupiter, odoriferous fruits, as nutmegs and cloves; to Mars, all odoriferous wood, as sanders, cypress, lignum balsam and lignum aloes; to the Sun, all gums, frankincense, mastic, benjamin, storax, ladanum, ambergris and musk; to Venus, sweet flowers, as roses, violets, saffron, and such like; to Mercury, all the peels of wood and fruit, as cinnamon, lignum cassia, mace, citron or lemon peel, and bayberries, and whatsoever seeds are odoriferous; to the Moon, the leaves of all vegetables, as the leaf indum, and the leaves of the myrtle and bay-tree.

Know, also, that according to the opinion of the magicians, in every good matter, as love, good will, and the like, there must be a good fume, odoriferous and precious; and in every evil matter, as hatred, anger, misery, and the like, there must be a stinking fume, that is of no worth.

The twelve Signs, also, of the Zodiac have their proper fumes, as Aries hath myrrh; Taurus, pepper-wort; Gemini, mastic; Cancer, camphor; Leo, frankincense; Virgo, sanders; Libra, galbanum; Scorpio, opopanax; Sagittarius, lignum aloes; Capricornus, benjamin; Aquarius, euphorium; Pisces, red storax. But Hermes describes the most powerful fume to be that which is compounded of the Seven Aromatics, according to the powers of the Seven Planets--for it receives from Saturn, pepper-wort; from Jupiter, nutmeg; from Mars, lignum aloes; from the Sun, mastic; from Venus, saffron; from Mercury, cinnamon; and from the Moon, the myrtle.

CHAPTER XLV. OF COLLYRIES, UNCTIONS, LOVE-MEDICINES, AND THEIR VIRTUES.

MOREOVER, collyries and unguents, conveying the virtues of things natural and celestial to our spirit, can multiply, transmute, transfigure, and transform it accordingly, as also transpose those virtues which are in them into it; that so, it cannot act only upon its own body, but also upon that which is near it, and affect that by visible rays, charms, and by touching it with some like quality. For because our spirit is the subtile, pure, lucid, airy, and unctuous vapor of the blood, it is therefore fit to make collyries of the like vapors, which are more suitable to our spirit in substance, for then, by reason of their likeness, they do the more stir up, attract, and transform the spirit. The like virtues have certain ointments and other confections. Hence by the touch sometimes sickness, poisonings, and love is induced; some things, as the hands or garments, being anointed. Also by kisses, some things being held in the mouth, love is induced; as in Virgil we read that Venus prays Cupid

That when glad Dido hugs him in her lap
At royal feasts, crown'd with the cheering grape,
When she, embracing, shall sweet kisses give,
Inspire hid flame, with deadly bane deceive,
He would----

Now the sight, because it perceives more purely and clearly than the other senses, and fastening in us the marks of things more acutely and deeply, doth most of all and before others, agree with the phantastic spirit, as is apparent in dreams, when things seen do more often present themselves to us than things heard, or any thing coming under the other senses. Therefore, when collyries or eye-waters transform visual spirits, that spirit doth easily affect the imagination, which indeed being affected with divers species and forms, transmits the same by the spirit unto the outward sense of sight; by which occasion there is caused in it a perception of such species and forms in that manner, as if it were moved by external objects, that there seem to be seen terrible images and spirits and such like. So there are made collyries, making us forthwith to see the images of spirits in the air or elsewhere; as I know how to make of the gall of a man, and the eyes of a black cat, and of some other things. The like is made also of the blood of a lapwing, of a bat, and a goat; and, they say, if a smooth, shining piece of steel be smeared over with the juice of mug-wort, and made to fume, it will make invoked spirits to be seen in it. So, also, there are some suffumigations, or unctions, which make men speak in their sleep, to walk, and to do those things which are done by men that are awake; and sometimes to do those things which men that are awake cannot or dare not do. Some there are that make us to hear horrid or delectable sounds, and such like. And this is the cause why maniacal and melancholy men believe they see and hear those things without which their imagination doth only fancy within; hence they fear things not to be feared, and fall into wonderful and most false suspicions, and fly when none pursueth them; are also angry and contend, nobody being present, and fear where no fear is. Such like passions also can magical confections induce, by suffumigations, by collyries, by unguents, by potions, by poisons, by lamps and lights, by looking-glasses, by images, enchantments, charms, sounds and music. Also by divers rites, observations, ceremonies, religions and superstitions; all which shall be handled in their places. And not only by these kind of arts are passions, apparitions and images induced, but also things themselves, which are really changed and transfigured into divers forms, as the poet relates of Proteus, Periclimenus, Acheloas, and Merra, the daughter of Erisichthon. So, also, Circe changed the companions of Ulysses; and of old, in the sacrifices of Jupiter Lycaeus, the men that tasted of the inwards of the sacrifices were turned into wolves which, Pliny saith, befell a certain man called Demarchus. The same opinion was Austin of, for, he saith, whilst he was in Italy, he heard of some women that by giving sorceries in cheese to travelers, turned them into working cattle, and when they had done such work as they would have them, turned them into men again; and that this befell a certain priest called Prestantius. The Scriptures themselves testify that Pharao's sorceries turned their rods into serpents and water into blood, and did other such like things.

CHAPTER XLVI. OF NATURAL ALLIGATIONS AND SUSPENSIONS.

WHEN the Soul of the World by its virtue doth make all things that are naturally generated or artificially made to be fruitful, by infusing into them celestial properties for the working of some wonderful effects, then things themselves--not only when applied by suffumigations, or collyries, or ointments, or potions, or any other such like way, but also when they, being conveniently wrapped up, are bound to or hanged about the neck, or in any other way applied, although by never so easy a contact--do impress their virtue upon us. By these alligations, therefore, suspensions, wrappings up, applications, and contacts, the accidents of the body and mind are changed into sickness, health, boldness, fear, sadness, and joy, and the like. They render them that carry them gracious or terrible, acceptable or rejected, honored and beloved or hateful and abominable. Now these kind of passions are conceived to be by the above said to be infused, and not otherwise, like what is manifest in the grafting of trees, where the vital virtue is sent and communicated from the trunk to the twig grafted into it by way of contact and alligation. So in the female palm-tree, when she comes near to the male her boughs bend to the male, and are bowed, which, the gardeners seeing, bind ropes from the male to the female, which becomes straight again, as if she had by this connection of the rope received the virtue of the male. In like manner we see that the cramp-fish, or torpedo, being touched afar off with a long pole, doth presently stupefy the hand of him that toucheth it. And if any shall touch the sea-hare with his hand or stick will presently run out of his wits. Also, if the fish called stella, or star-fish, as they say, being fastened with the blood of a fox and a brass nail to a gate, evil medicines can do no hurt to any in such house. Also, it is said, that if a woman take a needle and beray it with dung, and then wrap it up in earth in which the carcass of a man was buried, and shall carry it about her in a cloth which was used at the funeral, that she shall be able to possess herself so long as she hath it about her.

Now, by these examples, we see how, by certain alligations of certain things, as also suspensions, or by a simple contact, or the connection or continuation of any thread, we may be able to receive some virtues thereby. It is necessary that we know the certain rule of Alligation and Suspension, and the manner which the Art requires, viz., that they be done under a certain and suitable Constellation, and that they be done with wire, or silken threads, with hair, or sinews of certain animals. And things that are to be wrapped up must be done in the leaves of herbs, or the skins of animals, or fine cloths, and the like, according to the suitableness of things--as, if you would procure the Solary virtue of any thing, this being wrapped up in bay leaves, or the skin of a lion, hang it about thy neck with a golden thread, or a silken thread of a yellow color, whilst the Sun rules in the heaven--so thou shalt be endued with the Solary virtue of that thing. But if thou dost desire the virtue of any Saturnine thing, thou shalt in like manner take that thing whilst Saturn rules, and wrap it in the skin of an ass, or in a cloth used at a funeral (especially if you desire it for sadness), and with a black thread hang it about thy neck. In like manner we must conceive of the rest.

CHAPTER XLVII. OF MAGICAL RINGS AND THEIR COMPOSITIONS.

RINGS, also, which were always much esteemed of by the ancients, when they are opportunely made, do in like manner impress their virtue upon us, in as much as they do affect the spirit of him that carries them with gladness or sadness, and render him courteous or terrible, bold or fearful, amiable or hateful; in as much as they do fortify us against sickness, poisons, enemies, evil spirits, and all manner of hurtful things, or, at least, will not suffer us to be kept under them. Now, the manner of making these kinds of Magical Rings is this, viz.; When any Star ascends fortunately, with the fortunate aspect or conjunction of the Moon, we must take a stone and herb that is under that Star, and make a ring of the metal that is suitable to this Star, and in it fasten the stone, putting the herb or root under it--not omitting the inscriptions of images, names and characters, as also the proper suffumigations; but we shall speak more of these in another place, where we shall treat of Images and Characters.

So we read in Philostratus Jarchus that a wise prince of the Indies bestowed seven rings made after this manner (marked with the virtues and names of the seven planets) to Apollonius; of which he wore every day of the week one thereof, distinguishing them in their order according to the name of the days, as is set forth by astrologers, viz., Sunday, the ring marked with the virtues and inscribed with the name and seal of the Sun, that planet which ruleth over Sunday and from which the day taketh its name; Monday, the ring of the virtues, seal and name of the Moon; Tuesday, that inscribed unto Mars; Wednesday, that unto Mercury; Thursday, that inscribed unto Jupiter; Friday, that unto Venus, and Saturday, that unto the planet Saturn, seeing as Saturday is the last day of the week and hath correspondence with the last end of life, and is ruled by Saturn which carries the sickle of death; and, it is said, that Apollonius, by the benefit of these seven magical rings, lived above one hundred and thirty years, as also that he always retained the beauty and vigor of his youth. In like manner Moses, the lawgiver and ruler of the Hebrews, being skilled in the Magic of the Egyptians, is said by Josephus to have made rings of love and oblivion. There was also, as saith Aristotle, amongst the Cireneans, a ring of Battus which could procure love and honor. We read also that Eudamus, a certain philosopher, made rings against the bites of serpents, bewitchings, and evil spirits. The same doth Josephus relate of Solomon. Also we read in Plato that Gygus, the king of Lydia, had a ring of wonderful and strange virtues, the seal of which, when he turned it toward the palm of his hand, rendered him invisible; nobody could see him, but he could see all things; and, by the opportunity of which ring, he deceived the queen and slew the king, his master, and killed whomsoever he thought stood in his way; and in these villainies no one could see him; and, at length, by the benefit of this ring he became king of Lydia himself.

CHAPTER XLVIII. OF THE VIRTUE OF PLACES, AND WHAT PLACES ARE SUITABLE TO EVERY STAR.

THERE be wonderful virtues of places accompanying them, either from things there placed, or by the influences of the Stars, or in any other way. For, as Pliny relates of a cuckoo, in what place any one doth first hear him, if his right foot-print be marked about and that place dug up, there will no fleas be bred in that place where it is scattered. So they say that the dust of the track of a snake, being gathered up and scattered amongst bees, makes them return to their hives. So, also, that the dust in which a mule hath rolled himself, being cast upon the body, doth mitigate the heat of passion; and that the dust wherein a hawk hath rolled herself, if it be bound to the body in a bright red cloth, cures the quartan. So doth the stone taken out of the nest of a swallow, as they say, presently relieve those that have the falling sickness, and being bound to the party, continually preserves them, especially if it be rolled in the blood or heart of a swallow. And it is reported that if any one shall cut a vein, being fasting, and shall go over a place where any one lately fell with the fit of a falling sickness, that he shall fall into the same disease. And Pliny reports that to fasten an iron nail in that place where he that fell with a fit of the falling sickness first did pitch his head, will free him from his disease. So they say that an herb, growing upon the head of any image, being gathered, and bound up in some part of one's garment with a red thread, shall presently allay the headache; and that any herb gathered out of the brooks or rivers before Sunrising, and no body seeing him that gathers it, shall cure the tertian if it be bound to the left arm, the sick party not knowing what is done.

Amongst places that are appropriated to the Stars, all stinking places, and dark, underground, religious, and mournful places, as church-yards, tombs, and houses not inhabited by men; and old, tottering, obscure, dreadful houses; and solitary dens, caves, and pits; also fish-ponds, standing pools, sewers, and such like, are appropriated to Saturn. Unto Jupiter are ascribed all privileged places, consistories of noblemen, tribunals, chairs, places for exercise, schools, and all beautiful and clean places, and those sprinkled with divers odors. To Mars, fiery and bloody places, furnaces, bakehouses, shambles, places of execution, and places where there have been great battles fought and slaughters made, and the like. To the Sun, light places, the serene air, kings' palaces and princes' courts, pulpits, theaters, thrones, and all kingly and magnificent places. To Venus, pleasant fountains, green meadows, flourishing gardens, garnished beds, stews, and, according to Orpheus, the sea, the seashore, baths, dancing places, and all places belonging to women. To Mercury, shops, schools, warehouses, exchanges for merchants, and the like. To the Moon, wildernesses, woods, rocks, hills, mountains, forests, fountains, waters, rivers, seas, seashores, ships, highways, groves, granaries for corn, and such like. On this account they that endeavor to procure love are wont to bury for a certain time the instruments of their art, whether they be rings, images, looking-glasses, or any other, or hide them in a stew house, so that they will contract some virtue under Venus, the same as those things that stand in stinking places become stinking, and those in an aromatical place become aromatic and of a sweet savor.

The four corners of the earth also pertain to this matter. Hence they that are to gather a Saturnine, Martial, or Jovial herb must look towards the East or South, partly because they desire to be oriental from the Sun, and partly because of their principal houses, viz.: Aquarius, Scorpio and Sagittarius are Southern Signs, so also are Capricornus and Pisces. But they that will gather a Venereal, Mercury or Lunary herb must look towards the West because they delight to be western, or else they must look towards the North because their principal houses--viz., Taurus, Gemini, Cancer, Virgo--are Northern Signs. So in any Solary work we must look not only towards the East and South whilst plucking it, but also towards the Solary body and light.

CHAPTER XLIX. OF LIGHT, COLORS, CANDLES AND LAMPS, AND TO WHAT STARS, HOUSES AND ELEMENTS SEVERAL COLORS ARE ASCRIBED.

LIGHT also is a quality that partakes much of form, and is a simple act, and also a representation of the understanding. It is first diffused from the Mind of God into all things; but in God the Father, the Father of Light, it is the first true light; then in the Son a beautiful, overflowing brightness, and in the Holy Ghost a burning brightness, exceeding all Intelligences; yea, as Dyonisius saith of Seraphims, in angels it is a shining intelligence diffused, an abundant joy beyond all bounds of reason, yet received in divers degrees, according to the nature of the Intelligence that receives it. Then it descends into the celestial bodies, where it becomes a store of life and an effectual propagation; even a visible splendor. In the fire it is a certain natural liveliness, infused into it by the heavens. And, lastly, in men, it is a clear course of reason, an innate knowledge of divine things, and the whole rational faculty; but this is manifold, either by reason of the disposition of the body or by reason of him who bestows it, who gives it to every one as he pleaseth. From thence it passeth to the fancy, yet above the senses, but only imaginable; and thence to the senses, especially to the sense of the eyes. In them light is a visible clearness; and is extended to other perspicuous bodies, in which it becomes a color and a shining beauty; but in dark bodies it is a certain beneficial and generative virtue, and penetrates to the very center where its beams, being collected into a small place, become a dark heat, tormenting and scorching, so that all things perceive the vigor of the light according to their capacity--and all light, joining to itself an enlivening heat, and, passing through all things, doth convey its qualities and virtues to all things. Great is the power of light to mar or make enchantments. So a sick man, uncovered against the Sun or the Moon, their rays become charged with the noxious qualities of the sickness and, penetrating, convey them into the body of another, and affect that with a quality of the same kind. So that from the sick should be covered deep from the light, lest its occult quality doth infect the well. This is the reason why Enchanters have a care to cover their enchantments with their shadow. So the civet cat makes all dogs dumb with the very touch of her shadow.

Also, there are made, artificially, some Lights, by lamps, torches, candles, and such like, of some certain thing and fluids, opportunely chosen, according to the rule of the Stars, and composed amongst themselves according to their congruity, which, when they be lighted, and shine alone, are wont to produce some wonderful and celestial effects, which men many times wonder at. So Pliny reports, out of Anaxilaus, of a poison of mares which, being lighted in torches, doth monstrously represent a sight of horses' heads. The like may be done with flies, which being duly tempered with wax, and lighted, make a strange sight of flies; and the skin of a serpent, lighted in a proper lamp, maketh serpents appear. They say that when grapes are in their flower, if any one shall bind a vial full of oil to them, and shall let it alone until they be ripe, and then the oil be put in a lamp and lighted, it makes grapes to be seen; and so with other fruits. If centaury be mixed with honey, and the blood of a lapwing, and be put in a lamp, they that stand about will look much larger than they are wont; and if it be lit in a clear night the Stars will seem to scatter one from another. Such force, also, is in the ink of the cuttle-fish that it, being put into a lamp, makes blackamoors appear. It is also reported that a candle, made of some Saturnine things, being lighted, if it be extinguished in the mouth of a man newly dead, will afterwards, as oft as it shines alone, bring a feeling of sadness and great fear upon them that stand about it. Of such like torches and lamps doth Hermes speak more of, also Plato and Chyrannides, and of the latter writers, Albertus, in a certain treatise of this particular thing.

Colors, also, are a class of lights, which, being duly mixed with things, are wont to expose such things to the influence of those Stars to which the colors are agreeable. And we shall afterwards speak of some colors which are the Lights of the Planets, by which even the natures of Fixed Stars themselves are understood, which also may be applied to the flames of lamps and candles. But in this place we shall relate how the colors of inferior mixed things are distributed to divers planets. All colors as black, lucid, earthy, leaden, or brown, have relation to Saturn. Sapphire and airy colors, and those which are always green, clear, purple, darkish, golden, or mixed with silver, belong to Jupiter. Red colors, and burning, fiery, flaming, violet, purple, bloody, and iron colors, resemble Mars. Golden, saffron, purple, and bright colors, resemble the Sun. But all white, fair, curious, green, ruddy, betwixt saffron and purple, resemble Venus, Mercury and the Moon. Moreover, amongst the Signs of the Zodiac, known as the Houses of the Heaven, the first and seventh hath the color white; the second and twelfth, green; the third and eleventh, saffron; the fourth and the tenth, red; the fifth and ninth, a honey color; and the sixth and eighth, black.

The Elements, also, have their colors, by which natural philosophers judge of the complexion and property of their nature. For an earthy color, caused of coldness and dryness, is brown, and black, and manifests black choler and a Saturnine nature. Blue, tending towards whiteness, doth denote phlegm.

For cold makes white; moisture and dryness makes black. Reddish color shews blood; but fiery, flaming, burning hot, shews choler, which, by reason of its subtilty and aptness to mix with others, doth cause divers colors more; for if it be mixed with blood, and blood be most predominant, it makes a florid red; if choler predominate, it makes a reddish color: if there be an equal mixtion, it makes a sad red. But if adust choler be mixed with blood it makes a hempen color; and red, if blood predominate; and somewhat red if choler prevail; but if it be mixed with a melancholy humor it makes a black color; but with melancholy and phlegm together, in an equal proportion, it makes a hempen color. If phlegm abound, a mud color; if melancholy, a bluish; but if it be mixed with phlegm alone, in an equal proportion, it makes a citron color; if unequally, a pale or palish. Now, all colors are more prevalent when they be in silk, or in metals, or in perspicuous substances, or in precious stones, and in those things which resemble celestial bodies in color, especially in living things.

CHAPTER L. OF FASCINATION, AND THE ART THEREOF.

FASCINATION is a binding, which comes from the spirit of the witch, through the eyes of him that is so bewitched, and entering to his heart. Now the instrument of fascination is the spirit, viz., a certain pure, lucid, subtile vapor, generated of the purer blood by the heat of the heart. This doth always send forth, through the eyes, rays like to itself. Those rays, being sent forth, do carry with them a spiritual vapor, and that vapor a blood (as it appears in swollen and red eyes), whose rays, being sent forth to the eyes of him that looks upon them, carry the vapor of the corrupt blood together with itself; by the contagion of which it doth infect the eyes of the beholder with the like disease. So the eye, being opened and intent upon any one with a strong imagination, doth dart its beams (which are the vehiculum of the spirit) into the eyes of him that is opposite to him; which tender spirit strikes the eyes of him that is bewitched, being stirred up from the heart of him that strikes, and possesseth the breast of him that is stricken, wounds his heart and infects his spirit. Whence Apuleius saith, "Thy eyes, sliding down through my eyes into mine inward breast, stir up a most vehement burning in my marrow." Know, then, that men are most bewitched when, with often beholding, they direct the edge of their sight to the edge of the sight of those that bewitch them; and when their eyes are reciprocally intent one upon the other, and when rays are joined to rays and lights to lights, the spirit of the one is joined to the spirit of the other and fixeth its sparks. So are strong ligations made, and so most vehement loves are inflamed with only the rays of the eyes; even with a certain sudden looking on, as if it were with a dart or stroke, penetrating the whole body, whence then the spirit and amorous blood, being thus wounded, are carried forth upon the lover and enchanter, no otherwise than the blood and spirit of the vengeance of him that is slain are upon him that slays him. Whence Lucretius sang concerning those amorous bewitchings

The body smitten is, but yet the mind
 Is wounded with the darts of Cupid blind.
All parts do Sympathize i' th' wound, but know
 The blood appears in that which had the blow.

So, great is the power of fascination, especially when the vapors of the eyes are subservient to the affection. Therefore witches use collyries, ointments, alligations, and such like, to affect and corroborate the spirit in this or that manner. To procure love they use venereal collyries, as hippomanes, the blood of doves, or sparrows, and such like. To induce fear, they use martial collyries, as of the eyes of wolves, the civet cat, and the like. To procure misery or sickness, they use Saturnine things, and so of the rest.

CHAPTER LI. OF CERTAIN OBSERVATIONS, PRODUCING WONDERFUL VIRTUES.

THEY say that certain acts and observations have a certain power of natural things; that they believe diseases may be expelled, or brought thus and thus. So they say that quartanes may be driven away if the parings of the nails of the sick be bound to the neck of a live eel, in a linen cloth, and she be let go into the water. And Pliny saith that the parings of a sick man's nails of his feet and hands being mixed with wax, cure the quartan, tertian, and quotidian ague; and if they be before Sunrising fastened to another man's gate, will cure such like diseases. In like manner, let all the parings of the nails be put into the caves of ants, and the first ant that begins to draw at the parings must be taken and bound to the neck of the sick, and by this means will the disease be cured. They say that by wood, stricken with lightning, and cast behind the back with one's hands, any disease may be removed; and, in quartanes, a piece of a nail from a gibbet, wrapped up in wool, and hung about the neck, cures them; also, a rope doth the like that is taken from a gallows and hid under ground so that the Sun cannot reach it. The throat of him that hath a hard swelling, or imposthume, being touched with the hand of him that died by an immature death, will be cured thereby. They say, also, that a woman is presently eased of her hard labor if any one shall put into her bed a stone or dart with which a boar or a bear or man hath been killed with one blow. The same doth a spear that is pulled out of the body of a man, if it shall not first touch the ground; also, they say, that arrows, pulled out of the body of a man, if they have not touched the earth, taken and stealthily placed under any one lying down, will procure love. The falling sickness is cured by meat made of the flesh of a wild beast, slain in the same manner as a man is slain. A man's eyes that are washed three times with the water wherein he hath washed his feet shall never be sore or blear. It is said that some do cure diseases of the groin with thread taken out of a weaver's loom and tying into it seven or nine knots, the name of some widow being named at every knot. The spleen of cattle, extended upon painful spleens, cures them if he that applies it saith that he is applying a medicine to the spleen to cure and ease it. After this, they say, the patient must be shut into a sleeping room, the door being sealed up with a ring, and some verse be repeated over nineteen times. The water of a green lizard cures the same disease if it be hanged up in a vessel before the patient's bed-chamber so that he may, as he passes in and out, touch it with his hand. And a little frog climbing up a tree, if any one shall spit in his mouth, and then let him escape, is said to cure the cough. It is a wonderful thing, but easy to experience, that Pliny speaks of, that if any one shall be sorry for any blow that he hath given another, afar off or nigh at hand, if he shall presently spit into the middle of that hand with which he gave the blow, the party that was smitten shall presently be freed from pain. This hath been approved of in a four-footed beast that hath been sorely hurt. Some there are that aggravate the blow before they give it. In like manner, spittle carried in the hand, or to spit in the shoe of the right foot before it be put on, is good when any one passeth through a dangerous place. They say that wolves will not come to a field if one of them be taken and his blood let by little and little out of his legs, being unbroken, with a knife, and sprinkled about the outside of the field, and he himself be buried in that place from whence he was first drawn. The Methanenses, citizens of Trezenium, accounted it as a present remedy for preserving of vines from the wrong of the southern wind, having always found it by most certain experience, if, whilst the wind blows, a white cock should be pulled to pieces in the middle by two men, both of whom, each keeping his part, must walk each way around the vineyard, until both meet in the place from whence they began their circuit, and must in that place bury the pieces of the cock. Also, if any one shall hold a viper over a vapor with a staff, he shall prophesy, and that the staff wherewith a snake was beaten is good against female diseases. These things Pliny recites. It is said that in gathering roots and herbs we must draw three circles round about them first, with a sword, and then dig them up, meanwhile taking heed of any contrary wind. Also they say, that if any one shall measure a dead man with a rope, first from the elbow to the biggest finger, then from the shoulder to the same finger, and afterwards from the head to the feet, making thrice those mensurations; if any one afterwards shall be measured with the same rope, in the same manner, he shall not prosper, but be unfortunate and fall into misery and sadness. Albertus of Chyrannis saith, that if any woman hath enchanted thee to love her, take the gown she sleepeth in out of doors and spit through the right sleeve thereof, when the enchantment will be quitted. And Pliny saith, that to sit by women far with child, or when a medicine is given to any one of them, the fingers being joined together like the teeth of a comb, is a charm; so much the more if the hands be joined about one or both knees. Also, to sit cross legged is sorcery; therefore it was forbidden to be done in the counsels of princes and rulers, as a thing which hindered all acts. And, it is said, if any one shall stand before a man's chamber door, and call to him by name and the man answer, if then he fasten a knife or needle on the door, the edge or point being downward, and break it, he that be in the room shall be unable of his intention so long as those things shall be there.

CHAPTER LII. OF THE COUNTENANCE AND GESTURE, THE HABIT AND THE FIGURE OF THE BODY, AND TO WHAT STARS ANY OF THESE DO ANSWER--WHENCE PHYSIOGNOMY, AND METOPOSCOPY, AND CHIROMANCY, ARTS OF DIVINATION, HAVE THEIR GROUNDS.

THE countenance, gesture, motion, setting and figure of the body, being accidental to us, conduce to the receiving of celestial gifts and expose us to the superior bodies, which produce certain effects in us, like unto the effects following the methods of gathering hellebore, which, if thou pullest the leaf upward when gathering it, draws the humors upward and causeth vomiting; if downward, it causeth purging, drawing the humor downward.

How much also the countenance and gesture of one person doth affect the sight, imagination and spirit of another no man is ignorant. So they that are parents discover those impressions in their children of their previous conditions, and that which they did then do, form and imagine. So a mild and cheerful countenance of a prince in the city makes the people joyful; but if it be fierce or sad doth terrify them. So the gesture and countenance of any one lamenting, doth easily move to pity. So the shape of an amiable person doth easily excite to friendship. Thou must know that such like gestures and figures as harmonies of the body, do expose it no otherwise to the celestials, than odors, and the spirit of a medicine, and internal passions, also, do the soul. For as medicines and passions of the mind are by certain dispositions of the heaven increased, so also the gesture and motions of the body do get an efficacy by certain influences of the heavens. For there are gestures resembling Saturn which are melancholy and sad, as are beating of the breast or striking of the head; also such as are religious, as the bowing of the knee, and a fixed look downwards, as of one praying; also weeping, and such like, as are used by the austere and Saturnine man; such an one as a satirist describes:

With hang'd down head, with eyes fixed to the ground,
 His raging words bites in, and muttering sound
 He doth express with pouting lips.

A cheerful and honest countenance, a worshipful or noble gesture or bearing, clapping of the hands as of one rejoicing and praising, and the bending of the knee with the head lifted up, as of one that is worshiping, are ascribed to Jupiter.

A sour, fierce, cruel, angry, rough countenance and gesture are ascribed to Mars.

Solary are honorable and courageous gestures and countenances; also, walking abroad, a bending of the knee, as of one honoring a king with one knee bent.

Those under Venus are dances, embraces, laughters, and those of an amiable and cheerful countenance.

Those Mercurial are inconstant, quick, variable and such like gestures and countenances.

Those Lunary, or under the Moon, are such as are movable, poisonous, and childish and the like.

As we have spoken above of gestures so, also, are the shapes of men distinct, as follows:

Saturn bespeaks a man to be of a black and yellowish color, lean, crooked, of a rough skin, great veins, the body covered with hair, little eyes, of a frowning forehead, a thin beard, great lips, eyes intent upon the ground, of a heavy gait, striking his feet together as he walks, crafty, witty, a seducer and murderous.

Jupiter signifies a man to be of a pale color, darkish red, a handsome body, good stature, bold, of great eyes (not black altogether) with large pupils, short nostrils not equal, great teeth before, curled hair, of good disposition and manners.

Mars makes a man red, with red hair, a round face, yellowish eyes, of a terrible and sharp look, jocund, bold, proud and crafty.

The Sun makes a man of a tawny color, betwixt yellow and black dashed with red, of a short stature yet of a handsome body, without much hair and curly, of yellow eyes, wise, faithful and desirous of praise.

Venus signifies a man to be tending towards blackness, but more white, with a mixture of red, a handsome body, a fair and round face, fair hair, fair eyes, the blackness whereof is more intense, of good manners and honest love; also kind, patient and jocund.

Mercury signifies a man not much white, or black, of a long face, high forehead, fair eyes, not black, to have a straight and long nose, thin beard, long fingers, to be ingenious, a subtile inquisitor, a turncoat, and subject to many fortunes.

The Moon signifies a man to be in color white, mixed with a little red; of a fair stature, a round face, with some marks in it; eyes not fully black, frowning forehead, and kind, gentle and sociable.

The Signs, also, and the faces of Signs, have their figures and shapes which, he that would know, must seek them out in books of Astrology. Lastly, upon these figures and gestures, both Physiognomy and Metoposcopy, arts of divination, do depend; also Chiromancy, foretelling future events, not as causes but as signs, through like effects, caused by the same cause. And although these divers kinds of divinations may seem to be done by inferior and weak signs, yet the judgments of them are not to be slighted or condemned when prognostication is made by them, not out of superstition but by reason of the harmonical correspondency of all the parts of the body. Whosoever, therefore, doth the more exactly imitate the celestial bodies, either in nature, study, action, motion, gesture, countenance, passions of the mind, and opportunity of the season, is so much the more like to the heavenly bodies and can receive larger gifts from them.

CHAPTER LIII. OF DIVINATIONS, AND THE KINDS THEREOF.

THERE are some other kinds of divinations, depending upon natural causes, which are known to every one in his art and experience to be in divers things, by which physicians, husbandmen, shepherds, mariners, and others, do prognosticate out of the probable signs of every kind of divination. Many of these kinds of divination Aristotle made mention of in his book of Times, amongst which Auguria and Auspicia are the chiefest, which were in former time in such esteem amongst the Romans that they would do nothing that did belong to private or public business without the counsel of the Augures. Cicero in his Book of Divinations largely declares that the people of Tuscia would do nothing without this art. Now, there are divers kinds of Auspicias, for some are called Pedestria (i. e.), which are taken from four-footed beasts; some are called Auguria, which are taken from birds; some are Celestial, which are taken from thunderings and lightnings; some are called Caduca (i. e.), when any fell in the temple, or elsewhere; some were sacred, which were taken from sacrifices; some of these were called Piacula, and sad Auspicia, as when a sacrifice escaped from the altar, or, being smitten, made a bellowing, or fell upon another part of his body than he should. To these is added Exauguration, viz., when the rod fell out of the hand of the Augure with which it was the custom to view and take notice of the Auspicium.

Michael Scotus makes mention of twelve kinds of Auguries, viz., six on the right hand, the names of which, he saith, are Fernova, Fervetus, Confert, Emponenthem, Sonnasarnova, and Sonnasarvetus; and six on the left hand, the names of which are Confernova, Confervetus, Viaram, Herrenam, Scassarnova, and Scassarvetus. Expounding their names, he saith:

Fernova is an augury when thou goest out of thy house to do any business, and in going thou see a man or a bird going or flying, so that either of them set himself before thee upon thy left hand, that is a good signification in reference to thy business.

Fervetus is an augury when thou shalt go out of thy house to do any business, and in going thou find or see a bird or a man resting himself before thee on the left side of thee, that is an ill sign concerning thy business.

Viaram is an augury when a man or a bird in his journey, or flying, pass before thee, coming from the right side of thee, and, bending toward the left, go out of thy sight, that is a good sign concerning thy business.

Confernova is an augury when thou dost first find a man or a bird going or flying, and then rest himself before thee on thy right side, thou seeing of it, that is a good sign concerning thy business.

Confervetus is an augury when first thou find or see a man or a bird bending from thy right side, it is an ill sign concerning thy business.

Scimasarnova or Sonnasarnova is when a man or a bird comes behind thee and outgoeth thee, but before he comes at thee he rests, thou seeing of him on thy right side, it is to thee a good sign.

Scimasarvetus or Sonnasarvetus is when thou see a man or bird behind thee, but before he comes to thee he rests in that place, thou seeing of it, is a good sign.

Confert is an augury when a man or bird in journeying or flying shall pass behind thee, coming from the left side of thee, and, bending toward thy right, pass out of thy sight, and is an evil sign concerning thy business.

Scassarvetus is when thou see a man or a bird pass by thee, and resting in a place on thy left side, is an evil sign to thee.

Scassarnova is when thou see a man or a bird pass by thee, and resting in a place on thy right side, is an augury of good to thee.

Emponenthem is when a man or a bird, coming from thy left side, and passing to thy right, goeth out of thy sight without resting, and is a good sign.

Hartena or Herrenam is an augury that, if a man or a bird coming from thy right hand, shall pass behind thy back to thy left, and thou shall see him resting anywhere, this is in evil sign.

The ancients did also prognosticate from sneezings, of which Homer in the seventeenth book of his poem of the Odyssey makes mention, because they,

thought that they proceeded from a sacred place, viz., the head, in which the intellect is vigorous and operative. Whence, also, whatsoever speech came into the breast or mind of a man rising in the morning, unawares, is said to be some presage and an augury.

CHAPTER LIV. OF DIVERS CERTAIN ANIMALS, AND OTHER THINGS, WHICH HAVE A SIGNIFICATION IN AUGURIES.

ALL the Auspicia, or auspices, which first happen in the beginning of any enterprise are to be taken notice of. As, if in the beginning of thy work thou shalt perceive that rats have gnawn thy garments, desist from thy undertakings. If going forth thou shalt stumble at the threshhold, or if in the way thou shalt dash thy foot against any thing, forbear thy journey. If any ill omen happen in the beginning of thy business, put off thy undertakings, lest thy intentions be wholly frustrated, or accomplished to no purpose, but expect and wait for a fortunate hour for the dispatching of thy affairs with a better omen. We see that many animals are, by a natural power im-bred in them, prophetical. Doth not the cock by his crowing diligently tell you the hours of the night and morning, and, with his wings spread forth, chase away the lion? Many birds, with their singing and chattering, and flies, by their sharp pricking, foretell rain; and dolphins, by their often leaping above the water, warn of tempests. It would be too long to relate all the passages which the Phrygians, Cilicians, Arabians, Umbrians, Tuscians, and other peoples, which follow the auguries, have learned by birds. These they have proved by many experiments and examples. For in all things the Oracles of things to come are hid, but those are the chiefest which omenal birds shall foretell. These are those which the poets relate were turned from men into birds. Therefore, what the daw declares, hearken unto and mark, observing her setting as she sits; and her manner of flying, whether on the right hand or left; whether clamorous or silent; whether she goes before or follows after; whether she waits for the approach of him that passeth by, or flies from him, and which way she goes. All these things must be diligently observed. Arus Apollo saith in his Hieroglyphics that daws that are twins signify marriage, because this bird brings forth two eggs, out of which male and female must be brought forth; but if, which seldom happens, two males be generated, or two females, the males will not go with any other females, nor females with any other males, but will always live without a mate, and solitary. Therefore they that meet a single daw, divine thereby that they shall live a single life. The same also doth a black hen pigeon betoken, for after the death of her mate, she always lives single. Thou shall, also, as carefully observe crows, which are as significant as daws, yea, and in greater matters. It was Epictetus the Stoics' philosopher's judgment, who was a sage author, that if a crow did croak over against any one, it did betoken some evil, either to his body, fortune, honor, wife, or children. Then thou shall take heed to swans, who foreknow the secrets of the waters, for their cheerfulness doth presage happy events not only to mariners, but all other travelers, unless they be overcome by the coming over of a stronger bird, as of an eagle, who, by the most potent majesty of her sovereignty, makes null the predictions of all other birds if she speaks to the contrary; for she flies higher than all other birds, and is of more acute sight, and is never excluded from the secrets of Jupiter; she portends advancement and victory, but by blood, because she drinks no water but blood. An eagle flying over the Locresians, fighting against the Crotoniensians, gave them victory; an eagle setting herself unawares upon the target of Hiero, going forth to the first war, betokened that he should be king. Two eagles sitting all day upon the house at the birth of Alexander, of Macedonia, did portend to him an omen of two kingdoms, viz., Asia and Europe. An eagle, also, taking off the hat of Lucias Tarquinius Priscus, son to Demarathus the Corinthian (and, by reason of some discord, being come into Hetraria and going to Rome) and then flying high with it, and afterwards putting it upon his head again, did portend to him the kingdom of the Romans. Vultures signify difficulty, hardness, and ravenousness, which was verified in the beginning of the building of cities. Also they fortell the places of slaughter, coming seven days beforehand; and because they have most respect to that place where the greatest slaughter shall be, as if they gaped after the greatest number of the slain, therefore the ancient kings were wont to send out spies to take notice what place the vultures had most respect to. The phoenix promiseth singular good success, which being seen anew, Rome was built very auspiciously. The pelican because she hazards herself for her young, signifies that a man should, out of the zeal of his love, undergo much hardship. The painted bird gave the name to the city of Pictavia, and foreshowed the lenity of that people by its color and voice. The heron is an augury of hard things. The stork also is a bird of concord and makes concord. Cranes gives us notice of the treachery of enemies. The bird cacupha betokens gratitude, for she alone doth express love to her dam, being spent with old age. On the contrary, the hippopotamus, that kills his dam, doth betoken ingratitude for good turns, also injustice. The bird origis is most envious, and betokens envy. Amongst the smaller birds, the pie is talkative and foretells guests. The bird albanellus flying by anyone, it from the left to the right, betokens cheerfulness of entertainment; if contrariwise, betokens the contrary. The screech owl is always unlucky, so also is the horn owl, who, because she goes to her young by night, unawares, as death comes unawares, is therefore said to foretell death; yet, sometimes, because she is not blind in the dark of the night, doth betoken diligence and watchfulness, which she made good when she sat upon the spear of Hiero. And Dido, when she saw the unlucky owl, pitied Aeneas, whence the poet sang:

The Owl, sitting on top of the house alone,
 Sends forth her sad complaints with mournful tone.
And in another place,
The slothful Owl by mortals is esteemed
 A fatal omen--

The same bird sang in the capitol when the Roman affairs were low at Numantia and when Fregelia was pulled down for a conspiracy made against the Romans. Almadel says that owls and night-ravens, when they turn aside to strange countries, or houses, betoken the death of the men of that country and those houses, for those birds are delighted with dead carcasses and perceive them beforehand. For men that are dying have a near affinity with dead carcasses. The hawk is also a foreteller of contention, as Naso sings:

We hate the Hawk, because that arms amongst
 She always lives--

Lelius, the embassador of Pompey, was slain in Spain, amongst the purveyors, which misfortune, a hawk flying over the head, is said to foretell. And Almadel saith that these kinds of birds fighting amongst themselves, signify the change of a kingdom; but if birds of another kind shall fight with them and are never seen to come together again, it portends a new condition and state of that country. Also, little birds, by their coming to or departing from, foreshew that a family shall be increased or lessened; and their flight, by how much the more serene it is, by so much the more laudable shall the change be. Whence did Melampus, the Augure, conjecture at the slaughter of the Greeks by the flight of little birds, when he saith:

"Thou see now that no bird takes his flight in fair weather." Swallows, because when they are dying they provide a place of safety for their young, do portend a great patrimony or legacy after the death of friends. A bat, meeting any one running away, signifies an evasion; for, although she have no wings, yet she flies. A sparrow is a bad omen to one that runs away, for she flies from the hawk and makes haste to the owl, where she is in as great danger; yet in love she is fortunate, for being stirred up with affection she seeks her consort hourly. Bees are a good omen to kings, for they signify an obsequious people. Flies signify importunity and impudence because being oftentimes driven away they do continually return. Also domestic birds are not without some auguries, for cocks, by their crowing, promote hope, and the journey of him that is undertaking it. Moreover, Livia, the mother of Tiberius, when she was great with him, took a hen's egg and hatched it in her bosom, and at length came forth a cock chick with a great comb, which the auguries interpreted that the child that should be born of her should be a king. And Cicero writes that at Thebais, cocks, by their crowing all night, did presage that the Baeotians would obtain victory against the Lacedaemonians, and the reason is according to the augury's interpretations because that bird when he is beaten is silent, but when he himself hath overcome, crows. In like manner, also, omens of events are taken from beasts. For the meeting of a weasel is ominous; also, the meeting of a hare is an ill omen to a traveler, unless she be taken. A mule also is bad because barren. A hog is pernicious, for such is his nature, and therefore signifies pernicious men. A horse betokens quarrelings and fightings, whence Anchises, seeing of white horses, cries out in Virgil:

With war are Horses arm'd, yea, threaten war.

But when they are joined together in a chariot, because they draw with an equal yoke, they signify that peace is to be hoped for. An ass is an unprofitable creature, yet did Marius good, who, when he was pronounced an enemy to his country, saw an ass disdaining provender that was offered to him, and running to the water, by which augury he, supposing he saw a way of safety showed to him, entreated the aid of his friends that they would convey him to the sea, which being granted, he was set into a little ship, and so escaped the threats of Silla the conqueror. If the foal of an ass meet any one going to an augury, he signifies labor, patience and hinderances. A wolf meeting any one is a good sign, the effect whereof was seen in Hiero of Sicilia, from whom a wolf, snatching away a book whilst he was at school, confirmed to him the success of the kingdom, but yet the wolf makes him speechless whom he sees first. A wolf rent in pieces a watchman of P. Africanus and C. Fulvius at Minturn, when the Roman army was overcome by the fugitives in Sicilia. He signifies perfidious men, such as you can give no credit to, which was known in the progeny of Romans. For the faith which they long since sucked from their mother, the wolf, and kept to themselves from the beginning, as by a certain law of nature, passed over to their posterity. To meet a lion, seeing he is amongst animals the strongest and striking terror into all the rest, is good. But for a woman to meet a lioness is bad, because she hinders conception, for a lioness brings forth but once. To meet sheep and goats is good. It is read in the Ostentarian of the Tuscians, if this animal shall wear any unusual color, it portends to the emperor plenty of all things, together with much happiness. Whence Virgil to Pollio sings thus:

But, in the meadows, Rams shall scarlet bear,
And changing, sometimes golden fleeces wear.

It is good also to meet oxen treading out corn, but better to meet them plowing, which although breaking the way, hinder thy journey, yet by the favor of their Auspicium will recompense thee again. A dog in a journey is fortunate, because Cyrus, being cast into the woods, was nourished by a dog until he came to the kingdom; which, also, the angel, companion of Tobit, did not scorn as a companion. The castor, because he biteth himself sorely, so as to be seen by hunters, is an ill omen and portends that a man will injure himself. Also, amongst small animals, mice signify danger, for the same day that they did gnaw gold in the capitol, both the consuls were intercepted by Hannibal by way of ambush, near Tarentum. The locust making a stand in any place, or burning the place, hinders one from their wishes and is an ill omen; and on the contrary the grasshopper promotes a journey and foretells a good event of things. The spider weaving a line downwards, is said to signify hope of money to come. Also the ants, because they know how to provide for themselves, and to prepare safe nests for themselves, portend security and riches, and a great army. Hence, when the ants had devoured a tame dragon of Tiberius Caesar, it was advised that he should take heed of the tumult of a multitude. If a snake meet thee, take heed of an ill-tongued enemy; for this creature hath no power but in his mouth. A snake creeping into the palace of Tiberius, portended his fall. Two snakes were found in the bed of Sempronius Gracchus, wherefore a soothsayer told him, if he would let the male or the female escape, either he or his wife would shortly die; and he, preferring the life of his wife, killed the male and let the female go, and within a few days he died. So a viper signifies lewd women and wicked children; and an eel signifies a man displeased with everybody, for she lives apart from all other fishes, nor is ever found in the company of any. But, amongst all Auguries and Omens, there is none more effectual and potent than man himself, and none that doth signify the truth more clearly. Thou shalt, therefore, diligently note and observe the condition of the man that meeteth thee, his age, profession, station, stature, gesture, motion, exercise, complexion, habit, name, words, speech, and all such like things. For seeing there are in all other animals so many discoveries of presages, without all question these are more efficacious and clear which are infused into man's soul; which Tully himself testifies, saying, that there is a certain Auspicium naturally in men's souls of their eternity, for the knowing of the courses and causes of things. In the foundation of the city of Rome the head of a man was found with his whole face, which did presage the greatness of the empire, and gave the name to the Mountain of the Capitol. The Brutian soldiers fighting against Octavius and Antonius, found an Aethiopian in the gate of their castle, and though they slew him as a presage of ill success, yet they were unfortunate in battle, and both their generals, Brutus and Cassius, were slain.

The meeting of monks is commonly accounted an ill omen, and so much the rather if it be early in the morning, because these kind of men live for the most by the sudden death of men, as vultures do by slaughters.

CHAPTER LV. HOW AUSPICIAS ARE VERIFIED BY THE LIGHT OF NATURAL INSTINCT, AND OF SOME RULES OF FINDING IT OUT.

and Auguria, which foretell things to come by animals and birds, Orpheus, the divine, himself, as we read, did teach and show first of all, which afterwards were had in great esteem with all nations. Now they are verified by the light of natural instinct, as if from this some lights of divination may descend upon four-footed beasts, those winged, and other creatures, by which they are able to presage to us of the events of things; which Virgil seems to be sensible of when he sings:
Nor think I Heaven on them such knowledge states,
 Nor that their prudence is above the Fates.
Now, this Instinct of Nature, as saith William of Paris, is more sublime than all human apprehension, and very near, and most like to prophecy. By this instinct there is a certain wonderful light of divination in some animals naturally, as is manifested in some dogs, who know thieves by this instinct and men that are hid, unknown both to themselves and men, and find them out and apprehend them, falling upon them with a full mouth. By the like instinct vultures foresee future slaughters in battles, and gather together into places where they shall be, as if they foresaw the flesh of dead carcasses. By the same instinct partridges know their dam, whom they never saw, and leave the partridge which stole away her dam's eggs and sate upon them. By the same instinct, also, certain hurtful and terrible things are perceived, the soul being ignorant of them, whence terror and horror ceaseth when men think nothing of these things. So a thief, lying hid in a house, although no one knows or thinks of his being there, strikes fear and terror and a troublesomeness of mind into the inhabitants of that house, although, haply, not of all, because the brightness of this instinct is not common to all

men, yet possessed of some of them. So an evil person, being hid in some large building, is sometimes perceived to be there by some one that is altogether ignorant of their being there. It is mentioned in history that Heraiscus, a certain Egyptian, a man of a divine nature, could discern evil persons, not only by his eyes but also by their voice, he hearing them afar off, and thereupon did fall into a most grievous headache. William of Paris also makes mention of a certain woman in his time that, by the same instinct, perceived a man whom she loved coming two miles off. He relates, also, that in his time a certain stork was convicted of unchastity by the smell of the male, who, being judged guilty by a multitude of storks whom the male gathered together, discovering to them the fault of his mate, was, her feathers being pulled off, torn in pieces by them. The same doth Varro, Aristotle and Pliny relate concerning horses. And Pliny makes mention of a certain serpent, called the asp, that did such a like thing, for she, coming to a certain man's table in Egypt, was there daily fed, and she, having brought forth some young, by one of which a son of her host was killed, after she knew of it, killed that young one, and would never return to that house any more. Now, by these examples, you see how the lights of presage may descend upon some animals, as signs, or marks of things, and are set in their gesture, motion, voice, flying, going, meat, color, and such like. For, according to the doctrine of the Platonists, there is a certain power put into inferior things by which, for the most part, they agree with the superiors; whence also the tacit consents of animals seem to agree with divine bodies, and their bodies and affections to be affected with their powers, by the name of which they are ascribed to the deities. We must consider, therefore, what animals are Saturnine, what are Jovial and what Marital, and so of the rest; and, according to their properties, to draw forth their presages; so those birds which resemble Saturn and Mars, are all of them called terrible and deadly, as the screech owl, the hawlet, and others which we have mentioned before; also the horn owl, because she is a Saturnine, solitary bird, also nightly, and is reputed to be most unfortunately ominous, of which the poet saith:

The ugly Owl, which no bird well resents,
 Foretells misfortunes and most sad events.

But the swan is a delicious bird, under Venus, and dedicated to Phoebus, and is said to be most happy in her presages, especially in the auspices of mariners, for she is never drowned in water, whence Ovid Sings:

Most happy is the cheerful, singing Swan In her presages----

There are also some birds that presage with their mouth and singing, as the crow, pie, and daw, whence Virgil:

   This did foreshow
 Oft from the hollow holm that ominous Crow.

Now, the birds that portend future things by their flying are, viz., buzzards, the bone-breakers, vultures, eagles, cranes, swans, and the like, for they are to be considered in their flying, whether they fly slowly or swiftly; whether to the right hand or to the left; how many fly together. Upon this account, if cranes fly apace, they signify a tempest; and, when slowly, fair weather. When two eagles fly together, they are said to portend evil, because two is a number of confusion. In like manner thou shalt enquire into the reason of the rest, as this is shown by number. Moreover, it belongs to an artist to observe a similitude in these conjectures, as in Virgil, Venus, dissembling, teacheth her son, Aeneas, in these verses:

All this is not for naught,
Else me in vain my parents Augury taught;
Lo! twice six Swans in a glad company
Jove's bird pursued through the etherial Sky
In Heaven's broad tracks; now earth in a long train
They seem to take, or taken, to disdain;
As they return with sounding wings they sport,
And Heaven surrounding in a long consort.
Just so, I say, thy friends and fleet have gained
The port, or with full sails the Bay obtained.

Most wonderful is that kind of auguring of theirs, who hear and understand the speeches of animals, in which, as amongst the ancients, Melampus, , Thales, and Apollonius, the Tyanean, who, as we read, excelled, and whom, they report, had excellent skill in the language of birds; of whom Philostratus and Porphyrius speak, saying, that of old, when Apollonius sat in company amongst his friends, seeing sparrows sitting upon a tree, and one sparrow coming from elsewhere unto him, making a great chattering and noise, and then flying away, all the rest following him, he said to his companions that that sparrow told the rest that an ass, being burdened with wheat, fell down in a hole near the city and that the wheat was scattered upon the ground. Many, being much moved with these words, went to see, and so it was, as Apollonius said, at which they much wondered. Phorphyrius, the Platonist, in his third book of sacrifices, saith that there is certainly a swallow language, because every voice of every animal is significative of some passion of its soul, as joy, sadness, or anger, or the like, which voices, it is not so wonderful a thing, could be understood by men conversant about them. But Democritus himself declared this art, as saith Pliny, by naming the birds, of whose blood mixed together was produced a serpent, of which whosoever did eat should understand the voices of birds. And Hermes saith that if any one shall go forth to catch birds on a certain day of the Kalends of November, and shall boil the first bird that he catcheth with the heart of a fox, that all that shall eat of this bird shall understand the voices of birds and all other animals.

Also, the Arabians say that they can understand the meaning of brutes who shall eat the heart and liver of a dragon. Proclus, also, the Platonist, believed and wrote that the heart of a mole conduceth to presages. There were also divinations and auspices which were taken from the inwards of sacrifices, the inventor whereof was Tages, of whom Lucan sang:

And if the Inwards have no credit gained,
And if this Art by Tages was but feigned.

The Roman religion thought that the liver was the head of the inwards. Hence the soothsayers enquiring after future things in the inwards, did first look into the liver, in which were two heads, whereof the one was called the head for the city, the other for the enemy; and the heads of this, or another part, being compared together, they then gave judgment and pronounced for victory; as we read, in Lucan, that the inwards did signify the slaughter of Pompey's men and the victory of Caesar's, according to these verses:

In the inwards all defects are ominous
One part and branch of the entrails doth increase,
Another part is weak, and flagging lies,
Beats, and moves with quick pulse the arteries.

Then, the bowels being finished, they search the heart. Now, if there were a sacrifice found without a heart, or a head was wanting in the liver, these were deadly presages, and were called piacularia. Also, if a sacrifice fled from the altar, or, being smitten, made a lowing, or fell upon any part of his body than he ought to do, it was the like ominous. We read that when Julius Caesar on a day went forth to procession with his purple robe, and sitting in a golden chair and sacrificing, there was twice a heart wanting. When C. Marius Utica was sacrificing, there was wanting a liver. Also when Caius, the prince, and M. Marcellus, C. Claudius and L. Petellius Coss, were offering sacrifices, that the liver was consumed suddenly away and, not long after, one of them died of a disease, another was slain by men of Lyguria, the entrails foretelling so much; which was thought to be done by the power of the Gods, or help of the devil. Hence it was accounted a thing of great concernment amongst the ancients as oft as any thing unusual was found in the inwards, as when Sylla was sacrificing at Laurentum, the figure of a crown appeared in the head of the liver, which Posthumius, the soothsayer, interpreted to portend a victory with a kingdom, and therefore advised that Sylla should eat those entrails himself. The color, also, of the inwards is to be considered. Of these Lucan made mention:

Struck at the color Prophets were with fear,
For with foul spots pale entrals tinged were.
Both black and blue, with specks of sprinkled blood
They were

There was in times past such a venerable esteem of these arts that the most potent and wise men sought after them; yea, the senate and kings did nothing without the counsel of the Augures. But all these in these days are abolished, partly by the negligence of men and partly by the authority of the fathers.

CHAPTER LVI. OF THE SOOTHSAYINGS OF FLASHES AND LIGHTNINGS, AND HOW MONSTROUS AND PRODIGIOUS THINGS ARE TO BE INTERPRETED.

Now, the soothsayings of flashes and lightnings, and of wonders, and how monstrous and prodigious things are to be interpreted, the prophets and priests of Hetruscus have taught the art. For they have ordained sixteen regions of the heavens and have ascribed Gods to every one of them, besides eleven kinds of lightning, and nine gods which should dart them forth, by showing rules for understanding the signification of them. But as often as monstrous, prodigious and wondrous things happen, they do presage, as is most certain, some great matter. Now, their interpreter must be some excellent conjector of similitudes, as also some curious searcher, and of them who at that time are employed about the affairs of princes and provinces. For the celestials take such care only for princes, peoples and provinces that before the rest they might be prefigured and admonished by stars, by constellations and by prodigies. Now, if the same thing, or the like, hath been seen in former ages, we must consider that very thing and what happened after that, and according to these, to foretell the same, or the like, because the same signs are for the same things, and the like for like. So prodigies have come before the birth and death of many eminent men and kings, as Cicero makes mention of Midas, a boy, into whose mouth whilst he was sleeping, the ant put corns of wheat, which was an omen of great riches. So bees sat upon the mouth of Plato when he was sleeping in the cradle, by which was foretold the sweetness of his speech. Hecuba, when she was bringing forth Paris, saw a burning torch, which should set on fire Troy and all Asia. There appeared unto the mother of Phalaris the image of Mercury pouring forth blood upon the earth, with which the whole house was overflowed. The mother of Dionysius dreamed she brought forth a satyr, which prodigious dream the event that followed made good. The wife of Tarquinius Priscus, seeing a flame lick the head of Servius Tullius, foretold that he should have the kingdom.

In like manner, after Troy was taken, Aeneas disputing with Anchises, his father, concerning a fight, there appeared a flame licking the head of the crown of Ascanius and doing him no hurt. Which thing, seeing it did portend the kingdom to Ascanius, persuaded him to depart, for monstrous prodigies did forerun great and eminent destruction. So we read in Pliny that M. Attilius and C. Portius, being consuls, it rained milk and blood, which did presage that a very great pestilence should the next year overspread Rome. In Lucania it rained spongeous iron, and in the year before Marcus Crassus was slain in Parthia, with which, also, all the soldiers of Lucania, being a very numerous army, were slain. L. Paulus and C. Marcellus, being consuls, it rained wool about the castle of Corisanum, near which place, a year after, T. Annius was slain by Milus. And in the wars of Denmark, the noise of arms and the sound of a trumpet was heard in the air. And Livy, concerning the Macedonian wars, saith, in the year when Annibal died it rained blood for two days. Concerning the second Punic war, he saith that water mixed with blood came down from heaven like rain at the time when Annibal did spoil Italy. A little before the destruction of Leuctra, the Lacedemonians heard a noise of arms in the temple of Hercules, and at the same time in the temple of Hercules the doors that were shut with bars opened themselves, and the arms that were hanged on the wall were found on the ground. The like events may be prognosticated of other like things, as oftentimes in times past something hath been foretold of them. But concerning these, also, the judgments of the celestial influences must not be neglected, concerning which we shall more largely treat in the following chapters.

CHAPTER LVII. OF GEOMANCY, HYDROMANCY, AEROMANCY, AND PYROMANCY, FOUR DIVINATIONS OF ELEMENTS.

MOREOVER, the Elements themselves teach us fatal events; whence those four famous kinds of divinations, Geomancy, Hydromancy, Aeromancy, and Pyromancy, have got their names, of which the sorceress in Lucan seems to boast herself when she saith:
The Earth, the Aire, the Chaos, and the Skie,
The Seas, the Fields, the Rocks, and Mountains high
Foretell the truth----
The first, therefore, is Geomancy, which foreshows future things by the motions of the earth, as also the noise, the swelling, the trembling, the chops, the pits, and exhalation, and other impressions thereof, the art of which Almadel, the Arabian, sets forth. But there is another kind of Geomancy which divines by points written upon the earth by a certain power in the fall of it, which is not of present speculation, but of that we shall speak hereafter.

Now Hydromancy doth perform its presages by the impressions of waters, their ebbing and flowing, their increases, and depressions, their tempests, colors and the like; to which, also, are added visions which are made in the waters. A kind of divination found by the Persians, as Varro reports, was that of a boy who saw in the water the effigies of Mercury, which foretold, in a hundred and fifty verses, all the events of the war of

Mithridates. We read, also, that Numa Pompilius practiced Hydromancy, for in the water he called up the gods and learned of them things to come. Which art also Pythagoras, a long time after Numa, practiced. There was of old a kind of Hydromancy had in great esteem amongst the Assyrians, and it was called Lecanomancy, from a skin full of water, upon which they put plates of gold and silver and precious stones written upon with certain images, names and characters. To this may be referred that art by which lead and wax, being melted and cast into the water, do express manifest marks of images of those things we desire to know. There were also in former years fountains that did foretell things to come, as the fathers' fountain at Achaia, and that which was called the water of Juno, in Epidaurus; but of these more in the following chapter, where we shall speak of Oracles.

Hither also may be referred the divination of fishes, of which kind there was use made by the Lycians in a certain place which was called Dina, near the sea; in a wood dedicated to Apollo, was a hollow in the dry sand, into which he that went to consult of future things let down roasted meat, and presently that place was filled with water and a great multitude of fish and strange shapes, unknown to men, did appear; by the forms of which the prophet foretold what should come to pass. These things doth Atheneus more at large relate in the history of the Lycians.

After the same manner, also, doth Aeromancy divine by airy impressions, by the blowing of the winds, by rainbows, by circles round about the moon and stars, by mists and clouds, and by imagination in clouds and visions in the air.

So also Pyromancy divines by fiery impressions, and by stars with long tails, by fiery colors, by visions and imaginations in the fire. So the wife of Cicero foretold that he would be consul the next year because, when a certain man, after the sacrifice was ended, would look in the ashes, there suddenly broke forth a flame. Of this kind are those that Pliny speaks of-- that terrene, pale and buzzing fires presage tempests, circles about the snuffs of candles betoken rain, and if the flame fly, turning and winding, it portends wind. Also torches, when they strike the fire before them and are not kindled. Also when a coal sticks to a pot taken off from the fire, and when the fire casts off the ashes and sparkles; or when ashes are hard grown together on the hearth, and when a coal is very bright.

To these is also added Capnomancy, so called from smoke, because it searcheth into the flame and smoke; and thin colors, sounds and motions when they are carried upright, or on one side, or round, which we read of in these verses in Statius.

Let Piety be bound, and on the Altar laid,
Let us implore the Gods for divine aid.
She makes acute, red, towering flames, and bright,

Increas'd by th' aire, the middle being white;
And then she makes the flames without all bound
For to wind in and out, and to run round
Like a Serpent

Also in the Aethnean Caves and Fields of the Nymphs in Apollonia, auguries were taken from fires and flames--joyful, if they did receive what was cast into them, and sad, if they did reject them. But of these things we shall speak of in the following chapters, amongst the answers of the Oracles.

CHAPTER LVIII. OF THE REVIVING OF THE DEAD, AND OF SLEEPING OR HIBERNATING (WANTING VICTUALS) MANY YEARS TOGETHER.

THE Arabian philosophers agree that some men may elevate themselves above the powers of their body and above their sensitive powers; and, those being surmounted, they receive into themselves--by the perfection of the Heavens and the Celestial intelligences--A Divine Vigor. Seeing, therefore, that all the Souls of men are perpetual, and, also, that all the Spirits obey the perfect Souls, Magicians think that perfect men may, by the powers of their soul, repair their dying bodies (with other inferior souls, newly separated) and inspire them again: As a weasel, that is killed, is made alive again by the breath and cry of his dam; and as lions make alive their dead whelps by breathing upon them. And because, as they say, all like things, being applied to their like, are made of the same natures; and, also, every patient, subject, and thing that receives into itself the act of any agent is endowed with the nature of that agent and made conatural with it. Hence they think that to this vivification, or making alive, certain herbs, and Magical confections (such as, they say, are made of the ashes of the Phoenix and the cast skin of a Snake) do much conduce; which, indeed, to many may seem fabulous, and to some impossible, unless it could be accounted approved by an historical faith. For we read of some that have been drowned in water, others cast into the fire or put upon the fire, others slain in war, and others otherwise tried, and all these, after a few days were alive again, as Pliny testifies of Aviola, a man pertaining to the consul, of L. Lamia, Caelinus, Tubero, Corfidius, Gabienus, and many others. We read that Aesop, the tale-maker, Tindoreus, Hercules and Palicy, the sons of Jupiter, and Thalia, being dead, were raised to life again; also that many were, by physicians and magicians, raised from death again, as the historians relate of Aesculapius; and we have above mentioned, out of Juba, and Xanthus and Philostratus, concerning Tillo, and a certain Arabian, and Apollonius the Tyanean. Also we read that Glaucus, a certain man that was dead, the herb dragon-wort restored to life. Some say that he revived by the putting into his body a medicine made of honey, whence the proverb, Glaucus was raised from death by taking honey into his body. Apuleius, also, relating the manner of these kinds of restoring to life, saith of Zachla, the Egyptian prophet, that the prophet, being favorable, laid a certain herb upon the mouth of the body of a young man, being dead, and another upon his breast; then, turning toward the East, or rising of the propitious Sun, he prayed silently (a great assembly of people striving to see it), when, in the first place, the breast of the dead man did heave, then a beating in his veins, then his body filled with breath, after which the body rose and the young man spoke. If these accounts are true, the dying souls must, sometimes lying hid in their bodies, be oppressed with vehement extasies and be freed from all bodily action; so that the life, sense, and motion forsake the body, and also that the man is not yet truly dead, but lies astonied, and dead, as it were, for a certain time. And this is often found, that in times of pestilence many that are carried for dead to the graves to be buried, revive again. The same also hath often befell women by reason of fits of the mother. And Rabbit Moises, out of the book of Galen, which Patriarcha translated, makes mention of a man who was suffocated for six days, and did neither eat nor drink, and his arteries became hard. And it is said, in the same book, that a certain man, being filled with water, lost the pulse of his whole body, so that the heart was not perceived to move, and he lay like a dead man. It is also said that a man, by reason of a fall from a high place, or great noise, or long staying under the water, may fall into a swoon, which may continue forty-eight hours, and so may lay as if he were dead, his face being very green. And in the same place there is mention made of a man that buried a man, who seemed to be dead, seventy-two hours after his seeming decease, and so killed him because he buried him alive; and there are given signs whereby it may be known who are alive, although they seem to be dead, and, indeed, will die, unless there be some means to recover them, as phlebotomy, or some other cure. And these are such as very seldom happen. This is the manner by which we understand magicians and physicians do raise dead men to life, as they that were tried by the stinging of serpents, were, by the nation of the Marsi and the Psilli, restored to life. We may conceive that such kind of extasies may continue a long time, although a man be not truly dead, as it is in dormice and crocodiles and many other serpents, which sleep all winter, and are in such a dead sleep that they can scarce be awakened with fire. And I have often seen a dormouse dissected and continue immovable, as if she were dead, until she was boiled, and when put into boiling water the dissected members did show life. And, although it be hard to be believed, we read in some approved historians, that some men have slept for many years together; and, in the time of sleep until they awaked, there was no alteration in them so as to make them seem older. The same doth Pliny testify of a certain boy, whom, he saith, being wearied with heat and his journey, slept fifty-seven years in a cave. We read, also, that Epimenides Gnosius slept fifty-seven years in a cave. Hence the proverb arose--to outsleep Epimenides. M. Damascenus tells that in his time a certain countryman in Germany, being wearied, slept for the space of a whole autumn and the winter following, under a heap of hay, until the summer, when the hay began to be eaten up; then he was found awakened as a man half dead and out of his wits. Ecclesiastical histories confirm this opinion concerning the seven sleepers, whom they say slept 196 years. There was in Norvegia a cave in a high sea shore, where, as Paulus Diaconus and Methodius, the martyr, write, seven men lay sleeping a long time without corruption, and the people that went in to disturb them were contracted or drawn together, so that after a while, being forewarned by that punishment, they dared not disturb them. Xenocrates, a man of no mean repute amongst philosophers, was of the opinion that this long sleeping was appointed by God as a punishment for some certain sins. But Marcus Damascenus proves it, by many reasons, to be possible and natural, neither doth he think it irrational that some should, without meat and drink, avoiding excitements, and without consuming or corruption, sleep many months. And this may befall a man by reason of some poisonous potion, or sleepy disease, or such like causes, for certain days, months or years, according to the intention or remission of the power of the medicine, or of the passions of their mind. Physicians say that there are some antidotes, of which they that take too great a potion shall be able to endure hunger a long time; as Elias, in former time, being fed with a certain food by an angel, walked and fasted in the strength of that meat forty days. And John Bocatius makes mention of a man in his time, in Venice, who would every year fast four days without any meat; also, a greater wonder, that there was a woman in lower Germany, at the same time, who took no food till the thirteenth year of her age, which, to us, may seem incredible, but that he confirmed it. He also tells of a miracle of our age, that his brother, Nicolaus Stone, an Helvetian by nation, who lived over twenty years in the wilderness without meat till he died. That also is wonderful which Theoprastus mentions concerning a certain man, called Philinus, who used no meat or drink besides milk. And there are also grave authors who describe a certain herb of Sparta, with which, they say, the Scythians can endure twelve days' hunger, without meat or drink, if they do but taste it, or hold it in their mouth.

CHAPTER LIX. OF DIVINATION BY DREAMS.

THERE is also a certain kind of divination by dreams which is confirmed by the traditions of philosophers, the authorities of divines, the examples of histories and by daily experience. By dreams I do not mean vain and idle imaginations, for they are useless and have no divination in them, but arise from the remains of watchings, and disturbance of the body. For, as the mind is taken up about and wearied with cares, it suggests itself to him that is asleep. I call that a true dream which is caused by the celestial influences in the phantastic spirit, mind or body, being all well disposed. The rule of interpreting these is found amongst astrologers, in that part which is wrote concerning questions: but yet that is not sufficient, because these kinds of dreams come by use to divers men after divers manners, and according to the divers qualities and dispositions of the phantastic spirit. Wherefore, there cannot be given one common rule to all for the interpretation of dreams. But, according to the doctrine of Synesius, seeing there are the same accidents to things, and like befalls like, so he which hath often fallen upon the same visible thing, hath assigned to himself the same opinion, passion, fortune, action, and event. As Aristotle saith, the memory is confirmed by sense, and by keeping in memory the same thing, knowledge is obtained; as also, by the knowledge of many experiences, by little and little, arts and sciences are thus obtained. After the same account you must conceive of dreams. Whence Synesius commands that every one should observe his dreams and their events, and such like rules, viz., to commit to memory all things that are seen, and accidents that befall, as well in sleep as in watching, and with a diligent observation consider with himself the rules by which these are to be examined; for by this means shall a diviner be able, by little and little, to interpret his dreams, if so be nothing slip out of his memory. Now, dreams are more efficacious when the Moon overruns that Sign which was in the ninth number of the nativity, or revolution of that year, or in the ninth Sign from the Sign of Perfection. For it is a most true and certain divination, neither doth it proceed from nature or human arts, but from purified minds, by divine inspiration. We shall now discuss and examine Prophesying and Oracles.

CHAPTER LX. OF MADNESS, AND DIVINATIONS WHICH ARE MADE WHEN MEN ARE AWAKE, AND OF THE POWER OF A MELANCHOLY HUMOR, BY WHICH SPIRITS ARE SOMETIMES INDUCED INTO MEN'S BODIES.

IT happens also, sometimes, that not only they that are asleep, but also they that are watchful, do, with a kind of instigation of mind, divine; which divination Aristotle calls ravishment, or a kind of madness, and teacheth that it proceeds from a melancholy humor, saying in his treaties of divination: Melancholy men, by reason of their earnestness, do far better conjecture, and quickly conceive a habit, and most easily receive an impression of the celestials. And he, in his Problems, saith that the Sibyls, and the Bacchides, and Niceratus the Syracusan, and Ammon, were, by their natural melancholy complexion, prophets and poets. The cause, therefore, of this madness, if it be anything within the body, is a melancholy humor; not that which they call black choler, which is so obstinate and terrible a thing, that the violence of it is said, by physicians and natural philosophers (besides madness, which it doth induce), to draw or entice evil spirits to seize upon men's bodies. Therefore, we understand a melancholy humor here, to be a natural and white choler. For this, when it is stirred up, burns, and stirs up a madness conducing to knowledge and divination, especially if it be helped by any celestial influx, especially of Saturn, who (seeing he is cold and dry, as is a melancholy humor, hath his influence upon it) increaseth and preserveth it. Besides, seeing he is the author of secret contemplation, and estranged from all public affairs, and the highest of all the planets, he doth, as he withcalls his mind from outward business, so also make it ascend higher, and bestows upon men the knowledge and presages of future things. And this is Aristotle's meaning, in his book of Problems. By melancholy, saith he, some men are made, as it were, divine, foretelling things to come; and some men are made poets. He saith, also, that all men that were excellent in any science, were, for the most part, melancholy. Democritus and Plato attest the same, saying that there were some melancholy men that had such excellent wits that they were thought and seemed to be more divine than human. So also there have been many melancholy men at first rude, ignorant and untractable, as they say Tynnichus, Hesiod, Ion, Calcinenses, Homer, and Lucretius were, who on a sudden were taken with a madness and became poets, and prophesied wonderful and divine things, which they themselves scarce understood. Whence Plato, in Ion, saith that many prophets, after the violence of their madness was abated, do not well understand what they wrote, yet treated accurately of each art in their madness; as all artists, by reading of them, judge. So great also, they say, the power of melancholy is of, that, by its force, celestial spirits also are sometimes drawn into men's bodies, by whose presence and instinct, antiquity testifies, men have been made drunk and spake most wonderful things. And this thing, they think, happens under a three-fold difference, according to a three-fold apprehension of the soul, viz., imaginative, rational, and mental; they say, therefore, that when the mind is forced with a melancholy humor, nothing moderating the power of the body, and, passing beyond the bounds of the members, is wholly carried into imagination, it doth suddenly become a seat for inferior spirits, by which the mind oftentimes receives wonderful ways and forms of manual arts. So we see that any most ignorant man doth presently become an excellent painter, or contriver of building, and to become a master in any such art. But when these kinds of spirits portend to us future things they show those things which belong to the disturbing of the Elements and changes of times, as rain, tempests, inundations, earthquakes, slaughter, great mortality, famine, and the like. As we read in Aulus Gelius that his priest, Cornelius Patrarus, did, at the time when Caesar and Pompey were to fight in Thessalia, being taken with a madness, foretell the time, order and issue of the battle. But when the mind is turned wholly into reason it becomes a receptacle for middle world spirits. Hence it obtains the knowledge and understanding of natural and human things. So we see that a man sometimes doth on a sudden become a philosopher, physician, or an orator, and foretells mutations of kingdoms, and restitutions of ages, and such things as belong to them, as did the Sibyl to the Romans. But when the mind is wholly elevated into the understanding, then it becomes a receptacle of sublime spirits and learns of them the secrets of divine things, such as the Law of God, and the Orders of Angels, and such things as belong to the knowledge of things eternal and the ascent of souls. It foresees things which are appointed by predestination, such as future prodigies or miracles, the prophet to come, and the changing of the law. So the Sibyls prophesied of Christ a long time before his coming. So Virgil, understanding that Christ was at hand and remembering what the Sibyl, Cumaea, had said, sang thus to Pollio:

Last times are come, Cumaea's prophesie--
Now from high heaven springs a new progenie,
And times Great Order now again is born,
The Maid returns, Saturnian Realms return.

And, a little after, intimating that original sin shall be of no effect, he saith:

If any prints of our old vice remain'd
By thee they're void, and fear shall leave the Land;
He a God's life shall take, with Gods shall see
Mixt Heroes, and himself their object be;
Rule with paternal power th' appeased Earth
He shall----

Then he adds, that thence the fall of the Serpent, and the poison of the tree of death, or of the knowledge of good and evil, shall be nulled, saying:

The Serpent shall
And the deceitful Herb of Venom fall.

Yet he intimates that some sparks of original sin shall remain, when he saith:

Some steps of ancient fraud shall yet be found.

And at last with a most great hyperbole cries out to his child, as the offspring of God, adoring him in these words:

Dear race of Gods, great stock of Jupiter,
Behold! the World shakes on its ponderous axe,
See earth, and heavens immense, and Ocean tracts,
How all things at th' approaching Age rejoice!
O, that my life would last so long, and voice,

As would suffice thy actions to rehearse.

There are also some prognostics which are in the middle, betwixt natural and supernatural divination, as in those who are near to death, and, being weakened with old age, do sometimes foresee things to come, because, as saith Plato, by how much the more men are less hindered by their sense, so much the more accurately they understand, and because they are nearer to the place whither they must go (and their bonds being, as it were, a little loosed, seeing they are no more subject to the body) easily perceive the light of divine revelation.

CHAPTER LXI. OF THE FORMING OF MAN, OF THE EXTERNAL SENSES, ALSO THOSE INWARD, AND THE MIND; AND OF THE THREE-FOLD APPETITE OF THE SOUL, AND PASSIONS OF THE WILL.

IT IS the opinion of some divines that God did not immediately create the body of man, but by the assistance of the heavenly spirits compounded and framed him; which opinion Alcinous and Plato favor, thinking that God is the chief creator of the whole world, and of spirits, both good and bad, and therefore, immortalized them; but that all kinds of mortal animals were made only at the command of God; for, if he should have created them, they must have been immortal. The spirits, therefore, mixing Earth, Fire, Air, and Water together, made of them all, put together, one body, which they subjected to the service of the soul, assigning in it several provinces to each power thereof; to the meaner of them, mean and low places: as to anger, the midriff; to desire, the womb; but to the more noble senses, the head--as the tower of the whole body--and then the manifold organs of speech. They divide the senses into the external and internal. The external are divided into five, known to every one, to which there are allotted five organs, or subjects, as it were foundations; being so ordered that they which are placed in the more eminent part of the body, have a greater degree of purity. For the eyes, placed in the uppermost place, are the most pure, and have an affinity with the nature of Fire and Light; then the ears have the second order of place and purity, and are compared to the Air; the nostrils have the third order, and have a middle nature betwixt the Air and the Water. Then the organ of tasting, which is grosser, and most like to the nature of Water. Last of all the touching is diffused through the whole body, and is compared to the grossness of Earth. The more pure senses are those which perceive their objects farthest off, as seeing and hearing; then the smelling, then the taste, which doth not perceive but that which is nigh. But the touch perceives both ways, for it perceives bodies nigh; and as sight discerns by the medium of the Air, so the touch perceives, by the medium of a stick or pole, bodies hard, soft and moist.

Now the touch only is common to all animals. And it is most certain that man hath this sense, and, in this and taste, he excels all other animals; but in the other three, he is excelled by some animals, as by a dog, who hears, sees and smells more acutely than man; and the lynx and eagles see more acutely than all other animals and man. Now the interior senses are, according to Averrois, divided into four, whereof the first is called common sense, because it doth first collect and perfect all the representations which are drawn in by the outward senses. The second is the imaginative power, whose office is, seeing it represents nothing, to retain those representations which are received by the former senses, and to present them to the third faculty of inward sense, which is the phantasy, or power of judging, whose work is also to perceive and judge by the representations received, what, or what kind of thing that is of which the representations are; and to commit those things which are thus discerned and adjudged, to the memory to be kept. For the virtues thereof in general, are discourse, dispositions, persecutions, and fights, and stirrings up to action, but in particular, the understanding of intellectuals, virtues, the manner of discipline, counsel, and election. This is that which shows us future things by dreams, whence the fancy is sometimes named the phantastical intellect. For it is the last impression of the understanding, which, as saith Iamblicus, is that belonging to all the powers of the mind, and forms all figures, resemblances of species, and operations, and things seen, and sends forth the impressions of other powers unto others. And those things which appear by sense, it stirs up into an opinion; but those things which appear by the intellect, in the second place, it offers to opinion; but of itself it receives images from all, and by its property, doth properly assign them, according to their assimilation; it forms all the actions of the soul, and accommodates the external to the internal and impresses the body with its impression. Now these senses have their organs in the head, for the common sense and imagination take up the two forward cells of the brain, although Aristotle placeth the organ of the common sense in the heart; but the cogitative power possesseth the highest and middle part of the head; and, lastly, the memory the hindmost part thereof. Moreover, the organs of voice and speech are many, as the inward muscles of the breast betwixt the ribs, the breasts, the lungs, the arteries, the windpipe, the bowing of the tongue, and all those parts and muscles that serve for breathing. But the proper organ of speech is the mouth, in which are framed words and speeches, the tongue, the teeth, the lips, the palate and the like. Above the sensible soul, which expresseth its powers by the organs of the body, the incorporeal mind possesseth the highest place, and it hath a double nature--the one, which inquireth into the causes, properties, and progress of those things which are contained in the Order of Nature, and is content in the contemplation of the truth, which is, therefore called the contemplative intellect. The other is a power of the mind which, discerning by consulting what things are to be done and what is to be shunned, is wholly taken up in consultation and action, and is therefore called the active intellect. This order of powers, therefore, Nature ordained in man, that by the external senses we might know corporeal things, and by those internal the representations of bodies, as also things abstracted by the mind and intellect, which are neither bodies nor any thing like them. And, according to this three-fold order of the powers of the soul, there are three Appetites in the soul: The first is natural, and is an inclination of nature unto its end, as of a stone downward, which is in all stones; another is animal, which the sense follows, and it is divided into that irascible and that concupiscible; the third is intellectual, and is called the will, differing from the sensitive faculty in that the sensitive is, of itself, of those things which may be presented to the senses, desiring nothing unless in some manner comprehended. But the will, although it be of itself of all things that are possible, yet, because it is free by its essence, it may be also of things that are impossible, as it was in the devil (desiring himself to be equal with God) and, therefore, is altered and depraved with pleasure and with continual anguish, whilst it assents to the inferior powers. Whence, from its depraved appetite, there arise four passions in it, with which, in like manner, the body is affected sometimes. Whereof the first is called oblectation, which is a certain quietness or assentation of the mind or will, because it obeys, and not willingly consents to that pleasantness which the senses hold forth; which is, therefore, defined to be an inclination of the mind to an effeminate pleasure. The second is called effusion, which is a remission of, or dissolution of the power, viz., when beyond the oblectation, the whole power of the mind and intention of the present good is melted, and diffuseth itself to enjoy it. The third is vaunting and loftiness, thinking itself to have attained to some great good, in the enjoyment of which it prides itself and glorieth. The fourth and the last is envy, or a certain kind of pleasure or delight at another man's harm, without any advantage to itself. It is said to be without any advantage to itself, because, if any one should, for his own profit, rejoice at another man's harm, this would be rather out of love to himself than out of ill will to another. And all these four passions, arising from a depraved appetite for pleasure, the grief or perplexity itself doth also beget very many contrary passions, as horror, sadness, fear, and sorrow at another's good without his own hurt, which we call envy, or sadness at another's prosperity, just as pity is a certain kind of sadness at another's misery.

CHAPTER LXII. OF THE PASSIONS OF THE MIND, THEIR ORIGINAL SOURCE, DIFFERENCES, AND KINDS.

THE passions of the human mind are nothing else but certain motions or inclinations proceeding from the apprehension of any thing, as of good or evil, convenient or inconvenient. Now these kind of apprehensions are of three sorts, viz., Sensual, Rational, and Intellectual. According to these three are three sorts of passions in the soul; for when they follow the sensitive apprehension then they respect a temporary good or evil, under the notion of profitable or unprofitable, or delightful or offensive, and are called natural or animal passions. When they follow the rational apprehension, and so respect good or bad, under the notions of virtue or vice, praise or disgrace, profitable or unprofitable, or honest or dishonest, they are called rational or voluntary passions. When they follow the intellectual apprehension, and respect good or bad, under the notion of just or unjust, or true or false, they are called intellectual passions, or syncrisis, the faculty of choosing from comparison. Now, the subject of the passions of the soul is the concupitive power of the soul, and is divided into that concupiscible and that irascible, and both respect good and bad, but under a different notion. For when the concupiscible power respects good and evil absolutely, love or lust, or, on the contrary, hatred is caused. When it respects good, though absent, so desire is caused; or evil, though absent or at hand, and so is caused horror, flying from, or loathing; or, if it respects good, though present, then there is caused delight, mirth or pleasure; but if evil, though present, then sadness, anxiety, or grief; but the irascible power respects good or bad, under the notion of some difficulty, to obtain the one, or to avoid the other, and this sometimes with confidence. And so there is caused hope or boldness; but when with diffidency, then despair and fear. But when that irascible power riseth into revenge, and this be only about some evil past, as it were, of injury or hurt offered, there is caused anger. And so we find eleven passions in the mind, which are: love, hatred, desire, horror, joy, grief, hope, despair, boldness, fear, and anger.

CHAPTER LXIII. HOW THE PASSIONS OF THE MIND CHANGE THE PROPER BODY BY CHANGING ITS ACCIDENTS AND MOVING THE SPIRIT.

THE phantasy, or imaginative power, hath a ruling power over the passions of the soul when they follow the sensual apprehension. For this doth, of its own power, according to the diversity of the passions, first of all, change the proper body with a sensible transmutation, by changing the accidents in the body, and by moving the spirit upward or downward, inward or outward, and by producing divers qualities in the members. So in joy, the spirits are driven outward; in fear, drawn back; in bashfulness, are moved to the brain. So in joy, the heart is dilated outward, by little and little; in sadness, is constrained, by little and little, inward. After the same manner in anger or fear, but suddenly. Again anger, or desire of revenge, produceth heat, redness, a bitter taste and a looseness. Fear induceth cold, trembling of the heart, speechlessness and paleness. Sadness causeth sweat and a bluish whiteness. Pity, which is a kind of sadness, doth often ill affect the body of him that takes pity, though it seems to be the body of another man so affected. Also, it is manifest that amongst some lovers there is such a strong tie of love that what the one suffers the other suffers. Anxiety induceth dryness and blackness. And how great heats love stirs up in the liver and pulse, physicians know, divining by that kind of judgment the name of the one that is so beloved in an heroic passion. So Naustratus knew that Antiochus was taken with the love of Stratonica. It is also manifest that such like passions, when they are most vehement, may cause death. And this is manifest to all men, that with too much joy, sadness,love, hatred, men many times die, and are sometimes freed from a disease. And so we read that Sophocles, and Dionysius, the Sicilian tyrant, did both suddenly die at the news of a tragical victory. So a certain woman, also, seeing her son returning from the Canensian battle, died suddenly. Now, what sadness can do is known to all. We know that dogs oftentimes die with sadness because of the death of their masters. Sometimes, also, by reason of these like passions, long diseases follow, and are sometimes cured. So, also, some men looking from a high place, by reason of great fear, tremble, are dim-sighted and weakened, and sometimes lose their senses. So fears and falling-sickness sometimes follow sobbing. Sometimes wonderful effects are produced, as in the son of Croesus, whom his mother brought forth dumb, yet a vehement fear and ardent affection made him speak, which naturally he could never do. So with a sudden fall, oftentimes life, sense, or motion, on a sudden, leave the members, and presently again, are sometimes returned. And how much vehement anger, joined with great audacity, can do, Alexander the Great shows, who, being circumvented with a battle in India, was seen to send forth from himself lightning and fire; the father of Theodoricus is said to have sent forth out of his body sparks of fire, so that sparkling flames did leap out with a noise. And such like things sometimes appear in beasts, as in the horse of Tiberius, which was said to send forth a flame out of his mouth.

CHAPTER LXIV. HOW THE PASSIONS OF THE MIND
CHANGE THE BODY BY WAY OF IMITATION FROM SOME
RESEMBLANCE; OF THE TRANSFORMING AND
TRANSLATING OF MEN, AND WHAT FORCE THE
IMAGINATIVE POWER HATH, NOT ONLY OVER THE
BODY BUT THE SOUL.

THE foresaid passions sometimes alter the body by reason of the virtue which the likeness of the thing hath to change it, which power the vehement imagination moves, as in setting the teeth on edge at the sight or hearing of something, or because we see, or imagine, another to eat sharp or sour things. So he, which sees another gape, gapes also; and some, when they hear any one name sour things, their tongues waxeth tart. Also, the seeing of any filthy thing causeth nauseousness. Many, at the sight of a man's blood, fall into a swoon. Some, when they see bitter meat given to any, perceive a bitter spittle in their mouth. And William of Paris saith that he saw a man, that at the sight of a medicine, was affected as much as he pleased; when, as neither the substance of the medicine, nor the odor, nor the taste of it came to him, but only a kind of resemblance was apprehended by him. Upon this account, some that are in a dream think they burn and are in a fire, and are fearfully tormented, as if they did truly burn, when, as the substance of the fire is not near them, but only a resemblance apprehended by their imagination. And sometimes men's bodies are transformed, and transfigured, and also transported; and this oft times when they are in a dream, and sometimes when they are awake. So Cyprus, after he was chosen king of Italy, did very much wonder at and meditate upon the fight and victory of bulls, and in the thought thereof did sleep a whole night, and in the morning he was found horned, no otherwise than by the vegetative power, being stirred up by a vehement imagination, elevating cornific humors into his head and producing horns. For a vehement cogitation, whilst it vehemently moves the species, pictures out the figure of the thing thought on, which they represent in their blood, and the blood impresseth the figure on the members that are nourished by it; as upon those of the same body, so upon those of anothers. So the imagination of a woman with child impresseth the mark of the thing longed for upon her infant, and the imagination of a man, bit with a mad dog, impresseth upon his body the image of dogs. So men may grow gray on a sudden. And some, by the dream of one night, have grown up from boys into perfect men. Hereto, also, may be referred those many scars of King Dagobertus, and marks of Franciscus, which they received--the one, whilst he was afraid of correction, and the other, whilst he did wonderfully meditate upon the wounds of Christ. So, many are transported from place to place, passing over rivers, fires and unpassable places, viz., when the species of any vehement desire, or fear, or boldness, are impresed upon their spirits, and, being mixed with vapors, do move the organ of the touch in their original, together with phantasy, which is the original of local motion. Whence they stir up the members and organs of motion to motion, and are moved, without any mistake, unto the imagined place, not out of sight, but from the interior phantasy. So great a power is there of the soul upon the body, that whichever way the soul imagines and dreams that it goes, thither doth it lead the body. We read many other examples by which the power of the soul upon .the body is wonderfully explained, as like that which Avicen describes of a certain man, who, when he pleased, could affect his body with the palsy. They report of Gallus Vibius that he did fall into madness, not casually, but on purpose, for, whilst he did imitate madmen, he assimilated their madness to himself and became mad indeed. And Austin makes mention of some men who could move their ears at their pleasure, and some that could move the crown of their head to their forehead and could draw it back again when they pleased, and of another that could sweat at his pleasure. And it is well known that some can weep - at their pleasure, and pour forth abundance of tears; and there are some that can bring up what they have swallowed, when they please, as out of a bag, by degrees. And we see that in these days there are many who can so imitate and express the voices of birds, cattle, dogs, and some men, that they can scarce at all be discerned. Also Pliny relates, by divers examples, that women have been turned into men. Pontanus testifieth that in his time, a certain woman called Caietava, and another one called Aemilia, who, many years after they were married, were changed into men. Now, how much imagination can affect the soul no man is ignorant, for it is nearer to the substance of the soul than the sense is, and therefore acts more upon the soul than the sense doth. So women, by certain strong imaginations, dreams, and suggestions, brought in by certain magical arts, do often bind themselves into a strong affection for any one. So they say that Medea, by a dream, was filled with love for Jason. So the soul sometimes is, by a vehement imagination or speculation, altogether abstracted from the body, as Celsus relates of a certain presbyter, who, as often as he pleased, could make himself senseless and lay like a dead man, so that when any one pricked or burnt him he felt no pain, but lay without any motion or breathing; yet he could, as he said, hear men's voices, as it were, afar off, if they cried out aloud.

CHAPTER LXV. HOW THE PASSIONS OF THE MIND CAN WORK OF THEMSELVES UPON ANOTHER'S BODY.

THE passions of the soul which follow the phantasy when they are most vehement, cannot only change their own body, but also can transcend so as to work upon another body; so that some wonderful impressions are thence produced in elements and extrinsical things, and they can thus take away or bring some disease of the mind or body. For the passions of the soul are the chiefest cause of the temperament of its proper body. So the soul, being strongly elevated, and inflamed with a strong imagination, sends forth health or sickness, not only in its proper body, but also in other bodies. So Avicen is of the opinion that a camel may fall by the imagination of any one. So he who is bitten with a mad dog presently falls into a madness, and there appear in his body the shapes of dogs. So the longing of a woman with child doth act upon another's body when it signs the infant in the womb with the mark of the thing she longs for. So many monstrous generations proceed from monstrous imaginations of women with child, as Marcus Damascenus reports that at Petra Saneta, a town situated upon the territories of Pisa, there was a wench presented to Charles, king of Bohemia, who was rough and hairy all over her body, like a wild beast, whom her mother, affected with a religious kind of horror by the picture of John the Baptist (which was in the chamber she occupied), afterwards brought her forth after this fashion. And this, we see, is not only in men, but also is done among brute creatures. So we read that Jacob, the patriarch, with his speckled rods set in the watering places, did discolor the sheep of Laban. So the imaginative powers of peacocks, and other birds, whilst they be mating, impress a color upon their wings. Whence we produce white peacocks, by hanging white clothes round the places where they mate. Now, by the above examples, it appears how the affection of the phantasy, when it vehemently intends itself, doth not only affect its own proper body, but also anothers. So also the desire of witches to hurt doth bewitch men most perniciously with steadfast looks. To these things Avicen, Aristotle, Algazel, and Gallen assent. For it is manifest that a body may most easily be affected with the vapor of another's diseased body, which we plainly see in the plague and leprosy. Again, in the vapor of the eyes there is so great a power that they can bewitch and infect any that are near them, as the cockatrice or basilisk which kill men with their looks. And certain women in Scythia, amongst the Illyrians and Triballi, killed whomsoever they looked angry upon. Therefore, let no man wonder that the body and soul of one may, in like manner, be affected with the mind of another, seeing the mind is far more powerful, strong, fervent, and more prevalent in its motion than the vapors exhaling out of bodies; neither are there wanting mediums by which it should work, neither is another's body less subject to another's mind than to another's body. Upon this account, they say that a man, by his affection and habit only, may act upon another. Therefore, philosophers advise that the society of evil and mischievous men must be shunned, for their soul, being full of noxious rays, infects them that are near with a hurtful contagion. On the contrary, they advise that the society of good and fortunate men be endeavored after, because by their nearness they do us much good. For as the smell of musk doth penetrate, so something of either bad or good is derived from anything bad or good by those that are nigh to them; which may continue a long time. Now, if the foresaid passions have so great a power in the phantasy, they have certainly a greater power in the reason, in as much as the reason is more excellent than the phantasy; and, lastly, they have much greater power in the mind; for this, when it is fixed upon God for any good with its whole intention, doth oftentimes affect another's body, as well as its own, with some divine gift. By this means we read that many miracles were done by Apollonius, Pythagoras, Empedocles, Philolaus, and many prophets and holy men of our religion, which things we shall now consider.

CHAPTER LXVI. THAT THE PASSIONS OF THE MIND ARE HELPED BY A CELESTIAL SEASON, AND HOW NECESSARY THE CONSTANCY OF THE MIND IS IN EVERY WORK.

THE passions of the mind are much helped, and are helpful, and become most powerful by virtue of the Heavens, as they agree with the Heaven, either by any natural agreement or by voluntary election. For, as saith Ptolemy, he which chooseth that which is the better seems to differ nothing from him who hath this by nature. It conduceth, therefore, very much for the receiving of the benefit of the Heavens, in any work, if we shall, by the Heaven, make ourselves suitable to it in our thoughts, affections, imaginations, deliberations, elections, contemplations, and the like. For such like passions do vehemently stir up our spirit to the likeness of the Heavens and expose us and ours straightway to the Superior Significators of such like passions; and, also, by reason of their dignity and nearness to the Superiors do much more partake of the Celestials than any other material things. For our mind can, through imagination or by reason of a kind of imitation, be so conformed to any Star as suddenly to be filled with the virtues of that Star, as if it were a proper receptacle of the influence thereof. Now, the contemplating mind, as it withdraws itself from all sense, imagination, nature, and deliberation, and calls itself back to things separated, unless it exposeth itself to Saturn, is not of present consideration or enquiry. For our mind Both effect divers things by faith (which is a firm adhesion, a fixed intention, and a vehement application of the worker, or receiver) to him that cooperates in any thing, and gives power to the work which we intend to do. So that there is made, as it were, in us, the image of the virtue to be received, and the thing to be done in us, or by us. We must, therefore, in every work and application of things, affect vehemently, imagine, hope, and believe strongly, for that will be a great help. And it is verified amongst physicians, that a strong belief, and an undoubted hope and love towards the physician and medicine, conduce much to health; yea, more, sometimes, than the medicine itself. For the same that the efficacy and virtue of the medicine works, the same doth the strong imagination of the physician work, being able to change the qualities in the body of the sick, especially when the patient placeth much confidence in the physician, by that means disposing himself for the receiving of the virtue of the physician and physic. Therefore, he that works in Magic must be of a constant belief, be credulous, and not at all doubtful of obtaining the effect. For, as a firm and strong belief doth work wonderful things, although it be in false works, so distrust and doubting doth dissipate and break the virtue of the mind of the worker, which is the medium between both extremes; whence it happens that he is frustrated of the desired influence of the superiors, which could not be joined and united to our labors without a firm and solid virtue of our mind.

CHAPTER LXVII. HOW THE MIND OF MAN MAY BE JOINED WITH THE MIND OF THE STARS, AND INTELLIGENCES OF THE CELESTIALS, AND, TOGETHER WITH THEM, IMPRESS CERTAIN WONDERFUL VIRTUES UPON INFERIOR THINGS.

THE philosophers, especially the Arabians, say that man's mind, when it is most intent upon any work, through its passion and effects, is joined with the mind of the stars and intelligences; and, being so joined, is the cause of some wonderful virtue being infused into our works and things; and this, because there is in the mind an apprehension and power of all things, so all things have a natural obedience to it, and of necessity an efficacy; and more to that which desires them with a strong desire. And according to this is verified the art of characters, images, enchantments, and some speeches, and many other wonderful experiments as to everything which the mind affects. By this means, whatsoever the mind of him that is in vehement love, affects, hath an efficacy to cause love; and whatsoever the mind of him that strongly hates, dictates, hath an efficacy to hurt and destroy. The like is in other things, which the mind affects with a strong desire. For all those things which the mind acts and dictates by characters, figures, words, speeches, gestures, and the like, help the appetite of the soul and acquire certain wonderful virtues; as from the soul of the operator, in that hour when such a like appetite doth invade it, so from the opportunity and celestial influence, moving the mind in that manner. For our mind, when it is carried upon the great excess of any passion or virtue, oftentimes presently takes of itself a strong, better and more convenient hour or opportunity, which Thomas Aquinas, in his third book against the Gentiles, confesseth. So many wonderful virtues both cause and follow certain admirable operations by great affections in those things which the soul doth dictate in that hour to them. But know that such things confer nothing, or very little, to the author of them, and to him which is inclined to them, as if he were the author of them. And this is the manner by which their efficacy is found out. And it is a general rule in them, that every mind that is more excellent in its love and affection makes such like things more fit for itself, becoming efficacious to that which it desires. Every one, therefore, that is willing to work in Magic must know the virtue, measure, order, and degree of his own soul, in relation to the Power of the Universe.

CHAPTER LXVIII. HOW OUR MIND CAN CHANGE AND BIND INFERIOR THINGS TO THE ENDS WHICH WE DESIRE.

THERE is also a certain virtue in the minds of men of changing, attracting, hindering, and binding to that which they desire; and all things obey them when they are carried into a great excess of any passion or virtue, so as to exceed those things which they bind. For the superior binds that which is inferior, and converts it to itself; and the inferior is, by the same reason, converted to the superior, or is otherwise affected, and wrought upon. By this reason, things that receive a superior degree of any star, bind, or attract, or hinder things which have an inferior, according as they agree or disagree amongst themselves. Whence a lion is afraid of a cock, because the presence of the Solary virtue is more agreeable to a cock than to a lion. So a loadstone draws iron, because, in its order, it hath a superior degree of the Celestial Bear.

So the diamond hinders the loadstone, because, in the order of Mars, it is superior to it. In like manner any man, when he is opportunely exposed to the celestial influences (as by the affections of his mind and due applications of natural things), if he become stronger in a Solary virtue, he binds and draws the inferior into admiration and obedience--in the order of the Moon, to servitude or infirmities; in a Saturnine order, to quietness or sadness; in the order of Jupiter, to worship; in the order of Mars, to fear and discord; in a Venus order, to love and joy; in a Mercurial order, to persuasion and obsequiousness, and the like. The ground of such a kind of binding is the very vehement and boundless affection of the soul with the concourse of the celestial order. But the dissolutions or hinderances of such a like binding are made by a contrary effect, and that more excellent or strong; for as the greater excess of the mind binds, so, also, it looseth and hindereth. And, lastly, when the mind feareth Venus, it opposes Saturn; when Saturn or Mars, it opposes Venus or Jupiter; for astrologers say that these are most at enmity, and contrary the one to the other (i. e.), causing contrary effects in these inferior bodies. For in the Heavens, where there is nothing wanting, and where all things are governed with love, there can in no wise be hatred or enmity.

CHAPTER LXIX. OF SPEECH, AND THE OCCULT VIRTUE OF WORDS.

IT being shown that there is a great power in the affections of the soul, you must know, moreover, that there is no less virtue in words and the names of things, and greatest of all in speeches and motions; by which we chiefly differ from the brutes, and are called rational; not from reason, which is taken for that part of the soul which contains the affections (which Galen saith is also common to brutes, although in a less degree), but we are called rational from that reason which is, according to the voice, understood in words and speech, which is called Declarative Reason; by which part we do chiefly excel all other animals. For logos, in Greek, signifies reason, speech, and a word. Now, a word is twofold, viz., internal and uttered. An internal word is a conception of the mind and motion of the soul, which is made without a voice; as in dreams we seem to speak and dispute with ourselves, and whilst we are awake, we run over a whole speech silently. But an uttered word hath a certain act in the voice, and properties of locution, and is brought forth with the breath of a man, with opening of his mouth and with the speech of his tongue; in which nature hath coupled the corporeal voice and speech to the mind and understanding, making that a declarer and interpreter of the conception of our intellect to the hearers; and of this we now speak. Words, therefore, are the fittest medium betwixt the speaker and the hearer, carrying with them not only the conception of the mind, but also the virtue of the speaker, with a certain efficacy, unto the hearers; and this oftentimes with so great a power, that often they change not only the hearers but also other bodies and things that have no life. Now those words are of greater efficacy than others which represent greater things--as intellectual, celestial, and supernatural; as more expressly, so more mysteriously. Also those that come from a more worthy tongue, or from any of a more holy order; for these (as it were certain signs and representations) receive a power of celestial and supercelestial things, as from the virtue of things explained, of which they are the vehicle, and from a power put into them by the virtue of the speaker.

CHAPTER LXX. OF THE VIRTUE OF PROPER NAMES.

THAT the proper names of things are very necessary in Magical Operations, almost all men testify. For the natural power of things proceeds, first, from the objects to the senses, and then from these to the imagination, and from this to the mind, in which it is first conceived, and then is expressed by voices and words. The Platonists, therefore, say that in this very voice, or word, or name framed, with its articles, that the power of the thing, as it were some kind of life, lies under the form of the signification. First conceived in the mind, as it were through certain seeds of things, then by voices or words, as a birth brought forth; and lastly, kept in writings. Hence magicians say, that the proper names of things are certain rays of things, everywhere present at all times, keeping the power of things, as the essence of the thing signified, rules, and is discerned in them and know the things by them, as by proper and living images. For, as the great operator doth provide divers species and particular things by the influence of the Heavens, and by the elements, together with the virtues of planets, so, according to the properties of the influences, proper names result to things and are put upon them by him who numbers the multitude of the stars, calling them all by their names; of which names Christ in another place speaks, saying, "Your names are written in Heaven." Adam, therefore, that gave the first names to things, knowing the influences of the Heavens and properties of all things, gave them all names according to their natures, as it is written in Genesis, where God brought all things that he had created before Adam, that he should name them; and as he named any thing, so the name of it was; which names,indeed, contain in them wonderful powers of the things signified. Every voice, therefore, that is significative, first of all signifies by the influence of the celestial harmony; secondly, by the imposition of man, although oftentimes otherwise by this than by that. But when both significations meet in any voice or name, which are put upon them by the said harmony, or men, then that name is with a double virtue, viz., natural and arbitrary, made most efficacious to act as often as it shall be uttered in due place and time, and seriously, with an intention exercised upon the matter rightly disposed, and that can naturally be acted upon by it. So we read in Philostratus, that when a maid at Rome died the same day she was married, and was presented to Apollonius, he accurately inquired into her name, which being known, he pronounced some occult thing, by which she revived. It was an observation amongst the Romans, in their holy rites, that when they did besiege any city, they did diligently enquire into the proper and true name of it, and the name of that

God under whose protection it was; which being known, they did then with some verse call forth the Gods that were the protectors of that city, and did curse the inhabitants of that city, so at length, their Gods being absent, did overcome them, as Virgil sings:

That kept this Realm, our Gods
Their Altars have forsook, and blest abodes.

Now the verse with which the Gods were called out and the enemies were cursed, when the city was assaulted round about, let him that would know find it out in Livy and Marcrobius; but also many of these Serenus Samonicus, in his book of secret things, makes mention of.

CHAPTER LXXI. OF MANY WORDS JOINED TOGETHER, AS IN SENTENCES AND VERSES; AND OF THE VIRTUES AND ASTRICTIONS OF CHARMS.

BESIDES the virtues of words and names, there is also a greater virtue found in sentences, from the truth contained in them, which hath a very great power of impressing, changing, binding, and establishing, so that being used it doth shine the more, and being resisted is more confirmed and consolidated; which virtue is not in simple words, but in sentences, by which anything is affirmed or denied; of which sort are verses, enchantments, imprecations, deprecations, orations, invocations, obtestations, adjurations, conjurations, and such like. Therefore, in composing verses and orations for attracting the virtue of any star or deity, you must diligently consider what virtue any star contains, as, also, what effects and operations, and to infer them in verses, by praising, extolling, amplifying, and setting forth those things which such a kind of star is wont to cause by way of its influence, and by vilifying and dispraising those things which it is wont to destroy and hinder, and by supplicating and begging for that which we desire to get, and by condemning and detesting that which we would have destroyed and hindered; and after the same manner to make an elegant oration, and duly distinct, by articles, with competent numbers and proportions. Moreover, magicians command that we call upon and pray by the names of the same star, or name to them to whom such a verse belongs, by their wonderful things, or miracles, by their courses and ways in their sphere, by their light, by the dignity of their kingdom, by the beauty and brightness that is in it, by their strong and powerful virtues, and by such like things as these. As Psyche, in Apuleius, prays to Ceres, saying, "I beseech thee by thy fruitful right hand, I intreat thee by the joyful ceremonies of harvests, by the quiet silence of thy chests, by the winged chariots of dragons, thy servants, by the furrows of the Sicilian earth, the devouring wagon, the clammy earth, by the place of going down into cellars at the light nuptials of Proserpina, and returns at the light inventions of her daughter, and other things which are concealed in her temple in the city of Eleusis, in Attica." Besides, with the divers sorts of the names of the stars, they command us to call upon them by the names of the Intelligences ruling over the stars themselves, of which we shall speak more at large in their proper place. They that desire further examples of these, let them search into the hymns of Orpheus, than which nothing is more efficacious in Natural Magic, if they, together with their circumstances, which wise men know, be used according to a due harmony with all attention. But to return to our purpose. Such like verses, being aptly and duly made, according to the Rule of the Stars, and being full of signification and meaning, and opportunely pronounced with vehement affection (as according to the number and the proportion of their articles, so according to the form resulting from the articles) and, by the violence of imagination, do confer a very great power in the enchanter, and sometimes transfers it upon the thing enchanted, to bind and direct it to the same purpose for which the affections and speeches of the enchanter are intended. Now, the instrument of enchanters is a most pure, harmonical spirit--warm, breathing, living, bringing with it motion, affection, and signification; composed of its parts, endued with sense, and conceived by reason. By the quality, therefore, of this spirit, and by the celestial similitude, thereof (besides those things which have already been spoken of) verses, also, from the opportunity of time, receive from above most excellent virtues; and, indeed, are more sublime and efficacious than spirits, and. vapors exhaling out of the vegetable life, such as herbs, roots, gums, aromatical things, and fumes and such like. And, therefore, magicians enchanting things, are wont to blow and breathe upon them the words of the verse, or to breathe in the virtue with the spirit, that so the whole virtue of the soul be directed to the thing enchanted, being disposed for the receiving of said virtue. And here it is to be noted that every oration, writing and words, as they induce accustomed motions by their accustomed numbers, proportions, and form, so (besides their usual order) being pronounced, or wrote backwards, move unto unusual effects.

CHAPTER LXXII. OF THE WONDERFUL POWER OF ENCHANTMENTS.

THEY say that the power of enchantments and verses is, so great, that it is believed they are able to subvert almost all Nature. Apuleius saith that with a magical whispering, swift rivers are turned back, the slow sea is bound, the winds are breathed out with one accord, the Sun is stopped, the Moon is clarified, the Stars are pulled out, the day is kept back, the night is prolonged; and of these things Lucan writes:

The courses of all things did cease, the night

Prolonged was, 'twas long before 'twas light;
Astonied was the headlong World--all this
Was by the hearing of a verse.
And a little before:
Thessalian verse did into his heart so flow,
 That it did make a greater heat of love.
And elsewhere:
No dregs of poison being by him drunk;
 His wits decay'd enchanted----
Also Virgil, in Damon,
Charms can command the Moon down from the Skie;
 Circe's Charms chang'd Ulysses' company.
 A cold snake, being charm'd, burst----
And Ovid, in his untitled book, saith:
With charms doth with 'ring Ceres dye,
 Dried are the fountains all,
 Acorns from Okes, enchanted Grapes,
 And apples from trees fall.

If these things were not true, there would not be such strict penal statutes made against them that should enchant fruit. And Tibullus saith of a certain enchantress:

Her with Charms drawing Stars from Heaven, I,
 And turning the course of rivers, did espy;
 She parts the earth, and Ghosts from Sepulchres
 Draws up, and fetcheth bones away from th' fires,
 And at her pleasure scatters clouds i' th' Air,
 And makes it Snow in Summer hot and fair.

Of all which that enchantress seems to boast herself in Ovid, when she saith:

At will, I make swift streams retire
 To their fountains, whilst their Banks admire;
 Sea toss and smooth; clear Clouds with Clouds deform.
 With Spells and Charms I break the Viper's jaw,
 Cleave solid Rocks, Oakes from their seizures draw,
 Whole Woods remove, the lofty Mountains shake,
 Earth for to groan, and Ghosts from graves awake,
 And thee, O Moon, I draw----

Moreover, all poets sing, and philosophers do not deny, that by verses many wonderful things may be done, as corn to be removed, lightnings to be commanded, diseases to be cured, and the like. For Cato, himself, in country affairs, used some enchantments against the diseases of beasts, which as yet are extant in his writings. Also Josephus testifies that Solomon was skilled in those kinds of enchantments. Also Celsus Africanus reports, according to the Egyptian doctrine, that man's body, according to the number of the faces of the Zodiac Signs, was taken care of by so many, viz., thirty-six spirits, whereof each undertake and defend their proper part, whose names they call with a peculiar voice, which, being called upon, restore to health with their enchantments, the diseased parts of the body.

CHAPTER LXXIII. OF THE VIRTUE OF WRITING, AND OF MAKING IMPRECATIONS, AND INSCRIPTIONS.

THE use of words and speech is to express the inwards of the mind, and from thence to draw forth the secrets of the thoughts, and do declare the will of the speaker. Now, writing is the last expression of the mind, and is the number of speech and voice, as, also, the collection, state, end, continuing, and iteration, making a habit, which is not perfected with the act of one's voice. And whatsoever is in the mind, in voice, in word, in operation, and in speech, the whole and all of this is in writing also. And as nothing which is conceived in the mind is not expressed by voice, so nothing which is expressed is not also written. And, therefore, magicians command that in every work there be imprecations and inscriptions made, by which the operator may, express his affection; that if he gather an herb, or a stone, he declare for what use he doth it; if he make a picture, he say and write to what end he maketh it, with imprecations and inscriptions. Albertus, also, in his book, called the Speculum, doth not disallow this, without which all our works would never be brought into effect, seeing a disposition does not cause an effect, but the act of the disposition. We find, also, that the same kind of precepts was in use amongst the ancients, as Virgil testifies when he sings:
    I walk around
  First with these Threads--in number which three are--
  'Bout th' Altars, thrice I shall thy Image bear.
And a little after:
  Knots, Amaryllis, tie! of Colors three,
  Then say, "These bonds I knit for Venus be."
And in the same place:
  As with one fire this clay doth harder prove,
  The wax more soft; so, Daphnis, with our love.

CHAPTER LXXIV. OF THE PROPORTION, CORRESPONDENCY, AND REDUCTION OF LETTERS TO THE CELESTIAL SIGNS AND PLANETS, ACCORDING TO VARIOUS TONGUES, AND A TABLE THEREOF.

GOD gave to man a mind and speech, which (as saith Mercurius Trismegistus) are thought to be a gift of the same virtue, power, and immortality. The omnipotent God hath by his providence divided the speech of men into divers languages, which languages have, according to their diversity, received divers and proper characters of writing, consisting in their certain order, number, and figure, not so disposed and formed by hap or chance, nor by the weak judgment of man, but from above, whereby they agree with the celestial and divine bodies and virtues. But before all notes of languages, the writing of the Hebrews is, of all, the most sacred in the figures of characters, points of vowels, and tops of accents; or consisting in matter, form, and spirit.

The position of the Stars being first made in the seat of God, which is Heaven, after the figure of them (as the masters of the Hebrews testify) are most fully formed the letters of the Celestial Mysteries, as by their figure, form, and signification, so by the numbers signified by them, and also by the various harmonies of their conjunction. Whence the more curious Mecubals of the Hebrews do undertake--by the figure of their letters, the forms of characters, and their signature, simpleness or composition, separation, crookedness or directness, defect, abounding, greatness or littleness, crowning, opening or shutting, order, transmutation, joining together, revolution of letters, and of points, and tops, by the supputation of numbers, and by the letters of things signified--to explain all things; how they proceed from the first cause, and are again to be reduced into the same. Moreover, they divide the letters of the Hebrew alphabet, viz., into twelve simple, seven double, and three mothers, which, they say, signify as characters of things--the Twelve Signs, Seven Planets, and Three Elements, viz., Fire, Water, and Earth; for they account Air no element, but as the glue and spirit of the elements. To these, also, they appoint points and tops. As, therefore, by the aspects of planets and signs, together with the Elements (the working spirit and truth), all things have been and are brought forth. So, by these characters of letters and points, signifying those things that are brought forth, the names of all things are appointed, as certain Signs and vehicles of things explained, carrying with them everywhere their essence and virtues. The profound meanings and Signs are inherent in those characters, and figures of them, as also numbers, place, order, and revolution; so that Origenes, therefore, thought that those names, when translated into another idiom, do not retain their proper virtue. For only the original names, which are rightly imposed, because they signify naturally and have a natural activity. It is not so with them which signify at pleasure, which have no activity as they are signifying, as they are but certain natural things in themselves. Now, if there be any language whose words have a natural signification, it is manifest that this is the Hebrew; the order of which he that shall profoundly and radically observe, and shall know to resolve proportionably the letters thereof, shall have a rule exactly to find out any idiom. There are, therefore, two and twenty letters, which are the foundation of the world, and of creatures that are, and are named in it, and every saying and every creature are of them, and by their revolutions receive their name, being, and virtue.

He, therefore, that will find them out, must by each joining together of the letters so long examine them, until the voice of God is manifest, and the framing of the most sacred letters be opened and discovered; for hence voices and words have efficacy in magical works, because that in which Nature first exerciseth magical efficacy is the voice of God. But these are of more deep speculation than to be handled in this book. To return to the division of the letters: of these, amongst the Hebrews, are three mothers, viz., y, w, '; seven double, viz., th, r, p, k, d, n, b. The other twelve, viz., sh, q, tz, `, s, g, m, l, t, ch, z, h, are simple. The rule is the same amongst the Chaldeans, and, by the imitation of those above, also the letters of other tongues are distributed to the Signs, Planets, and Elements, after their order. For the vowels in the Greek tongue answer to the Seven Planets, and the others are attributed to the Twelve Signs of the Zodiac, the Four Elements, and the Spirit of the World. Amongst the Latins there is the same signification of them. For the five vowels A, E, I, O, U, and J and V, consonants, are ascribed to the Seven Planets, and the consonants, B, C, D, F, G, L, M, N, P, R, S, T, are answerable to the Twelve Signs. The rest, viz., K, Q, X, Z, make the Elements. H the aspiration, represents the Spirit of the World. Y, because it is a Greek, and not a Latin character, and serving only to Greek words, follows the nature of its idiom.

But this you must not be ignorant of, that it is observed by all wise men, that the Hebrew letters are the most efficacious of all, because they have the greatest similitude with celestials and the world, and that the letters of the other tongues have not so great an efficacy because they are more distant from them. Now the disposition of these the following table will explain. Also all the letters have double numbers of their order, viz., extended, which simply express of what number the letters are, according to their order; and collected, which re-collect with themselves the numbers of all the preceding letters. Also they have integral numbers, which result from the names of letters, according to their various manners of numbering. The virtues of which numbers, he that shall know, shall be able in every tongue to draw forth wonderful mysteries by their letters, as also to tell what things have been past, and foretell things to come. There are also other mysterious joinings of letters with numbers, but we shall abundantly discourse of all these in the following books. Wherefore we will now put an end to this first book.

HENRY MORLEY'S CRITICISM.

LITTLE disguised by Hebrew admixture, and little by the speculations of the Platonists of Alexandria, Philo the Jew, Plotinus, and Iamblichus, whom the young student quotes most frequently, we have again the Attic Moses, Plato, speaking through a young and strong heart to the world. Very great was the influence of Plato in this period of wakening to thought. Nothing was known by experience of Nature, for little had been learnt since the time when Plato, theorising upon Nature, owned it to be impossible to arrive at any certain result in our speculations upon the creation of the visible universe and its authors; "wherefore," he said, "even if we should only advance reasons not less probable than those of others, you should still be content." In this spirit alone Cornelius Agrippa taught his age: "There are these marvels well accredited; there is this cumbrous and disjointed mass of earthly, sensible experience, which there is no way of explaining left to me but one. I accept the marvels, foolish as they seem; they are as well accredited as things more obviously true. With God all things are possible. In God all things consist. I will adopt Plato's belief, that the world is animated by a moving soul, and from the soul of the world I will look up to its Creator. I cannot rest content with a confused mass of evidence; I will animate with my own soul, and a faith in its divine origin, the world about me. I will adopt the glorious belief of Plato, that we sit here as in a cavern with our faces held from looking to the cavern's mouth, down which a light is streaming and pours in a flood over our heads, broken by shadows of things moving in the world above. We see the shadows on the wall, hear echoes, and believe in all as the one known truth of substance and of voice, although these are but the images of the superiors. I also will endeavor to climb up out of the cave into the land flooded with sunlight. I connect all that we see here with Plato's doctrine of superior ideas, I subdue matter to spirit, I will see true knowledge in apparent foolishness, and connect the meanest clod with its divine Creator. I will seek to draw down influences, and to fill my soul with a new strength imparted by the virtue of ideas streaming from above. The superior manifest in the inferior is the law of Nature manifested in the thing created. My soul is not sufficient for itself; beyond it and above it lie eternal laws, subtle, not having substance or form, yet the cause of form and substance. I cannot hope to know them otherwise than as ideas; to unborn generations they will be revealed, perhaps; to me they are ideas, celestial influences, working intelligences. I believe in them, and I desire to lay open my soul to their more perfect apprehension. They are not God, though God created them; they are not man, though they have by divine ordainment formed him. The more I dwell upon their qualities, the more I long for the divine, the more shall I be blessed by the reception of their rays. The more intensely I yearn heavenward, the more shall I bring down heaven to dwell in my soul."

So we may hear, if we will, the spirit of the young inquirer pleading to us from across the centuries, and if our own minds ever yearned for an escape from the delusions of the grosser sense and the restriction set by crowds on free inquiry, there is no true heart that will not say: "You labored well, my brother."

AGRIPPA AND THE ROSICRUCIANS.

THE secrets to be talked over between Cornelius and his friend related to that study of the mysteries of knowledge in which the Theosophists assisted one another. Secret societies, chiefly composed of curious and learned youths, had by this time become numerous, and numerous especially among the Germans. Not only the search after the philosopher's stone, which was then worthy to be prosecuted by enlightened persons, but also the new realms of thought laid open by the first glance at Greek literature, and by the still more recent introduction of a study of the Hebrew language, occupied the minds of these associated scholars. Such studies often carried those who followed them within the borders of forbidden ground, and therefore secrecy was a condition necessary to their freedom of inquiry. Towards the close of the sixteenth century such associations (the foundation of which had been a desire to keep thought out fetters) were developed into the form of brotherhoods of Rosicrucians: Physician, Theosophist, Chemist, and now, by the mercy of God, Rosicrucian, became then the style in which a brother gloried. The brotherhoods of Rosicrucians are still commonly remembered, but in the social history of Europe they are less to be considered than those first confederations of Theosophists, which nursed indeed mystical errors gathered from the Greeks and Jews, but out of whose theories there was developed much of a pure spiritualism that entered into strife with what was outwardly corrupt and sensual in the body of the Roman Church, and thus prepared the way for the more vital attacks of the Reformers.

When first Greek studies were revived, the monks commonly regarded them as essentially adverse to Roman interests, and the very language seemed to them infected with the plague of heresy. In the Netherlands it became almost a proverb with them that to be known for a grammarian was to be reputed heretic. Not seldom, indeed, in later times, has John Reuchlin, who, for his Greek and Hebrew scholarship was called, after the manner of his day, the Phoenix of Germans, and who was the object of an ardent hero worship to men like Cornelius Agrippa, been called also the Father of the Reformation. Certainly Luther, Erasmus, and Melancthon had instruction from him; by him it was that Schwartzerd had been taught to call himself Melancthon; and many will remember how, after his death, Erasmus, in a pleasant dialogue, raised his old friend to the rank of saint, and prayed to him, "Oh, holy soul, be favorable to the languages; be favorable to those that love honorers of the languages; be propitious to the sacred tongues." But Reuchlin--for the taste of smoke in it, Reuchlin quasi Reeki, his name was turned into the Greek form, Capnio,--Reuchlin, or Capnio, never passed as a reformer beyond detestation of the vices of the priesthood. Like Cornelius, who begun his life before the public as a scholar by an act of homage to his genius, Reuchlin loved liberty and independence, cherished the idol of free conscience, but never fairly trusted himself to its guidance. To the last an instinct of obedience to the church governed his actions, and the spiritual gold he could extract from Plato, Aristotle, or the wonderful Cabala of the Jews, was in but small proportion to the dross fetched up with it from the same ancient mines.

A contemporary notion of the Reformation, not without some rude significance in this respect, is said to have been obtruded upon Charles V. by a small body of unknown actors, who appeared before him in 1530, when he was in Germany. He had been dining with his brother Ferdinand, and did not refuse their offer to produce a comedy in dumb show. One dressed as a scholar, labelled Capnio, brought before the emperor a bundle of sticks--some crooked and some straight--laid them down in the highway, and departed. Then entered another, who professed to represent Erasmus, looked at the sticks, shook his head, made various attempts to straighten the crooked ones, and finding that he could not do so, shook his head over them again, put them down where he had found them, and departed. Then came an actor, labelled Luther, with a torch, who set all that was crooked in the bundle blazing. When he was gone entered one dressed as an emperor, who tried in vain to put the fire out with his sword. Last came Pope Leo X., to whom, grieving dismally over the spectacle before him, there were two pails brought; one contained oil, the other water. His holiness, to quell the fire, poured over it the bucketful of oil, and while the flame attracted all eyes by the power, beyond mastery, with which it shot up towards heaven, the actors made their escape undetected.

Now, it was over the crooked sticks of Capnio, and many other matters difficult of comprehension, that Cornelius and his confederates were bent in curious and anxious study. "The bearer of the letters," said Landulph, in excusing himself on the plea of illness, from a winter journey to a friend at Avignon--"the bearer of these letters is a German, native of Nuremberg, but dwelling at Lyons; and he is a curious inquirer after hidden mysteries, a free man restrained by no fetters, who, impelled by I know not what rumor concerning you, desires to sound your depths." That the man himself might be sounded, as one likely to have knowledge of some important things, and that if it seemed fit, he should be made a member of their brotherhood, was the rest of the recommendation of this person by Landulph to his friend Agrippa.

At Lyons were assembled many members of his league, awaiting the arrival of the young soldier-philosopher. His early taste for an inquiry into mysteries had caused him to take all possible advantage, as a scholar, of each change of place and each extension of acquaintance among learned men who were possessors of rare books. He had searched every accessible volume that might help him in the prosecution of the studies that had then a fascination, not for him only, but for not a few of the acutest minds in Christendom. At that time there was, in the modern sense, no natural science; the naturalists of ancient Greece and Rome being the sole authorities in whom the learned could put trust. Of the miraculous properties of plants and animals, and parts of animals, even at the close of the sixteenth century, careful and sober men placed as accepted knowledge many extravagant ideas on record. At the beginning of the century, when a belief in the influences of the stars, in the interferences of demons, and in the most wonderful properties of bodies, was the rule among learned and unlearned--Luther himself not excluded from the number--an attempt to collect and group, if it might be, according to some system, the most recondite secrets of what passed for the divine ordering of Nature, was in no man's opinion foolish, though in the opinion of the greater number criminal. Belief in the mysteries of magic, not want of belief, caused men to regard with enmity and dread researches into secrets that might give to those by whom they were discovered subtle and superhuman power, through possessing which they would acquire an influence, horrible to suspect, over their fellow-creatures. Detaching their search into the mysteries of the universe from all fear of this kind, the members of such secret societies as that to which Cornelius belonged gathered whatever fruit they could from the forbidden tree, and obtained mutual benefit by frank exchange of information. Cornelius had already, by incessant search, collected notes for a complete treatise upon magic, and of these not a few were obtained from Reuchlin's Hebrew-Christian way of using the Cabala.

From Avignon, after a short stay, Cornelius Agrippa went to Lyons, and remaining there some weeks, compared progress with his friends, and no doubt also formally divested himself of any further responsibility connected with the Spanish enterprise. Towards the end of this year, a friend at Cologne, Theodoric, Bishop of Cyrene, wrote, expressing admiration of him, as of one among so many thousand Germans who at sundry times and places had displayed in equal degree power to labor vigorously as a man at arms as well as man of letters. Who does not know, the bishop asks, how few of many thousands have done that' He envies those who can thus earn the wreath of Mars without losing the favor of Minerva, and calls the youth "in arms a man, in scholarship a teacher." To escape the soldier's life of bondage seems to be now the ambition of the scholar. With the world before him, in the twenty-third year of his age, well born, distinguished among all who knew him for the rare extent of his attainments, Cornelius, attended by his servant, Stephen, quitted his friends at Lyons, and rode to Authun, where he was received in the abbey of a liberal and hospitable man, physician, theologian, and knight by turns, M. Champier, who, having been born at Saint Saphorin-le-Chateau, near Lyons, was called Symphorianus Champier, or Campegius, and who, not content with his own noble ancestry, assigned himself, by right of the Campegius, to the family of the Campegi of Bologna, and assumed its arms. He studied at Paris Litera humaniora, at Montpellier medicine, and practiced at Lyons. He lived to obtain great fame, deserving title, and losing after his death all. It was not until five years after this visit from Cornelius Agrippa that Symphorianus, acting as body physician to the Duke of Lorraine, was knighted on the battle-field of Marignano. Among his writings, those which most testify his sympathy with the inquiries of Cornelius, are a book on the Miracles. of Scripture, a Life of Arnold of Villeneuve, and a French version of Sibylline oracles. This Champier then sympathized with the enthusiasm of the young theosophist, and under his roof the first venture of Cornelius before the world of letters seems to have been planned. In the last week of May, we find that he has sent Stephen to fetch DeBrie from Dole, has summoned Antonius Xanthus from Niverne, and wishes, in association with Symphorianus, to arrange a meeting with Landulph, at any convenient place and time. He has something in hand concerning which he wishes to take counsel with his comrades. A few days afterwards he and Landulph are at Dole together; and while Cornelius has left Dole for a short time to go to Chalon (sur Saone), his friend sends word to him that he has engaged on his behalf the interest of the Archbishop of Besancon (Antony I., probably not an old man, since he was alive thirty years afterwards), who desires greatly to see him, and boasts that he can give information of some things unknown perhaps even to him. The archbishop is impatient to see the person who has stored up from rare books, even those written in Greek and Hebrew, so great a number of the secrets of the universe. Landulph, to content him, antedates the time appointed for his friend's return, and while reporting this, adds that there are many at Dole loud in the praise of Cornelius, and none louder than himself. The influence of his associates is evidently at work on his behalf among the magnates of the town and university of Dole, and learned men in the adjoining towns of Burgundy, for it is at Dole that he has resolved to make his first public appearance as a scholar, by expounding in a series of orations Reuchlin's book on the Mirific Word. At Chalon, however, Cornelius fell sick of a summer pestilence, from which he was recovering on the eighth of July. As soon as health permitted he returned to Dole, where there was prepared for him a cordial reception.

Dole is a pretty little town, and at that time possessed the university which was removed in after years to Besancon. Its canton was called, for its beauty and fertility, the Val d'Amour; and when Besancon was independent of the lords of Burgundy, Dole was their capital. A pleasant miniature capitol, with not four thousand inhabitants, a parliament, a university, a church of Notre Dame whereof the tower could be seen from distant fields, a princely residence--Dole la Joyeuse they called it until thirty years before Cornelius Agrippa declaimed his orations there; but after it had been, in 1479, captured and despoiled by a French army, it was called Dole la Dolente.

Mistress of Dole and Burgundy was Maximilian's daughter, Margaret of Austria, who, in this year of Agrippa's life, was twenty-nine years old. She was already twice a widow. When affianced twice--once vainly to France, a second time to Spain, and likely to perish in a tempest before reaching her appointed husband--she had wit to write a clever epitaph upon herself. Her Spanish husband died almost after the first embrace, and she had since, after four years of wedded happiness, lost her true husband, Philibert of Savoy. She was twenty-four years old when that happened, and resolved to make an end of marrying.

In 1506, after the death of Archduke Philip, her father Maximilian being guardian of his grandson Charles the Fifth, made Margaret his governor over the Netherlands, and appointed her to rule also over Burgundy and the Charolois. Thus she came to be, in the year 1509, mistress at Dole. A clever, lively woman, opposed strongly to France, and always mindful of the interests of that house of Austria, to which the family of young Agrippa was attached, Margaret was well known for her patronage of letters and her bounty towards learned men. It would be, therefore, a pleasant transfer of his loyalty, Agrippa, thought, from Maximilian to Margaret, if he could thereby get rid of what he regarded as camp slavery under the one, and earn the favor of the other in the academic grove. To earn Margaret's goodwill and help upon the royal road to fortune was one main object of Cornelius when he announced at Dole that he proposed to expound Reuchlin's book, on the Mirific Word, in orations, to which, inasmuch as they were to be delivered in honor of the most serene Princess Margaret, the whole public would have gratuitous admission.

Poor youth! he could not possibly have made a more genuine and honest effort, or one less proper to be used by evil men for the damnation of his character. Margaret was the princess to whom of all others he was able to pay unaffected homage, and Reuchlin, then the boast of Germans, was the scholar of whom before every other, he, a German youth, might choose to hold discourse to the Burgundians. Of Reuchlin, Aegidius, chief of the Austin Friars, wrote, that he "had blessed him and all mortals by his works." Philip Beroaldus, the younger, wrote to him: "Pope Leo X. has read your Pythagorean book, as he reads all good books, greedily; then it was read by the Cardinal de' Medici, and I am expecting next to have my turn." This book, which had been read by the Pope himself with eager pleasure, was a wonder of the day, and was in the most perfect unison with the whole tone of Agrippa's mind; he really understood it deeply, it was most dear to him as a theosophist, and he was not to be blamed if he felt, also that of all books in the world there was none of which the exposition would so fully serve his purpose of displaying the extent and depth of his own store of knowledge.

EXPOSITION OF THE CABALA.

MAINLY upon what was said and written by Cornelius Agrippa in this twenty-third year of his age has been founded the defamation by which, when he lived, his spirit was tormented and the hope of his existence miserably frustrated--by which, now that he is dead, his character comes down to us defiled. This victim, at least, has not escaped the vengeance of the monks, and his crime was that he studied vigorously in his salad days those curiosities of learning into which, at the same time, popes, bishops, and philosophers, mature of years, inquired with equal faith and almost equal relish, but less energy or courage. For a clear understanding of the ground, and of the perils of the ground, now taken by Cornelius Agrippa, little more is necessary than a clear notion of what was signified by Reuchlin's book on the Mirific Word; but what has to be said of Reuchlin and his book, as well as of other matters that will hereafter concern the fortunes of Cornelius, requires some previous attention to a subject pretty well forgotten in these days by a people rich in other knowledge; we must recall, in fact, some of the main points of the Cabala.

This account of the Cabala is derived from German sources, among which the chief are Brucker's Historia Philosophae and the Kabbala Denudata, a collection of old cabalistical writings arranged and explained by Christian Knorr von Rosenroth. The traditions, or Cabala, of the Jews, are contained in sundry books, written by Hebrew Rabbis, and consist of a strange mixture of fable and philosophy varying on a good many points, but all adhering with sufficient accuracy to one scheme of doctrine. They claim high and remote origin. Some say that the first Cabala were received by Adam from the angel Raziel, who gave him, either while he yet remained in Paradise, or else at the time of his expulsion, to console and help him, a book full of divine wisdom. In this book were the secrets of Nature, and by knowledge of them Adam entered into conversation with the Sun and Moon, knew how to summon good and evil spirits, to interpret dreams, foretell events, to heal, and to destroy. This book, handed down from father to son, came into Solomon's possession, and by its aid Solomon became master of many potent secrets. A cabalistic volume, called the Book of Raziel, was, in the middle ages, sometimes to be seen among the Jews.

Another account said that the first cabalistical book was the Sepher Jezirah, written by Abraham; but the most prevalent opinion was, that when the written law was given on Mount Sinai to Moses, the Cabala, or mysterious interpretation of it, was taught to him also. Then Moses, it was said, when he descended from the mountain, entered Aaron's tent, and taught him also the secret powers of the written word; and Aaron, having been instructed, placed himself at the right hand of Moses, and stood by while his sons, Eleazar and Ithamar, who had been called into the tent, received the same instruction. On the right and left of Moses and Aaron then sat Ithamar and Eleazar, when the seventy elders of the Sanhedrim were called in and taught the hidden knowledge. The elders finally were seated, that they might be present when all those among the common people who desired to learn came to be told those mysteries; thus the elect of the common people heard but once what the Sanhedrim heard twice, the sons of Aaron three times, and Aaron four times repeated of the secrets that had been made known to Moses by the voice of the Most High.

Of this mystical interpretation of the Scripture no person set down any account in writing, unless it was Esdras; but some Jews doubt whether he did. Israelites kept the knowledge of the doctrine by a pure tradition; but about fifty years after the destruction of Jerusalem, Akiba, a great rabbi, wrote the chief part of it in that book, Sepher-Jezireh, or the Book of the Creation, which was foolishly ascribed by a few to Abraham. A disciple of the Rabbi Akiba was Rabbi Simeon ben Jochai, who wrote more of the tradition in a book called Zoar.

The truth probably is, that the literature of cabalism, which is full of suggestion derived from the Neoplatonics of Alexandria, began with the Jews of Alexandria under the first Ptolemys. In the book of Simeon ben Schetach it went to Palestine, where it at first was little heeded; but after the destruction of Jerusalem it gained importance, and then Rabbis Akiba and Simeon ben Jochai extended it. It is indisputable that Aristotle had been studied by the writer of the Sepher-Jezireh, the oldest known book of the Cabalists. The Cabala went afterwards with other learning to Spain, and that part of it at least which deals with Hebrew anagrams cannot be traced to a time earlier than the eleventh century. Many rabbis--Abraham ben David, Saudia, Moses Botril, Moses bar Nachman, Eliezer of Garmiza, and others--have written Hebrew books for the purpose of interpreting the system of the Cabala; but it was, perhaps, not before the eighth century that it had come to receive very general attention from the Jews.

The Cabala consisted of two portions, the symbolical and the real; the symbolical Cabala being the means by which the doctrines of the real Cabala were elicited.

In the Hebrew text of the Scriptures, it was said, there is not only an evident, but there is also a latent meaning; and in its latent meaning are contained the mysteries of God and of the universe. It need scarcely be said that a belief in secret wisdom has for ages been inherent in the Oriental mind, and in the Scriptures, it was reasoned by the later Jews, all wisdom must be, of necessity, contained. Of divine authorship, they cannot be like ordinary works of men. But if they were taken only in the natural sense, might it not be said that many human works contain marvels not less surprising and morality as pure. No, it was said, as we have entertained angels, and regarded them as men, so we may entertain the words of the Most High, if we regard only their apparent sense and not their spiritual mystery. And so it was that through a blind excess of reverence the inspired writings were put to superstitious use.

The modes of examining their letters, words, and sentences, for hidden meaning, in which wholly consisted the symbolical Cabala, were three, and these were called Gemantria, Notaricon, Themura.

Gemantria was arithmetical when it consisted in applying to the Hebrew letters of a word the sense they bore as numbers, letters being used also for figures in the Hebrew as in the Greek. Then the letters in a word being taken as numbers and added up, it was considered that another word, of which the letters added up came to an equal sum, might fairly be substituted by the arithmetical gemantria. Figurative gemantria deduced mysterious interpretations from the shapes of letters used in sacred writing. Thus, in Numbers x., 35, Beth means the reversal of enemies. This kind of interpretation was known also by the name of Zurah. Architectonic gemantria constructed words from the numbers given by Scripture when describing the measurements of buildings, as the ark, or temple.

By Notaricon more words were developed from the letters of a word, as if it had consisted of so many abbreviations, or else first and last letters of words, or the first letters of successive words, were detached from their places and put side by side. By Themura, any word might be made to yield a mystery out of its anagram; these sacred anagrams were known as Zeruph. By the same branch of the symbolical Cabala three systems were furnished, in accordance with which words might be transformed by the substitution of one letter for another. The first of the systems, Albam, arranged the letters of the alphabet in two rows, one below another; the second, Athbath, gave another couple of rows; the third, Athbach, arranged them by pairs in three rows--all the pairs in the first row being the numerical value ten, in the second row a hundred, in the third a thousand; any one of these forms might be consulted, and any letter in a word exchanged for another standing either in Albam, Athbath, or Athbach, immediately above it or below it, or on the right hand of it or the left.

This was the symbolical Cabala, and the business of it was to extract, by any of the means allowed, the hidden meaning of the Scriptures. The real Cabala was the doctrine in this way elicited. It was theoretical, explaining divine qualities, the ten sephiroth, the fourfold cabalistical worlds, the thirty-two footprints of wisdom, the fifty doors to prudence, Adam Kadmon, &c.; or it was practical, explaining how to use such knowledge for the calling of spirits, the extinguishing of fires, the banishing of disease, and so forth.

The theoretical Cabala contained, it was said by

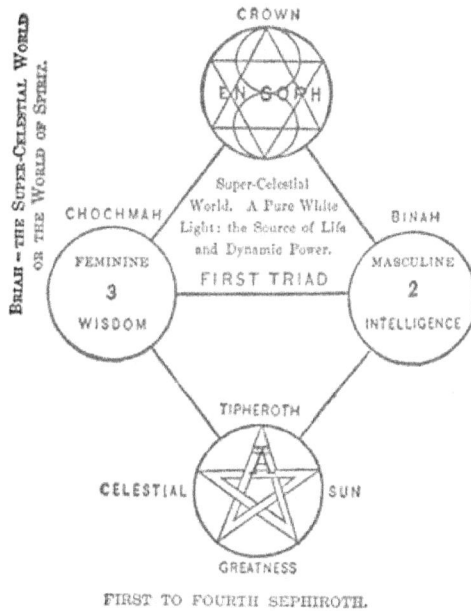

FIRST TO FOURTH SEPHIROTH.

FIRST TO FOURTH SEPHIROTH.

Christian students, many references to the Messiah. Its main points were: 1--The Tree; 2--The Chariot of Ezekiel; 3--The Work of Creation; 4--The Ancient of Days mentioned in Daniel. It concerns us most to understand the Tree. The Chariot of Ezekiel, or Maasseh Mercabah, was a description of prefigurements concerning ceremonial and judicial law. The doctrine of Creation, in the book Levischith, was a dissertation upon physics. The Ancient of Days treated of God and the Messiah in a way so mystical that cabalists generally declined to ascribe any meaning at all to the direct sense of the words employed. Of these things we need say no more, but of the Cabalistical Tree it will be requisite to speak in more detail.

It was an arrangement of the ten sephiroth. The word Sephiroth is derived by some rabbis from a word meaning to count, because they are a counting of the divine excellence. Otherwise it is considered an adaptation of the Greek word Sphere, because it represents the spheres of the universe which are successive emanations from the Deity.

In the beginning was Or Haensoph, the eternal light, from whose brightness there descended a ray through the first-born of God, Adam Kadmon, and presently, departing from its straight course, ran in a circle, and so formed the first of the sephiroth, which was called Kethei, or the crown, because superior to all the rest. Having formed this circle, the ray resumed its straight course till it again ran in a circle to produce the second of the ten sephiroth, Chochma, wisdom, because wisdom is the source of all. The same ray of divine light passed on, losing gradually, as it became more distant from its holy source, some of its power, and formed presently, in like manner, the third of the sephiroth, called Binah, or understanding, because understanding is the channel through which wisdom flows to things below--the origin of human knowledge. The fourth of the sephiroth is called Gedolah or Chesed, greatness or goodness, because God, as being great and good,

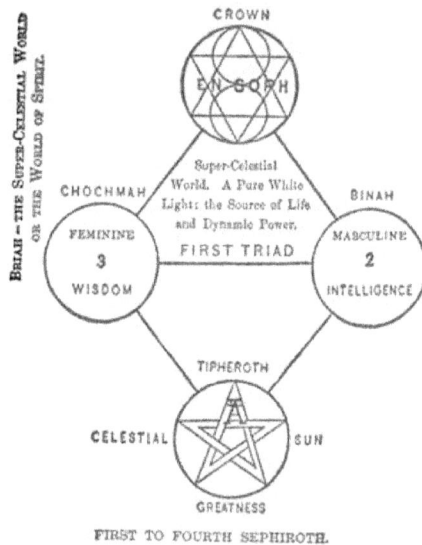

FIRST TO FOURTH SEPHIROTH.

FOURTH TO NINTH SEPHIROTH.

created all things. The fifth is Geburah, strength, because it is by strength that He maintains them, and because strength is the only source of justice in the world. The sixth of the sephiroth, Thpereth, beauty or grace, unites the qualities of the preceding. The four last of the sephiroth are successively named Nezach, victory; Hod, honor; Jesod, or Schalom, the foundation or peace; and finally, Malcuth, the kingdom. Each of the ten has also a divine name, and their divine names, written in the same order, are Ejeh, Jah, Jehovah (pronounced Elohim), Eloah, Elohim, Jehovah (pronounced as usual), Lord Sabaoth, Jehovah Zebaoth, Elchai (the living God), Adonai (the Lord). By these circles our world is surrounded, and, weakened in its passage through them, but able to bring down with it powers that are the character of each, divine light reaches us. These sephiroth, arranged in a peculiar manner, form the Tree of the Cabalists; they are also sometimes arranged in the form of a man, Adam Kadmon, according to the idea of the Neoplatonics that the figure of the world was that of a man's body. In accordance with another view derived from the same school, things in this world were supposed to be gross images of things above. Matter was said by the cabalists to have been formed by the withdrawal of the divine ray, by the emanation of which from the first source it was produced. Everything created was created by an emanation from the source of all, and that which being most distant contains least of the divine essence is capable of gradual purification; so that even the evil spirits will in course of time become holy and pure, and be assimilated to the brightest of the emanations from Or Haensoph. God, it was said, is all in all; everything is part of the divine essence, with a growing, or perceptive, or reflective power, one or all, and by that which has one all may be acquired. A stone may become a plant; a plant, a

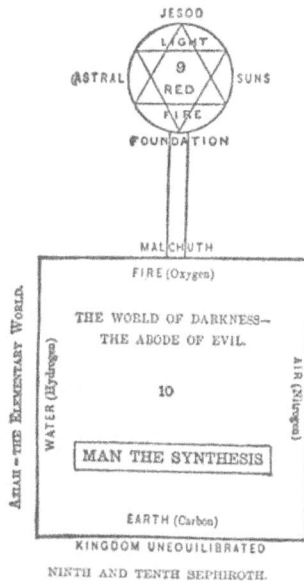

NINTH AND TENTH SEPHIROTH.

beast; a beast, a man; a man, an angel; an angel, a creator.

This kind of belief, which was derived also from the Alexandrian Platonists led to that spiritual cabalism by which such Christians as Reuchlin and Agrippa profited. It connected them by a strong link with the divine essence, and they, feeling perhaps more distinctly than their neighbors that they were partakers of the divine nature, and might, by a striving after purity of soul and body win their way to a state of spiritual happiness and power, cut themselves off from all communion with the sensuality that had become the scandal of the Church of Rome, and keenly perceived, as they expressed strongly, their sense of the degraded habits of the priests. It was in this way that the Christian Cabalists assisted in the labors of the Reformation.

Little more has to be said about their theory, and that relates to the four Cabalistical Worlds. These were placed in the four spaces between the upper sephiroth. Between the first and second was placed Aziluth, the outflowing, which contained the purest beings, the producers of the rest. Between the second and third sephiroth was the world Briah, or the thrones, containing spirits less pure, but still not material. They were classed into wheels, lightnings, lions, burning spirits, angels, children of God, cherubim. Their prince was called Metatron. The world in the next interspace, called Jezireh, angels, approached more nearly to a material form; and the fourth, Asiah, was made wholly material. From this point density increases till our world is reached. Asiah is the abode of the Klippoth, or material spirits striving against God. They travel through the air, their bodies are of dense air, incorruptible, and they have power to work in the material world. With Catoriel, Adam Belial, Esau, Aganiel, Usiel, Ogiel, Thomiel, Theumiel, for captains, they fight in two armies under their chiefs Zamiel and Lilith. Their enemies are the angels, who contend against them with two armies, led by Metatron and Sandalphon. Lilith is the begetter of the powers striving against light.

The nature of man's soul, said Cabalists, is threefold--vegetative, perceptive, intellectual--each embracing each. It emanates from the upper sephiroth, is composed of the pure elements--for the four elements, either in their pure and spiritual or their gross form, enter into all things--is expansive, separates after death, so that the parts return each to its own place, but reunite to praise God on the Sabbaths and new moons. With each soul are sent into the world a guardian and an accusing angel.

THE MIRIFIC WORD.

NOW, as the creative light runs round each upper world before coming to ours, it comes to us charged with supernal influence, and such an idea lies at the foundation of cabalistical magic. By what secret to have power over this line of communication with superior worlds it is for practical cabalism to discover.

The secret consisted chiefly in the use of names. God, it was said, gave to all things their names; He could have given no name that was not mystically fit; every such name, therefore, is a word containing divine power, and especially affecting that thing, person or spirit to which it belongs. The Scripture tells us that there are names written in heaven; why, it was said, should they be written there, if they be useless. Through the knowledge of such divine names, it is affirmed, Moses overcame the sorcerers of Egypt, Elias brought fire from heaven, Daniel closed the mouths of lions. But of all names by which wonders can be wrought, the Mirific Word of Words (here we come to the main thought of Reuchlin's book, and to the central topic of the oratory of Cornelius) was the concealed name of God--the Schem-hammaphoraseh. Whoever knows the true pronunciation of the name Jehovah--the name from which all other divine names in the world spring as the branches from a tree, the name that binds together the sephiroth--whoever has that in his mouth has the world in his mouth. When it is spoken angels are stirred by the wave of sound. It rules all creatures, works all miracles, it commands all the inferior names of deity which are borne by the several angels that in heaven govern the respective nations of the earth. The Jews had a tradition that when David was on the point of fighting with Goliath, Jaschbi, the giant's brother, tossed him up into the air, and held a spear below, that he might fall upon it. But Abishai, when he saw that, pronounced the holy name, and David remained in the air till Jaschbi's spear no longer threatened him. They said, also, that the Mirific name was among the secrets contained in the Holy of Holies, and that when any person having entered that shrine of the temple learnt the word of power, he was roared at as he came out by two brazen lions, or bayed by brazen dogs, until through terror he lost recollection of it. Some Jews accounted also by a fable of this nature for our Savior's miracles. They said that, having been admitted within the Holy of Holies, and having learnt the sacred mystery, he wrote it down upon a tablet, cut open his thigh, and having put the tablet in the wound, closed the flesh over it by uttering the name of wonder. As he passed out the roaring lions caused the secret to pass from his mind, but afterwards he had only to cut out the tablet from his thigh, and, as the beginning of miracles, heal instantly the wound in his own flesh by pronouncing the Mirific Word. Such Jewish details were, of course, rejected by the Christians, who accepted the essential principles of the Cabala.

As the name of all power was the hidden name of God, so there were also names of power great, though limited, belonging to the angels and the evil spirits. To discover the names of the spirits, by applying to the Hebrew text of Scripture the symbolical Cabala, was to acquire some of the power they possessed. Thus, it being said of the Sodomites that they were struck with blindness, the Hebrew word for blindness was translated into Chaldee, and the Chaldee word by one of the symbolical processes was made to yield the name of a bad angel, Schabriri, which, being written down, was employed as a charm to cure ophthalmia. A common mode of conjuration with these names of power was by the use of amulets, pieces of paper or parchment on which, for certain purposes, certain names were written. At his first entrance into the world such an amulet, with the names "Senoi Sansenoi, Semongeloph," upon it was slipped round the neck of the new-born child, so that the infant scarcely saw the light before it was collared by the genius of superstition.

Another mode of conjuration consisted in the use, not of names, but of the Psalms of David. Whole volumes were written upon this use of the Psalms. The first of them, written on doeskin, was supposed to help the birth of children; others could, it was thought, be so written as to make those who carried them invisible; others secured favors from princes; others extinguished fires. The transcription of a psalm for any such purpose was no trifling work, because, apart from the necessary care in the formation of letters, some having a mystical reason for being larger than others, it was necessary for the copyist, as soon as he had written down one line, to plunge into a bath. Moreover, that the charm might be the work of a pure man, before beginning every new line of his manuscript, it was thought necessary that he should repeat the plunge.

REUCHLIN THE MYSTIC.

SUCH were the mysteries of the Hebrew Cabala, strangely blending a not unrefined philosophy with basest superstition. It remains for us to form some just opinion of the charm they had for many Christian scholars in the first years of the sixteenth century. Reuchlin, or Capnio, was of such scholars the leader and the type; as such, indeed, he was accepted by the young Cornelius Agrippa. He was the greatest Hebrew scholar of his day, and had become so by his own natural bent. Born at Pfortzheim, of the poorest parents, two and thirty years before Agrippa came into the world, taught Latin at the town school, and winning in his youth a ducal patron by his tunable voice as chorister in the court chapel at Baden, by his quick wit, and his serene, lively, amiable temper, he never afterwards lacked powerful assistance.

The life of Reuchlin is the story of the origin of Greek and Hebrew studies among learned Europeans. He was sent with the Margrave's son, afterwards Bishop of Utrecht, to Paris. The fall of Constantinople, in 1453, had caused fugitive Greeks to betake themselves to many European cities, where they sometimes gave instruction in their language. Reuchlin, at Paris, learned Greek from a Spartan, who gave him instruction also in caligraphy and made him so clever a workman with his pen, that he could eke out his means and buy books with money earned as a Greek copyist. He studied Aristotle with the Spartan. Old John Wessel, of Groningen, a disciple of Thomas a Kempis, taught him Hebrew, and invited him to a direct study of the Bible. At the age of twenty he was engaged by publishers to write a Latin dictionary, which he called Breviloquus. At the age of twenty he taught Greek publicly, laying his main stress on a study of the grammar; the good sense he spoke emptied the benches of the sophisters around him, and produced complaints from old-fashioned professors. It was then urged that all the views disclosed in Greek books were essentially opposed to the spirit and belief of Rome. The monks had no commerce with the language; and when they came to a Greek quotation in a book that they were copying, were used to inscribe the formula "Graeca sunt, non leguntur." Reuchlin maintained his ground, at twenty-five wrote a Greek grammar, lectured at Poictiers, and was made licentiate of civil law. His notion of law studies was expressed in a formula that has been applied in other terms to other things: In his first year the young lawyer knows how to decide all causes, in the second begins to be uncertain, in the third acknowledges that he knows nothing, and then first begins to learn. In the last of these stages of progress the licentiate of Poictiers repaired to Tubingen, and practiced as an advocate with such success that he made money and married. At Tubingen, Reuchlin won the confidence of Eberhard of the Beard, became his private secretary and one of his privy-councillors, and went with him to Rome in 1482, his age then being eight and twenty. At Rome he distinguished himself as an orator before the Pope, and was considered to speak Latin wonderfully well for a German. After his return to Germany, John Reuchlin remained with Eberhard in Stuttgard, became assessor of the Supreme Court at the age of thirty, and a year afterwards was elected proctor for the body of the Dominicans throughout all Germany, which unpaid office he held for nearly thirty years. At the age of thirty-one he received at Tubingen his doctorate, and in the year following, that is to say, in the year of Cornelius Agrippa's birth, he was sent with two others to Frankfort, Cologne, and Aix-la-Chapelle, on the occasion of the coronation of Maximilian as Roman emperor. Then it was that Maximilian first became acquainted with him. Reuchlin had then a house at Stuttgard, and was known as a great cultivator of the learned languages, while he was also high in the favor of his own prince, and in constant request as a practitioner of law. In 1490 he was sent to Rome on another mission, and on his way through Florence enjoyed personal intercourse with Giovanni Pico di Mirandola, the scholar who, although a determined antagonist to the astrologers, was a great friend to cabalism and the introducer of the cabalistic mysteries into the favor of Italian scholars. By him Reuchlin was further stimulated to the love of Hebrew lore. When, two years afterwards, Reuchlin was at Linz on state business with the Emperor Frederic III., it was something, indeed, that the base-born scholar was raised to the dignity of court palatine, but it was more to Reuchlin that the court physician was a learned Jew, Jehiel Loans, who perfected his intimacy with the Hebrew. His aim then was, above all things, first to study the original text of the Old Testament, and secondly to read the writings of the Cabalists. The emperor, whose life was then about to close (he died while Reuchlin was at Linz), saw here another way of gratifying the agreeable and kindly scholar, for he not only made Reuchlin a count palatine (his arms were a golden altar, from which smoke arose, with the inscription "Ara Capnionis"), but he also presented to him a very ancient Hebrew Bible, written carefully on parchment, a treasure then worth three hundred gold crowns, which is to be seen still in the library of the Grand Duke of Carlsruhe, where it is regarded as the oldest of its kind in Europe. With the knowledge imparted by Jehiel Loans, and the actual text in which all mysteries lay hidden, Reuchlin went home enriched as much as he had been ennobled. Hebrew writing was at that time very rare, and was to be met with chiefly in the hands of Jews. At Hebrew Reuchlin labored, collecting Hebrew books and works expounding the Cabala, whenever possible; and eventually he gave life in Germany, as Giovanni Pico di Mirandola was giving life in Italy, to the cabalistical philosophy, the great impulse to this German revival being the publication of the book on the Mirific Word. It first appeared at Basle, in the year 1495, the author's age then being forty-one. It was not published at Tubingen till 1514. The book was regarded as a miracle of heavenly wisdom. Philip Beroaldus told of the Pope's enjoyment, and wrote word also to its author that he had caused not only men of letters, but even statesmen and warriors, to betake themselves to studying the mysteries of the Cabala.

The death of Reuchlin's patron, Eberhard the elder, soon after his elevation to the rank of duke in 1495, was followed by a period of misrule in the little state. One of the first acts of Eberhard the younger was to release his favorite, a dissolute priest, named Holzinger, from the prison in which he had been kept by the good counsel of Reuchlin; and for the further discomfiture of the scholar this man was appointed chancellor over the university of Tubingen. Reuchlin of course resigned. He had been long wanted at Heidelberg, and went there to be cherished by a new patron in the Elector Palatine. He showed, as usual, his lively energy by the establishment of a Greek chair, which the monks pronounced upon the spot to be a heresy; and by venting his wrath against Holzinger in a Latin comedy, denouncing dissolute priests, which he called Sergius, or the Head of the Head. It was written to be acted by the students. A Latin comedy was then a rare thing in the land; and the news that John Reuchlin had written one was noised abroad. Prudent friends counseled him to beware of such unscrupulous and powerful enemies as he would make if he attacked abuses of the priesthood; he submitted to advice, and as he was notoriously answerable for a comedy, and gossip must be satisfied, he suddenly composed a substitute for that first written. When, therefore, the day of the performance came, it was found that the Greek professor had composed a comedy against abuses in his own profession; it was a castigation of dishonest advocates. Scenica Progymnastica the piece was called.

After two years of misrule Eberhard the younger took its consequences; he was then deposed, and Holzinger, the monk, sent back to prison. "When the bricks are doubled, Moses comes," said Reuchlin, and returned to his old post at Tubingen. Hitherto his life of study had not been unprofitable, nor, much benefit as he received through patronage, was it a life wanting independence. "Whatever," he says, "I spent in learning, I acquired by teaching."

An anecdote of this good-humored scholar may be here interpolated, which displays his character in half a dozen points of view. He was detained once in an inn when it was raining very heavily, and of course had his book with him. The rain had driven into the common room a large number of country people, who were making a great noise. To quiet them Reuchlin called for a piece of chalk, and drew with it a circle on the table before which he sat. Within the circle he then drew a cross, and also within it, on the right side of the cross, he placed with great solemnity a cup of water, on the left he stuck a knife upright. Then placing a book--doubtless a Hebrew one--within the mysterious circle, he began to read, and the rustics who had gathered round him, with their mouths agape, patiently waited for the consequence of all this conjuration. The result was that Reuchlin finished comfortably the chapter he was reading without being distressed even by a whisper of disturbance.

In the year 1502 Reuchlin was elected to the post of general judge of alliance under the terms of the Suabian league. His office was to adjudicate in all matters of dispute among confederates and vassals, concerning the interests of the emperor as Archduke of Austria, the electors and princes. There was a second judge for prelates, counts, and nobles, a third for imperial cities. This post he held during eleven years; he was holding it, therefore, at the time when the young Cornelius Agrippa undertook to comment publicly at Dole upon his book concerning the Mirific Word, Reuchlin then being fifty-five years old, and at the summit of his fame, high, also, in the good esteem of Maximilian. Three years before this date, notwithstanding the great mass of legal business entailed on him by his judicial office, Reuchlin had, to the great help of all students, published a volume of the Rudiments of Hebrew, which included both a grammar and a dictionary. This book, he wrote, "cost me the greatest trouble, and a large part of my fortune." Cornelius no doubt had learnt his Hebrew by the help of it, and was already deep in studies which a few years afterwards brought the monks of Cologne into array against Reuchlin himself, their hostility somewhat embittered by an inkling of the Latin comedy that was not to be quite suppressed. Cornelius, however, was the first to feel the power of such enemies. By the Epistolae Obscurorum Virorum the monks were destined to come off much worsted from their battle against Reuchlin and the scholars who defended his fair name. Of their fortune in the battle fought against Cornelius Agrippa it is one part of this history to tell.

Reuchlin wrote at a later period (1517) a book upon the cabalistic art. If it is written God created heaven and earth, he interpreted that to mean spirit and matter, the spirit consisting of the angels and ministers by whom the ways of man are influenced. Magic, he said, dealt with evil spirits, but the true Cabala only with the good. He believed in astrology; and so, indeed, did Luther and Melancthon; Giovanni Pico di Mirandola at Florence, while adopting the Cabala, was very singular in his hostility to a belief in influences of the stars. His own faith in cabalism Reuchlin enforced thus: God, out of love to his people, has revealed the hidden mysteries to some of them, and these could find in the dead letters the living spirit. For Scripture consists of single letters, visible signs, which stand in a certain connection with the angels, as celestial and spiritual emanations from God. By the pronunciation of the one, the others also are affected; but with a true Cabalist, who penetrates the whole connection of the earthly with the heavenly, these signs, rightly placed in connection with each other, are a way of putting him into immediate union with the spirits, who through that are bound to satisfy his wishes.

In his book called Capnio, or the Mirific Word, expounded at Dole by Cornelius Agrippa, Reuchlin placed the Christian system in the center of old heathen philosophies, considering many of the doctrines of Pythagoras and Plato as having been taken from, not introduced into, the wisdom of the Cabalists. The argument is stated in the form of dialogue, which is immediately preceded by a summary of its intention that may very well suffice here for a summary of its contents: "Receive, then, in this book the argument on the Mirific Word of three philosophers, whom I have feigned to be holding such dispute among themselves as the controversies proper to their sects would occasion, as to the best elucidation of the hidden properties of sacred names. Out of which, great as they are in number and importance, occasion will at last be the more easily afforded for selecting one name that is above all names supremely mirific and beatific. And this you may know the whole matter in brief. Sidonius, at first ascribed to the school of Epicurus, but found afterwards, nullius jurare in verba magistri, an unfettered philosopher, travels about to satisfy his thirst for knowledge, and after many experiences enters Suabia, where he meets in the town of Pfortzheim" (Reuchlin's birthplace) "two philosophers--Baruch, a Jew, and Capnio" (Reuchlin himself), "a Christian, with whom he disserts upon many systems, and presently upon the knowledge itself of divine and human things, upon opinion, faith, miracles, the powers of words and figures, secret operations, and the mysteries of seals. In this way question arises concerning the sacred names and consecrated characters of all nations which have anything excellent in their philosophy, or not unworthy in their ceremonies; an enumeration of symbols is made by each speaker zealously on behalf of the rites cherished in his sect, until at last Capnio, in the third book, collects out of all that is holy one name, Jehosua, in which is gathered up the virtue and power of all sacred things, and which is eternally, supremely blessed."

AGRIPPA EXPOUNDS REUCHLIN.

HERE was a vast theme for the oratory of a youth of twenty-three, and it was one also that enabled him to display the whole range of his learning. The newly recovered treasures of Greek literature; the study of Plato, that had lately been revived by Marsilius Ficinus in Italy; the study of Aristotle, urged and helped in France by Faber Stapulensis (d'Etapies), appeared to bring the fullest confirmation of the principles of the Cabala to men ignorant, as all were then, of the Greek source of more than half the later mysticism of the Hebrews, which attributed to itself an origin so ancient. That he had acquired so early in his life Hebrew and Greek lore, that he was deeply read in studies which were admired from afar only by so many scholars of his day, and, thus prepared, that he discussed mysteries about which men in all ages feel instinctive curiosity, and men in that age reasoned eagerly, would alone account sufficiently for the attention paid to the young German by the university of Dole. Moreover, while fulfilling his own private purpose, he appeared also to the loyalty of the Burgundians, by delivering his orations to all corners , for the honor of the Princess Margaret, their ruler, and opening them with her panegyric. The young orator being also remarkable for an effective manner of delivery, the grave and learned men who came to his prelections honored him by diligent attendance. The exposition was made from the pulpit of the gymnasium, before the parliament and magistracy of Dole, the professors and the readers of the university. Simon Vernet, vice-chancellor of the university, dean of the church, and doctor in each faculty, was not once absent. The worthy vice-chancellor, or dean, appears, indeed, to have taken an especial interest in the fame of their visitor. He had himself a taste for public declamation, and to a friend who was urging on Cornelius that he should seek durable fame rather by written than by spoken words, expressed a contrary desire on his behalf. He preferred orator to author. When Cornelius had complied with the request of another friend, who wished to translate into the vernacular his panegyric upon Margaret, praising his oratory for the perfect fitness of each word employed in it, and its complete freedom from verbiage, and desiring that through a translation the illustrious princess might be informed how famously Cornelius had spoken in her honor, and so be the more disposed to reward him with her favor, the translation came back with a note, saying that the vice-chancellor had been its censor and corrector. Vernet was diligent, in fact, on the young scholar's behalf, and his interests were seconded by the Archbishop of Besancon. Not a syllable was whispered about heresy. The friend who urged Cornelius, in spite of the dean's contrary counsel, to become an author, gave a familiar example from his own experience of the vanity of spoken words. He had declaimed publicly from memory, and without one hitch, upwards of two thousand two hundred verses of his own composition, yet, because they were not printed, earned only a temporary local fame. Of the value of the written word evidence very soon afterwards was enclosed to Cornelius by that other friend who had translated his oration. Zealous to do good service, he had caused a copy of the panegyric to proceed, by way of Lyons, on the road to royal notice, and delighted the aspirant after patronage by enclosing to him flatteries from John Perreal, a royal chamberlain, probably the same learned Frenchman who became known twenty or more years later as Johannis Perellus, translated into Latin Gaza on the Attic Months, and wrote a book about the Epacts of the Moon.

To the youth flushed with triumph as a scholar there came also reminders of the military life he was so ready to forsake. A correspondent sent him news of a defeat of the Venetians by the French, near Agnadello, the first fruits of the discreditable league of Cambray. The French, it will be remembered, won this victory while Maximilian, their new ally, was still perplexed by the dissatisfaction of his subjects evidenced during the late diet at Worms. Agrippa's friend wished to have in return for his news any knowledge that his relation to the emperor might give him of intentions that might be disclosed at an approaching diet. His real intentions were to break a pledge by marching against the Venetians; his fate, to retire ere long, defeated, from before the walls of Padua. He was renewing with his enemy, the King of France, the treaty of Cambray, and sending a messenger to

Spire to burn the book in which he had recorded all the injuries and insults suffered by his family, or empire, at the hands of France. Cornelius cared little for France or Padua; his hopes as a scholar were with Margaret at Ghent, though she, too, being another member of the league, could have employed him as a soldier. Other hopes, as a man, he was directing towards a younger and a fairer mistress. He desired not only to prosper but to marry.

The little university of Dole favored the young man heartily. His prelections had excited great attention, and procured for him the admiration of the neighborhood. From the university they won for him at once the degree of doctor of divinity, together with a stipend.

THE NOBILITY OF WOMAN.

ANGLING for private patronage was in the sixteenth century correlative to the habit not very uncommon in these days of using baits to catch the public favor. Men who once lived by the help of princes now owe their support to the whole people, and the pains bestowed upon the cultivation of the good-will of the people in these days are neither less nor more to be reprehended than the pains taken by scholars of past time to procure a safe means of subsistence through the good-will of a prince. It may be said, with a fair approximation to the truth, that as much as a man may do now, with the intention of deserving popularity, and not discredit himself in his own eyes or those of the great number of his neighbors, he might have done with as little discredit in the sixteenth century with the design of earning favor from the great. We have seen how, in the case of Reuchlin, a poor chorister was fostered at first by small princes of Germany, afterwards even by the emperor, and enabled to develop into a great Hebrew scholar, when one patron died having another ready to befriend him, and enjoying dignity and wealth with a complete sense of independence. That age was, in fact, as far removed as this is from the transition period, during which the patronage of letters by the great, extinct as a necessity, survived as a tradition, and the system that had once been vigorous and noble became imbecile and base.

Nobody at Dole was ignorant that the design of Cornelius Agrippa was to earn the patronage of Margaret, a liberal encourager of learning. Nobody considered it dishonorable to seek this by showing that it was deserved. The prevalent feeling was so far removed from any such impression, that from many quarters the young man was urged to magnify his claim on Margaret's attention by devoting not only the orations, but also some piece of writing to her honor. Even the cordial vice-chancellor, desirous to advance the interests of the young orator, set aside his predilection for the spoken word, and was among the foremost in admonishing Cornelius to write. Not slow to profit by advice that ran the same course with his inclinations, the new doctor of divinity set himself to display his powers as a theologian in the true manner of the day, and with theological acuteness to combine a courtier's tact, by dedicating to the most conspicuous example of his argument a treatise on the Nobility and Pre-excellence of the Female Sex. As I have hinted, too, there was a private example of it known to his own heart.

Angling for patronage shown from another point of view!--mean arts used by mean spirits to compel the favor of the rich and base. But to secure the favor of the rich and noble the arts used were not to be accounted mean.

Now let us trace in a brief summary the argument for the Nobility of the Female Sex and the Superiority of Woman over Man, written at Dole, in the year 1509, by a doctor of divinity, aged twenty-three. He sets out with the declaration that when man was created male and female, difference was made in the flesh, not in the soul. He quotes Scripture to show that after the corruption of our bodies difference of sex will disappear, and that we shall all be like angels in the resurrection. As to the soul, then, man and woman are alike; but as to everything else the woman is the better part of the creation.

In the first place, woman being made better than man, received the better name. Man was called Adam, which means Earth; woman Eva, which is by interpretation Life. By as much as life excels earth woman therefore excels man. And this, it is urged, must not be thought trivial reasoning, because the maker of those creatures knew what they were before he named them, and was One who could not err in properly describing each. We know, and the Roman laws testify, that ancient names were always consonant with the things they represented, and names have been held always to be of great moment by theologians and jurisconsults. It is written thus of Nabal: "As his name is, so is he; Nabal is his name, and folly is with him." (1 Samuel, xxv., 25.) Saint Paul, also, in his Epistle to the Hebrews, speaks of his Lord and Master, as "made so much better than the angels, as he hath obtained a more excellent name than they." (Heb., i., 4.) The reader's memory will at once supply the next passage of Scripture quoted, I do not like to cite it. Agrippa then dilates, as well he may, on the immense importance of words, according to the practice of all jurists, he tells how Cyprian argued against the Jews that Adam's name was derived from the initials of the Greek words meaning east, west, north, and south, because his flesh was made out of the earth, though that derivation was at variance with Moses, who put only three letters in the Hebrew name. For this, however, adds Agrippa, Cyprian was not to blame, since, like many saints and expounders of the sacred text, he had not learnt the Hebrew language.

Upon the word Eva it is further maintained that it suggests comparison with the mystic symbols of the Cabalists, the name of the woman having affinity with the ineffable Tetragrammaton, the most sacred name of the Divinity; while that of the man differed entirely from it. All these considerations, however, Agrippa consents to pass over, as matters read by few and understood by fewer. The pre-eminence of the woman can be proved out of her constitution, her gifts, and her merits.

The nature of woman is discussed, however, from the theologian's point of view. Things were created in the order of their rank. First, indeed, incorruptible soul, then incorruptible matter, but afterwards, out of that matter, more or less corruptible things, beginning with the meanest. First minerals, then herbs, and shrubs, and trees, then zoophytes, then brutes in their order, reptiles first, afterwards fishes, birds, quadrupeds. Lastly, two human beings, but of these first the male, and finally the female, in which the heavens and the earth and their whole adornment were perfected. The divine rest followed, because the work was consummated, nothing greater was conceived; the woman was thus left the most perfect and the noblest of the creatures upon earth, as a queen placed in the court that had been previously prepared for her. Rightly, therefore, do all beings round about her pay to this queen homage of reverence and love.

The difference between the woman and the man is yet more strongly marked, says the deeply read theologian, because the man was made like the brutes in open land outside the gates of paradise, and made wholly of clay, but the woman was made afterwards in paradise itself; she was the one creation. Presently there follow Scripture arguments to show that the place of their birth was a sign to men of honor or dishonor. The woman, too, was not made of clay, but from an influx of celestial matter; since there went into her composition nothing terrestrial except only one of Adam's ribs, and that was not gross clay, but clay that had been already purified and kindled with the breath of life.

The theological demonstrations Cornelius next confirms by the evidence of some natural facts equally cogent and trustworthy, which were held in that day by many wise men to be equally true. It is because she is made of purer matter that a woman, from whatever height she may look down, never turns .giddy, and her eyes never have mist before them like the eyes of men. Moreover, if a woman and man tumble together into water, far away from all external help, the woman floats long upon the surface, but the man soon sinks to the bottom. Is there not also the divine light shining through the body of the woman, by which she is made often to seem a miracle of beauty Then follows a clever inventory of all a woman's charms of person, written with due reserve, which might be here translated, if the English language had the terseness of the Latin. In short, woman is the sum of all earth's beauty, and it proved that her beauty has sometimes inspired even angels and demons with a desperate and fatal love. Then follows a chain of Scripture texts honoring female beauty, which all lead up to the twenty thousand virgins, solemnly celebrated by the church, and the admiration of the beauty of the Virgin Mary by the Sun and Moon.

Texts follow that must be omitted, and then the argument takes anatomical grounds of the most ingenious character, and shows how every difference of structure between the man and the woman gives to woman the advantage due to her superior delicacy. Even after death nature respects her inherent modesty, for a drowned woman floats on her face, and a drowned man upon his back. The noblest part of a human being is the head; but the man's head is liable to baldness, woman is never seen bald. The man's face is often made so filthy by a most odious beard, and so covered with sordid hairs, that it is scarcely to be distinguished from the face of a wild beast; in woman, on the other hand, the face always remains pure and decent. For this reason women were, by the laws of the twelve tables, forbidden to rub their cheeks lest hair should grow and obscure their blushing modesty. But the most evident proof of the innate purity of the female sex is, that a woman having once washed is clean, and if she wash in second water will not soil it; but that a man is never clean, though he should wash in ten successive waters, he will cloud and infect them all.

Some other marvellous peculiarities I must omit, and pass to Agrippa's appreciation of the woman's predominance in the possession of the gift of speech, the most excellent of human faculties, which Hermes Trismegistus thought equal to immortality in value, and Hesiod pronounced the best of human treasures. Man, too, receives this gift from woman, from his mother or his nurse; and it is a gift bestowed upon woman herself with such liberality that the world has scarcely seen a woman who was mute. Is it not fit that women should excel men in that faculty, wherein men themselves chiefly excel the brutes?

The argument again becomes an edifice of Scripture text, and it is well to show the nature of it. though we may shrink from the misuse of sacred words, because it is well thoroughly to understand how Scripture was habitually used by professed theologians in the sixteenth century, and from this light example to derive a grave lesson, perhaps, that may be, even to the people of the nineteenth century, not wholly useless.

Solomon's texts on the surpassing excellence of a good woman of course are cited, and a cabalistic hint is given of the efficacy of the letter H, which Abram took away from his wife Sarah, and put into the middle of his own name, after he had been blessed through her. Benediction has come always by woman, law by man. We have all sinned in Adam, not in Eve; original sin we inherit only from the father of our race. The fruit of the tree of knowledge was forbidden to man only, before woman was made; woman received no injunction, she was created free. She was not blamed, therefore, for eating, but for causing sin in her husband by giving him to eat; and she did that not of her own will, but because the devil tempted her. He chose her as the object of temptation, as St. Bernard says, because he saw with envy that she was the most perfect of creatures. She erred in ignorance because she was deceived; the man sinned knowingly. Therefore our Lord made atonement in the figure of the sex that had sinned, and also for more complete humiliation came in the form of a man, not that of a woman, which is nobler and sublimer. He humbled himself as man, but overcame as a descendant of the woman; for the seed of the woman, it was said, not the seed of man, should bruise the serpent's head. He would not, therefore, be born of a man; woman alone was judged worthy to be the earthly parent of the Deity. Risen again, he appeared first to woman. Men forsook him, women never. No persecution, heresy, or error in the Church ever began with the female sex. They were men who betrayed, sold, bought, accused, condemned, mocked, crucified the Lord. Peter denied him, his disciples left him. Women were at the foot of the cross, women were at the sepulchre. Even Pilate's wife, who was a heathen, made more effort to save Jesus than any man among believers. Finally, do not almost all theologians assert that the Church is maintained by the Virgin Mary?

Aristotle may say that of all animals the males are stronger and wiser than the females, but St. Paul writes that weak things have been chosen to confound the strong. Adam was sublimely endowed, but woman humbled him; Samson was strong, but woman made him captive; Lot was chaste, but woman seduced him; David was religious, but woman disturbed his piety; Solomon was wise, but woman deceived him; Job was patient, and was robbed by the devil of fortune and family; ulcerated, grieved, oppressed, nothing provoked him to anger till a woman did it, therein proving herself stronger than the devil. Peter was fervent in faith, but woman forced him to deny his lord. Somebody may remark that all these illustrations tend to woman's shame; not to her glory. Woman, however, may reply to man as Innocent III. wrote to some cardinal, "If one of us is to be confounded, I prefer that it be you." Civil law allows a woman to consult her own gain to an-other's hurt; and does not Scripture itself often extol and bless the evil deeds of the woman more than the good deeds of the man? Is not Rachel praised who deceived her fathers Rebecca, because she obtained fraudulently Jacob's benediction? Is not the deceit of Rahab imputed to her as justice? Was not Jael blessed among women for a treacherous and cruel deed? What could be more iniquitous than the counsel of Judith? what more cruel than her wiles? what worse than her perfidy? Yet for this she is blessed, lauded, and extolled in Scripture, and the woman's iniquity is reputed better than the goodness of the man. Was not Cain's a good work when he offered his best fruits in sacrifice and was reproved for it? Did not Esau well when he hunted to get venison for his old father, and in the meantime was defrauded of his birthright, and incurred the divine hate? Other examples are adduced, and robust scholars, ingenious theologians, are defied to find an equal amount of evidence in support of the contrary thesis, that the iniquity of the man is better than the goodness of the woman. Such a thesis, says Agrippa, could not be defended.

From this point to the end Agrippa's treatise consists of a mass of illustrations from profane and Scripture history, classified roughly. Some are from natural history. The queen of all birds, he says, is the eagle, always of the female sex, for no male eagles have been found. The phoenix is a female always. On the other hand, the most pestilent of serpents, called the basilisk, exists only as a male; it is impossible for it to hatch a female.

All evil things began with men, and few or none with woman. We die in the seed of Adam and live in the seed of Eve. The beginning of envy, the first homicide, the first parricide, the first despair of divine mercy was with man; Lamech was the first bigamist, Noah was the first drunkard, Nimrod the first tyrant, and so forth. Men were the first to league themselves with demons and discover profane hearts. Men have been incontinent, and had, in innumerable instances, to each man many wives at once; but women have been continent, each content with a single husband, except only Bathsheba. Many women are then cited as illustrations of their sex in this respect, or for their filial piety, including Abigail, Lucretia, Cato's wife, and the mother of the Gracchi, the vestal Claudia, Iphigenia. If any one opposes to such women the wives of Zoilus, Samson, Jason, Deiphobus, and Agamemnon, it may be answered that these have been unjustly accused, that no good man ever had a bad wife. Only bad husbands get bad wives, or if they get a good one, are sometimes able to corrupt her excellence. If women made the laws, and wrote the histories and tragedies, could they not justly crowd them with testimony to the wickedness of men? Our prisons are full of men, and slain men cumber the earth everywhere, but women are the beginners of all liberal arts, of virtue and beneficence. Therefore the arts and virtues commonly have feminine names. Even the corners of the world receive their names from women--the nymph Asia; Europe, the daughter of Agenior; Lybia, the daughter of Epaphus, who is called also Aphrica.

Illustrations follow of the pre-eminence of woman in good gifts, and it is urged that Abraham, who by his faith was accounted just, was placed in subjection to Sarah his wife, and was told, "In all that Sarah hath said unto thee, harken unto her voice." (Gen., xxi., 12.)

There follows a host of other illustrations of the excellence of women, drawn from all sources; among others, illustrations of her eminence in learning. "And," adds Agrippa, "were not women now forbidden to be literary, we should at this day have most celebrated women, whose wit would surpass that of men. What is to be said upon this head, what even by nature women seem to be born easily superior to practiced students in all faculties? Do not the grammarians entitle themselves masters of right speaking? Yet we learn this far better from our nurses and our mothers than from the grammarians. For that reason Plato and Quintilian so solicitously urged a careful choice of children's nurses, that the children's language might be formed on the best model. Are not the poets in the invention of their whims and fables, the dialecticians in their contentious garrulity, surpassed by women? Was ever orator so good or so successful, that a courtesan could not excel his powers of persuasion? What arithmetician by false calculation would know how to cheat a woman in the payment of a debt? What musician equals her in song and in amenity of voice 3 Are not philosophers, mathematicians, and astrologers often inferior to country women in their divinations and predictions, and does not the old nurse very often beat the doctor?" Socrates himself, the wisest of men, did not disdain to receive knowledge from Aspasia, nor did Apollo the theologian despise the teaching of Priscilla.

Then follows a fresh string of illustrations by which we are brought to a contemplation of the necessity of women for the perpetuation of any state, and the cessation of the human race that may be consequent on her withdrawal. Through more examples we are brought then to consider the honor and precedence accorded by law and usage to the female sex. Man makes way for woman on the public road, and yields to her in society the highest places. Purple and fine linen, gold and jewels are conceded as the fit adornments of her noble person, and from the sumptuary laws of the later emperors women were excepted. Illustrations follow of the dignity and privileges of the wife, and of the immunities accorded to her by the law. Reference is made to ancient writers, who tell how, among the Getulians, the Bactrians, and others, men were the softer sex, and sat at home while women labored in the fields, built houses, transacted business, rode abroad, and went out to do battle. Among the Cantabrians men brought dowries to their wives, brothers were given in marriage by their sisters, and the daughters of a household were the heirs. Among the Scythians, Thracians, and Gauls, women possessed their rights, but among us, said Agrippa, "the tyranny of men prevailing over divine right and the laws of nature, slays by law the liberty of woman, abolishes it by use and custom, extinguishes it by education. For the woman, as soon as she is born, is from her earliest years detained at home in idleness, and as if destitute of capacity for higher occupations, is permitted to conceive of nothing beyond needle and thread. Then when she has attained years of puberty she is delivered over to the jealous empire of a man, or shut up for ever in a shop of vestals. The law also forbids her to fill public offices. No prudence entitles her to plead in open court." A list follows of the chief disabilities of women, "who are treated by the men as conquered by the conquerors, not by any divine necessity, for any reason, but according to custom, education, fortune, and the tyrant's opportunity."

A few leading objections are then answered. Eve was indeed made subject to man after the fall, but that curse was removed when man was saved. Paul says that "wives are to be subject to their husbands,and women to be silent in the church," but he spoke of temporal church discipline, and did not utter a divine law, since "in Christ there is neither male nor female, but a new creature." We are again reminded of the text subjecting Abraham to Sarah, and the treatise closes then with a short recapitulation of its heads. "We have shown," Agrippa says, "the pre-eminence of the female sex by its name, its order and place of creation, the material of which it was created, and the dignity that was given to woman over man by God, then by religion, by nature, by human laws, by various authority, by reason, and have demonstrated all this by promiscuous examples. Yet we have not said so many things but that we have left more still to be said, because I came to the writings of this not moved by ambition, or for the sake of bringing myself praise, but for the sake of duty and truth, lest, like a sacrilegious person, I might seem, if I were silent, by an impious taciturnity (and as it were a burying of my talent) to refuse the praises due to so devout a sex. So that if any one more curious than I am should discover any argument which he thinks requisite to be added to this work, let him expect to have his position not contested by me, but attested, in as far as he is able to carry on this good work of mine with his own genius and learning. And that this work itself may not become too large a volume, here let it end."

Such was the treatise written by Cornelius at Dole for the more perfect propitiation of the Princess Margaret. Many years before it was printed and presented to the princess; doubtless, however, the youth read the manuscript to his betrothed very soon after it was written. Towards the close of the year a friend in Cologne wrote to Agrippa of the impatience of his parents for their son's return, but at the close of November another friend in Cologne, Theodoric, Bishop of Cyrene, asking as an especial favor for his views upon judicial astrology so hotly opposed by Pico di Mirandola, says that his expression on the subject had appeared to him ambiguous when they conversed together. Probably he had then been offering to the embrace of his parents not a son only, but a son and daughter, for it is said to have been in the year 1509, when all was honor for him in the present, all hope in the future, that Cornelius von Nettesheim married Jane Louisa Tyssie, of Geneva, a maiden equal to him in rank, remarkable for beauty, and yet more remarkable for her aspirations and her worth. She entered with her whole soul into the spirit of her husband's life, rejoiced in his ambition, and knew how to hold high converse with his friends. The marriage was in every respect a happy one; there was a world of gentleness and loving kindness in Agrippa's heart. We shall have revelation of it as the narrative proceeds. The tenderness of his nature mingles strangely, sadly, with his restlessness, his self-reliance, and his pride,

So, full of hope and happiness, at the age of twenty-three, he took to wife a maiden who could love him for his kindliness, and reverence him for his power. He was no needy adventurer, but the son of a noble house, who was beginning, as it seemed, the achievement of the highest honors. He was surrounded by admirers, already a doctor of divinity, hereafter to attain he knew not what. Fostered by Maximilian's daughter, what might not his intellect achieve?

Poor youth, even in that year of hope the blight was already settling on his life! While he was writing praise of womanhood at Dole to win the smiles of Margaret, Catilinet, a Franciscan friar, who had been at the adjacent town of Gray when Reuchlin was expounded, mediated cruel vengeance on the down-chinned scholar. At Ghent, as preacher before the Regent of the Netherlands and all her court,

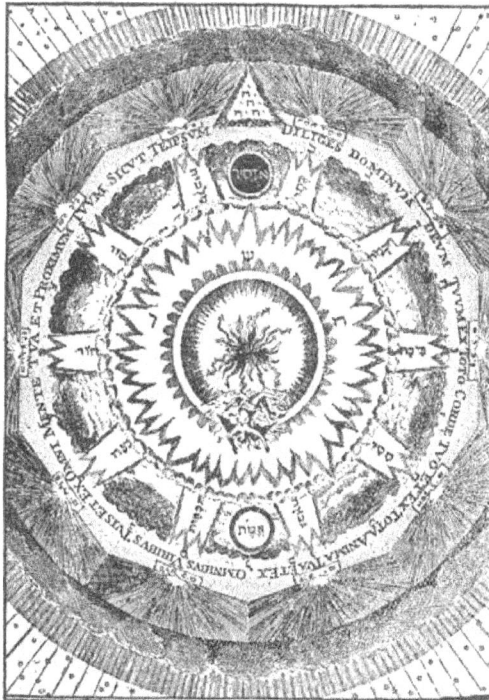

System of the Interior or Empyrean Heaven showing the fall of Lucifer

155

Catilinet was to deliver in the Easter following the Quadragesimal Discourses. Against the impious Cabalist he was preparing to arouse the wrath of Margaret during those same days which were spent by the young student in pleasant effort to deserve her kindness.

Now it was that Agrippa wrote his book on Magic.

ORDER OF THE EMPYREAN HEAVEN.

THERE is a God, all-powerful, all-intelligent and supremely perfect; eternal and infinite; omnipotent and omniscient; who endures from eternity to eternity, and is present from infinity to infinity.

But though, from the nature and perfections of the Deity, he is invisibly present in all places and nothing happens without his knowledge and permission; yet it is expressly revealed in Scripture, and admitted by all wise and intelligent authors, that he is visibly present with the angels and spirits, and blessed souls of the departed, in those mansions of bliss called Heaven. There he is pleased to afford a nearer and more immediate view of himself, and a more sensible manifestation of his glory, and a more adequate perception of his attributes, than can be seen or felt in any other parts of the universe; which place, for the sake of pre-eminent distinction, and as being the seat and center, from whence all things flow and have their beginning, life, light, power, and motion, is called the interior or Empyrean Heaven.

The position and order of this interior heaven, or center of the Divinity, has been variously described, and its locality somewhat disputed among the learned; but all agree as to the certainty of its existence. Hermes Trismegistus defines heaven to be an intellectual sphere, whose center is everywhere, and circumference nowhere, but by this he meant no more than to affirm, what we have done above, that God is everywhere, and at all times, from infinity to infinity, that is to say, without limitation, bounds, or circumference. Plato speaks of this internal heaven in terms which bear so strict a resemblance with the books of Revelation, and in so elevated and magnificent a style, that it is apparent the heathen philosophers, notwithstanding their worshiping demi or false gods, possessed an unshaken confidence in one omnipotent, supreme, overruling power, whose throne was the center of all things, and the abode of angels and blessed spirits.

To describe this interior heaven, in terms adequate to its magnificence and glory, is utterly impossible. The utmost we can do is to collect, from inspired writers, and from the words of Revelation, assisted by occult philosophy, and a due knowledge of the celestial spheres, that order and position of it, which reason and the divine lights we have, bring nearest to the truth. That God must be strictly and literally the center from whence all ideas of the Divine Mind flow, as rays in every direction, through all spheres and through all bodies, cannot admit of a doubt. That the inner circumference of this center is surrounded, filled or formed, by arrangements of the three hierarchies of angels, is also consonant to reason and Scripture, and forms what may be termed the entrance or inner gate of the empyrean heaven, through which no spirit can pass without their knowledge and permission, and within which we must suppose the vast expanse or mansions of the Godhead, and glory of the Trinity, to be. This is strictly conformable to the idea of all the prophets and evangelical writers. From this primary circle, or gate of heaven, Lucifer, the grand Apostate, as Milton finely describes it, was hurled into the bottomless abyss; whose office, as one of the highest orders of angels, having placed him near the eternal throne, he became qcompetitor for dominion and power with God himself.

The circles next surrounding the hierarchies, are

Symbol of the Universal Spirit of Nature

composed of the ministering angels and spirits and messengers of the Deity. In positions answering to the ideas of the holy Trinity, and intersecting all orders of angels, are seated, in fullness of glory and splendor, those superior angels, or intelligent spirits, who answer to the divine attributes of God, and are the pure essences or stream through which the will or fiat of the Godhead is communicated to the angels and spirits, and instantaneously conducted to the Anima Mundi. Round the whole, as an atmosphere round a planet, the Anima Mundi, or universal Spirit of Nature, is placed; which, receiving the impressions or ideas of the Divine Mind, conducts them onward, to the remotest parts of the universe; to infinity itself; to, and upon, and through, all bodies, and to all God's works. This Anima Mundi is therefore what we understand of Nature, of Providence, of the presence of God, and the fountain or seat of all second causes, being, as it were, the Eye of God, or medium between God and all created things. Next to the Anima Mundi, is that vast region or expanse, called the ethereal heaven, or firmament, wherein the fixed stars, planets, and comets, are disposed; and wherein the celestial bodies, and the comets, move freely in all directions, and towards all parts of the heavens.

To illustrate what has been stated above a plate is here inserted of the Interior Heaven, with the different orders of the Spirits and Essences of the Divine Mind, distinguished by their proper names and characters, in the original Hebrew and Iberian text, as pointed out in the manuscripts of ancient and learned philosophers. This plate shows in what manner the rays or beams of Divine Providence pass from the center or seat of the Godhead, through all the different orders of angels and spirits, to the Anima Mundi, and from thence to all the celestial bodies planets, and stars; to our earth, and to the remotest parts of infinite space, constituting what is termed celestial influx, or that faculty in nature by which the quality and temperature of one body is communicated to another.

Theologists have divided angels into different ranks or classes, which they term Hierarchies, a word signifying to rule in holy things. Ancient authors give nine orders of these celestial spirits--Cherubim, Seraphim, Thrones, Dominions, Principalities, Powers, Virtues, Angels, and Archangels--and these they class into Three Hierarchies, appointing them their respective offices in the performance of the word and will of God.

The rabbis and cabalistical writers have defined one rank of angels--or the Intelligences--as superior to all the foregoing nine orders of spirits, and which answer to and are contained in the ten distinguishing names of God, and are the pure essences of the Supreme Spirit, or the Divine Diffusion through which the mirific Word and Will are communicated to the angels and blessed spirits, and through which providence extends to the care and protection of Nature.

The first of these divine essences is Jehovah, and is peculiarly attributed to God the Father, being the pure and simple essence of the Supreme Divinity, flowing through Hajoth Hakados, to the angel Metratton, and to the ministering spirit Reschith Hagalalim, who guides the Primum Mobile, and bestows the gift of being upon all things. To this spirit is allotted the office of bringing the souls of the faithful departed into heaven; and by him God spake to Moses.

The second is Jah, and is attributed to the Person of the Messiah, whose power and influence descend through the angel Masleh into the sphere of the celestial Zodiac. This is the Spirit of Nature, the Soul of the World, or the Omnific Word which actuated the chaos and divided the unwrought matters into three portions: Of the first and most essential part was the Spiritual World composed; of the second was made the visible heavens or the Celestial World; and of the third part was formed the Terrestrial World, out of which was drawn the elemental quintessence, or first matter of all things, which produced the four elements of Fire, Water, Air, and Earth, and all the creatures which inhabit them, by the agency of a particular spirit called Raziel, who was the ruler of Adam.

The third is Ehjeh, and is attributed to the Holy Spirit, whose divine light is received by the angel Sabbathi, and communicated from him through the sphere of Saturn. This is the principium generationis, the beginning of the ways of God, or the manifestations of the Father and the Son's light in the supernatural generation. And from hence flow down all living souls, entering the inanimate body, and giving form to unsettled matter.

The fourth is El, through the light of whom flows grace, goodness, mercy, piety, and munificence, to the angel Zadkiel, and, thence, passing through the. sphere of Jupiter, fashioneth the images of all bodies, bestowing clemency, benevolence, and justice on all.

The fifth is Elohi, the upholder of the sword, and left hand of God, whose influence penetrates the angel Geburah, and thence descends through the sphere of Mars, giving fortitude in war and affliction.

The sixth is Tsebaoth, who bestoweth his mighty power through the angel Raphael into the sphere of the Sun, giving motion, heat, and brightness to it, and thence producing metals.

The seventh is Elion, who rules the angel Michael, and descends through the sphere of Mercury, giving benignity, motion, intelligence, and eloquence.

The eighth is Adonai, whose influence is received by the angel Haniel, and communicated through the sphere of Venus, giving zeal, fervency, and righteousness of heart, and producing vegetables.

The ninth is Shaddai, whose influence is conveyed by cherubim to the angel Gabriel, and falls into the sphere of the Moon, causing increase and decrease of all things, like unto the tides of the sea, and governing the genii and natural protectors of man.

The tenth is Elohim, who extends his beneficence to the angel Jesodoth, into the sphere of the Earth, and dispenseth knowledge, understanding, and wisdom.

The three first of these ten names--Jehovah, Jah, and Ehjeh--express the essence of God, and are proper names; but the other seven are only expressive of his attributes. The only true name of God, according to the cabala, is the name of four letters--the Tetragrammaton--Yod-he-vau-he.

In the exterior circle of the celestial heaven, occupied by the fixed stars, the Anima Mundi hath her particular forms, answering to the ideas of the Divine Mind; and this situation approaching nearest to the Empyrean Heaven, the seat of God, receives the spiritual powers and influences which immediately proceed from him. Hence they are diffused through the spheres of the planets and heavenly bodies, and communicated to the inmost center of the Earth by means of natural law, or the Spirit of the World, that rules the terrestrial world.

While many ancient authors have contended on the definition and meaning of the word Nature, yet they all in reality mean one and the same thing, only giving different explanations of the same ideas; and if their arguments are closely pursued and compared with each other, they will all tend to show that the Anima Mundi and the Soul of the Universe is what they mean by Nature.

SYMBOLS OF THE ALCHEMISTS.

THIS volume would be incomplete without the symbols of the Alchemists, as they naturally pertain to Natural Magic, and occasionally prove of great value. The London Pharmaceutical Journal, an excellent authority, gives the symbols we here introduce.

Nowadays chemists write their formulas and work out their processes by means of symbols, and the alchemists used also signs and hieroglyphics to represent the then known elements, metals, and other substances in common use.

The so-called elements--Fire, Water, Air, Earth--were represented by special symbols, here represented. The metals were supposed to be influenced by the planets to a certain degree, and were represented by the corresponding signs of the Zodiac. Various other articles also had their symbols, which served as a means of shorthand at a period when caligraphy was little known or employed. Gold, for instance, was associated with the Sun because of its brightness and perfection, for it was always held to be the noblest of metals. The symbol applied to it embodies these qualities. Silver resembles the Moon in lustre, and the origin of the crescent needs no explanation. Iron was dedicated to Mars, being the metal from which implements of war were made, Mars being the god of war, probably owing to the blood-red color of the planet. Saturn was the slowest of the planets, and lead, being the dullest and most despised of metals, was therefore accorded to Saturn. Quicksilver was, of course, most appropriate to Mercury, the messenger of the gods.

Dr. Pereira derives all these symbols from gold and the Greek cross, taken to represent acrimony the supposititious substance, which, combined with gold, produced other metals. Copper, for instance, has the sign of gold on top, and that of acrimony underneath. Quicksilver derived its symbol from that of silver on the top, because of its color, that of acrimony beneath, and gold between, because gold was supposed to lurk in all metals. Iron was supposed to contain acrimony of a different nature from that of the other metals, being represented in this symbol by the barbed spearhead. Fire and Water being antagonistic are represented by the same symbol, one being inverted. Air, which was supposed to be a modification of fire, has a modified fire symbol, whilst the fourth hypothetical element has for its symbol that of air inverted. These are based on Aristotle's doctrine, which taught that the four elements had each two qualities, one of which was common to some other elements.

SYMBOLS OF THE ALCHEMISTS AND THEIR SIGNIFICATIONS.

Sal Ammoniac.   Sulphur.   Tartar.   A Covered Pot.   To Sublime.   To Precipitate.

Spirits of Wine.   Roman Symbol for Denarius.   To Digest.   To Distill.   Aqua Fortis.

Aqua Regalia.   Brick.   To Calcine.   Camphire.   Ashes.   Cerusse.

Lime.   Quicklime.   Cinnabar.   Wax.   Hartshorn.

A Crucible.   Crystal.   A Gum.   Oil.

Steel Filings.   Litharge.   To Lute.   Sublimated Mercury.   Precipitated Mercury.   Nitre.

Realgar.   Sand.   Soap.   Sal Alkali.   Sal Ammoniac.

Salt.   Tallow.   Vinegar.   Verdigris.   Vitriol.   Urine.   Day.   Night.

SYMBOLS OF THE ALCHEMISTS, CONTINUED

A MESSAGE FROM THE STARS.

I stood at eventime. The never-ending plain
All empty looked and void. Yet, as I gazed again
An army bivouacked. Unnumbered points of light
Bespoke a force Supreme--invincible for Right.

THE ETERNAL PRINCIPLE.

BY DR. L. W. DE LAURENCE.

The struggle between light and darkness, between good and evil, is as old as the world, and yet there is no principle of evil; whatever degrades is evil, whatever elevates is good.

Evil or so-called sin is simply undeveloped good. Good and evil are the light and shadow of the one eternal principle of life, and each is necessary for the existence of the other.

The struggle between light and shadow is life, and there can be no life without a struggle.

Matter transmits force, but does not originate force. It is for a time the receptacle of power, but not the power. All essence of power belongs to Spirit. All pure force is invisible.

Matter and Spirit may be one to the Absolute and Infinite Being, but that one is Spirit. In human speech, matter is only the name of an effect whose cause is wrapped in mystery.

It remains for the human to penetrate the veil and solve the mystery. And the solution of this problem of mind and matter discovers man unto himself, and binds him in loving union forever with the Infinite "I am," the Spirit of all.

Absence of feeling and of suffering only shows that the process of death has begun, or that the animal has taken full possession. Pain is not an element to be most dreaded; for, as gold is refined by fire, the Soul is refined by pain, and only through the death of suffering does the human Soul rise into eternal life.

If selfishness and the animal instinct have full sway, the Soul shrivels toward decay, while all its noble powers are congealed, its sensibilities benumbed, its vision blinded, its intellect dimmed, and from the once clear mirror the reflection of a noble Soul shines no more where the innermost temple might have been radiant with truth and virtue.

DEATH--Is death more to be feared because it is an enigma the mysteries of which western dull minds, because obscured by theology, cannot fathom, or their weak fancy cannot comprehend?

The human Soul is the anchorage or place of ideas. The Astral body or star magno is the mirror that reflects and records them, human thoughts being simply the clothing of these ideas. The spirit is the self-acting energy that produces the Idea.

A MESSAGE TO ALL MYSTICS.

THE HINDU MAGIC MIRROR.

BY DR. L. W. DE LAURENCE.

Copyright, 1910, by de Laurence, Scott & Co., Publishing Department.

A sincere and true message to all faithful Brother Mystics and those who may wish to join this Occult Organization which exists here and in the Astral or unseen world.

Given under and by the direction of the great Occult Organization and Brotherhood of Magic for the never ending advancement of human souls through Dr. L. W. de Laurence, whose supreme desire is to educate capable and sincere brothers and sisters to act in concert with our Brotherhood of unseen Mystics and teach them the work that they must do preparatory thereto.

I, Dr. L. W. de Laurence, do hereby state, truly, and positively, that I know that the existence of a powerful Occult Organization and Brotherhood of Mystics, both here and in the great unseen world, to be an incontestable truth; and, furthermore, that I KNOW that the Science and Art of Magic as operated by these Mystics is worthy of faithful investigation.

Furthermore, be it known to all the world, and especially so unto him or her into whose hands this message may come, not by reason of their own solicitation, or by advertisement, but by their own Astral influence and Occult magnetism, that the hereinafter simple message to Brother Mystics and those who desire to rid themselves of the bonds and shackles of gross ignorance, theology, superstition and materialism, regarding the famous "Magic Mirror," that wonderful Astral Instrument so long used by leading Mystics, Adepts, and Occult workers for communication and preparatory development for communication between the two worlds, will help all who heed.

This message hereinafter written I have given verbatim as it has come to me, under the direction of the great Brotherhood of Mystics from the unseen Astral world.

Every soul will rest at some mile-post in life
 Those never ending, unnumbered, unknown points
 All void, vacant, and dark.
 Yet, be still, for as it looks once more
 A multitude assembled;
 Unnumberable Astral souls reveal a force Supreme,

Invincible for human advancement,
The annulment of man-made law;
The concert uplifting and educating of humanity.
Listen, Oh ye capable brothers, for out of darkness
Comes this Mystic Message.

THE MESSAGE.

Part One.

TO THOSE MYSTICS STILL IN EARTH LIFE, THE ASTRAL BROTHERHOOD OF MAGIC, AN OCCULT ORGANIZATION, SENDS GOOD WILL, LIGHT AND GREETINGS.

UNTIL YOU, BROTHER AND SISTER "KNOW THYSELF" AND THE POSSIBILITIES OF "THYSELF," BY AND THROUGH THE UNDERSTANDING OF "SELF," AND ARE ABLE TO kindle the Astral fire within, there is labor for us to perform in assisting you in your preparatory work thereto.

The shackles and chains of centuries, of cycles of ages, of antiquity, are riven at length by their own corroding and heart-eating rust (materialism).

* * * * * * *

Let ye, oh brother and sister listen most attentively, for no shackle or bond that comes of theology, darkness or superstition, or gross ignorance, can ever endure the full light of inner truth nor the full dawn of the day.

To carry this work onward to its and your own full success we must have true, faithful, sincere and capable brothers on the Earth Plane who have common sense (sense that is not common), and who will act in full concert with us for the uplifting and Occult Education of humanity.

No city code, or man-made law, can overthrow, annul or set aside the laws of God (SELF, NATURE).

The progressive Mystic who has received his or her Occult Education will always act unselfishly, for they have by their education become Nature's (GOD'S) own legitimate and true instrument in human advancement.

They have steadfastly met and overthrown error, superstition, theology, ignorance, and arrogance in high and so-called holy places, and have thus denied the so-called Divine right of Kings, Ministers and Priests, and those who would scoff at spiritism.

They have without hesitation uprooted and overthrown the rule of despot and tyrant, have led true brothers and sisters with the potent weapon of mental thought and Astral force, to triumph over superstition and ignorance, and will finally be the means of ending the reign of the beasts of materialism and selfishness who can exist only for a time, and times, and half time.

166

Before the truths of our Brotherhood and Occult Organization the bonds and shackles of fettered humanity are destined to melt as snow beneath the Sun of Aries.

Do not be so foolish as to ask whether you are a Mystic or whether you can develop sufficiently to become identified with this great Occult Organization and ultimately communicate directly and personally with the unseen Brotherhood.

Each and every sensible and true soul possesses within itself these possibilities which are simply the attributes of Divine Soul Powers. Of course you may suppress and crucify them, or permit them to lie dormant, but only to your own loss and sorrow; or you can allow them to thrive and bloom, like the lotus blossoms on the river Nile, to a beauty and power that will allow you to outstep those who have devoted themselves to more inferior studies and pursuits.

Are you superstitious? Are you orthodox? Are you stingy? Are you selfish? Are you a doubting Tom? Ask yourself these questions.

These are the deep, treacherous, underlying false conditions you must combat and overcome. Can you lay aside these selfish or superstitious instincts and work for the good and uplifting of all worthy Brothers and Sisters instead of the aggrandizement of self? If you can, then you are welcome to our Astral Organization and great Occult Brotherhood.

If such you are, then we stretch out to you a helping hand over the infinite spaces, from the dim, forgotten centuries, and recognize you as a true brother or sister and comrade. You may rest assured, and the future will prove the truth of this statement, that the reign of truth and absolute justice and absolute unselfishness ultimately will come to every planet. To such culmination the progress of earth life is marked with every vicissitude that change and man-made laws may imply.

When such a condition has been brought about the planetary forces that previously indicated so much sorrow and suffering are discovered to be essential to perfect social organization.

'Tis thus the condition of adversity is turned into the force of perpetuity; the disappointments of failures and obstruction and slow decay are turned into a condition of sure, safe advancement.

Infinite force and infinite intelligence are infinitely good. If what you read here stirs the soul and smoldering forces within you it is the responding cry of your true spiritual self--your true Ego--the Astral self, recognizing and responding to the desires and vibrations of the eternal SELF.

It rests entirely with you whether this warning and recognition bears fruit or not. If you decide to act, ponder and consider well our advice. "BE SILENT." "Be ye wise as serpents but harmless as doves." A seed before it sprouts lies concealed, secret and silent in the dark earth.

It is in this condition that it finds its real and only opportunity for growth and development.

Antagonistic elements can only sweep over it while it lies concealed; its work, growth and development goes silently on. Such must be your self-development. So must your Astral and Soul Forces develop while silently hid in yourself.

Neither money nor position will buy true knowledge, nor can they destroy true knowledge.

Astral Powers, and Soul Forces, cannot be measured with money. Your Magical powers and great Astral possibilities must spring to life within yourself. Jesus, the greatest Master that ever lived, said: "Seek ye the Kingdom of God within you." We admonish you likewise.

See well to it that you heed. You may be so orthodox as to think that you should not heed and investigate, believing that the esoteric should not be investigated, or that your development should not be accelerated.

There is no subject, be it esoteric or exoteric, that is too sacred for true investigation, and it is the peculiar province of the True Mystic to desire to reason on all bidden and Astral forces with the utmost care.

The health of body, the energy and confidence that an ardor for truth and power inspires, mark his progress. No doubters, no laggard, no dotard, charlatan, no miser, no selfish one may ever hope to succeed, or ever overtake the fleeting feet of true Occultism and esoteric truths.

The true Master, Adept or Mystic must possess a will and intelligence that develops and brightens with attrition.

No scoffer, no obstacle, should daunt him, no condition should bar him, nothing should hinder or discourage him in his Astral development and search after truth.

He must acquire secret Knowledge and Mystic powers as a miser does his wealth to hold--his soul his strong-box; but, unlike the miser, he can give of his store and yet retain his all.

Steadfastness and purity of purpose and self are a necessary requisite while traveling the rugged path of Occultism and Mystic development.

* * * * * * *

We cannot enter into diseased or sensual conditions.

We may and desire to set those Astral forces in operation that will assuage deep-seated sorrow and physical suffering, but we cannot be expected to bring sweet music out of inharmonious notes.

To attempt to do so would of course be foolish and result in deep injury to ourselves. So we say, BE PURE, save your vital forces and preserve them long into old age.

The true Mystic and real Master never dissipates his physical or sex forces. The dissolute, sensual man does. The unspent and preserved sex and germinal forces surrounds you with a beautiful purple aura, which envelops you always greatly to your honor as well as being conducive to your development.

This beautiful aura and strength-giving element is dissipated and destroyed by sensual acts and animal instincts. When this purple Astral Aura is preserved and its supply constantly increased from day to day by pure acts and thoughts you will possess the means necessary for your development and the practice of true Occultism and Magic.

Heed thee, then, that your Aura remains purple, unimpaired and preserved. For this reason children are many times clairvoyant and possess Spirit and Astral Sight when their parents do not.

CONDITION ESSENTIAL FOR SPIRIT CO-ORDINATION AND COMMUNICATION.

It now becomes our province to direct and indicate the way and manner best suited for communication with the unseen world.

Try and fulfill all the requirements that we have indicated in the fore part of this communication and those which hereinafter follow, especially those relating to the preparation and use of the MAGIC MIRROR.

However, should you fail, do not be discouraged or cast down.--BE FAITHFUL. Faithfulness and application are all that will ever accelerate your development.

Persevere. To "him or her who is faithful much help and assistance will be given. At some future time, should you decide to become a brother or sister of this Occult Organization, you will know our meaning of the above; for we assure you we know full well how to handle this problem that has vexed so many who insist in developing in their own foolish way.

However, after you start, should no apparent results be obtained, keep on, be faithful, persevere, if necessary, for many years, yea, a lifetime.

Results and your capacity for work and perseverance will indicate the degree of your development and advancement as a true brother and faithful Mystic, while the cardinal principles of true Co-ordination will promote and signify the progress of your development and communication.

Of course, if you really wish to identify yourself with our Occult Organization and enter into such a relationship with us that you can communicate, you must place yourself, of your own free will and accord, in harmony and accord with those vibratory Astral forces which Co-ordinate with our own.

To obtain this class of vibratory forces you should read, then carefully re-read, this message many times until you thoroughly understand its real esoteric meaning.

Next most carefully decide and fix in your mind just the kind of an ideal life you think a true Mystic should live. Examine yourself as you would a peck of wheat, seeking both the inferior and superior grains or qualities.

Take heed of each inferior quality and virtue you possess. Then, like a true man or woman, decide to live what you believe to be the true ideal Mystical life.

After you do this see to it that you live the ideal life and you will bless the day and hour that this message came unsolicited by you.

Until you so live the ideal life, do not expect to co-ordinate with us. Should you decide upon an ideal Mystical life many questions will come to you.

Anticipating this there follows here the answer to all important ones. First--Good, pure, unselfish thoughts are absolutely essential and demanded. Remember, you seek to identify yourself with the greatest and really only true Occult Organization in the world.

A pure mind keeps away all vain fancies and mental delusions. Seek and you will find.

Aspire and you will be inspired. Perform any good deed you can; do not defer a good deed nor a laudable ambition.

The proper time to do anything is when ambition inspires you to do it. Then your energy is sustained by a free and natural ardor and desire, and you are assisted by a clear conception, unclouded by procrastination, which acts most effectively for success.

By living a pure mental and physical condition, and rounding out your existence by constantly keeping before you the ideal life of the advanced Mystic, you should rapidly advance to a degree of spiritual light and Astral coordination where we may be able to establish intelligent communication with you.

But remember, it all depends upon your faithfulness and capacity to persevere until you have advanced to a point where you can place yourself in a sphere of vibratory Astral forces that will admit of perfect coordination.

WHEN TO USE A MAGIC MIRROR.

Now if you have begun to live the ideal life and have arisen to a degree where we can cooperate with you through your Aura, you are now in a state where you can seek coordination, communication and relationship with us through a Magic Mirror.

Every wise Mystic constructs his own Opaque Magic Mirror, not because it could not be made for him, but because, if he constructs it himself, it will be more certain to serve the occult purpose for which it was made.

It will also more fully co-equal with his own cloisteral and monastic personality.

A Magic Mirror made under these circumstances, with an intense desire in the Disciple to succeed, will not be a means of preventing sodality and exclusive association between himself and the Astral world, as would one constructed by another, impregnated and perverted with their selfish corporeal magnetism and depressed lustreless Aura, which always serves as a bar to your complete coalesce and association with those in spirit life.

If you wish to succeed, disassociate yourself with any individual whose sole object and pursuit is financial gain, or who is of a mercenary nature.

If you make it a rule in life to disassociate yourself with any person who has a parsimonious, stingy nature and who is always curmudgeonly in his dealings, you will be better off.

Stay entirely away from those of a churlish, penurious disposition, as they will surround you with a muddy, mottled Aura or magnetism which will hold you back like a heavy fog or dismal vapor.

For this reason, unless you are careful, it is best to always live a sequestered and monastic life as far as your business and earthly pursuits will allow.

Far better that you remain untrammeled than to have to do with the close-handed and niggardly. Never get intimate or confidential with them or their kind.--Have no dealings with them, as they are surrounded with an Aura that means death to your hopes.

Shun them as you would an abominable, odious, damnable thing, for if you could see them in their true light, as the Mystic can, you would shrink and recoil from them as you would from something that was loathsome and nauseating--accursed.

Now, should you be interested enough to follow further, and it is purely your own affair whether you do or not, you are going to be told that if you were in a position to see clearly, that is to say, if your spiritual or Astral sight was developed, you would be able to observe many things which are low and unbecoming in those around you.

SPIRIT SIGHT AT WILL.

If you doubt this, it's because it is concealed from you owing to the fact that you only possess the physical sight. These things can only be observed by those who have Spirit Sight at will.

Does not your so-called Christian Bible, the toy and the mystery which the material minister and priest exhort over like a clod-pate of a jack-a-dandy, tell you to "develop the inner or spiritual sight"?

Common sense should indicate that it is your plain duty to possess Astral or Spirit Sight, which the ancients called the inner or spiritual sight.

If you wish to own a real, genuine Opaque Magic Mirror and be able to make it exactly as it was made by famous ancient Mystics so that it will possess Occult Virtue and become infused with Astral Auras, then proceed as hereinafter instructed, in this message, by this prerogative court and Brotherhood of Mystics.

Foremost, procure unto thyself the following materials from Messrs. de Laurence, Scott & Co., with which to make your own Opaque Magic Mirror.

One Convexo-Concave superior transparent glasswhich has a perfect and complete sphericity of form on the properly indicated side; manufactured by a certain secret process and formed by infusing silicious matter with fixed alkalies; but so constructed that it possesses none of the qualities of the lens, so that rays of Astral light passing through it are not made to change their direction or to magnify or diminish objects at a certain distance, as does the crystalline humour of the human eye.

In other words, this exclusive Convexo-Concave superior transparent glass must be so made by a special process that it has no mitigating, assuasive or lenitive qualities whatsoever.

Its exact size must be 5 9/16 * 7 10/16 inches.

Next obtain a sufficient amount of a secret bituminiferous substance like that used by the ancient mystics and old philosophers for this very purpose.

Also one small brush; very fine. The entire cost of the above materials, securely packed and sent in a special mailing case to any postoffice address in the world, should not exceed the amount of $3.00.

The materials referred to above were positively, previous to this communication, not obtainable anywhere in the world arranged ready for instant use.

Next obtain a box with a lid on to hold your mirror. Next procure one yard of new cloth. These are special materials from which you can make a genuine superior Opaque Magic Mirror.

The material for making a Superior Magic Mirror, that is, the Convexo-Concave transparent non-magnifying superior glass, 5 9/16 * 7 10/16 inches, and the secret bituminiferous substance to be used for coating your Magic Mirror, and the fine brush also to be used to apply the coating, you must obtain as told above, of Messrs. de Laurence, Scott & Co.

The box for holding the Magic Mirror, the yard of cloth and the pint of turpentine which you will also need, you of course can easily obtain yourself at a nominal cost from the stores where you reside.

These Convexo-Concave superior glasses for making the Magic Mirrors are prepared especially for this purpose and are only sold by Messrs. de Laurence, Scott & Co., who are the biggest and only official dealers in these materials as well as standard Occult, Spiritual and Magical books and Temple Incense in the world.

They are also official and direct importers, maintaining permanent offices and connections in India and the Orient for the importing of such materials as Temple Incense and costly essences which are used by the Priests and Mystics in the Orient and Hindu Occult Chambers.

* * * * * * * *

These particular superior transparent glasses, from which a Magic Mirror can be made, can not be obtained of anyone in the world outside of Messrs. de Laurence, Scott & Co., notwithstanding that after the publication and circulation of this Message others may offer them for sale.

So, unless you know that your dealer obtains them from this firm direct, you have no assurance they are genuine. Unless they are genuine and made after the special process as above, they will fail to serve the purpose for which you have obtained them.

To prevent this, obtain materials direct from this firm, or tell your dealer to do so. To prevent the sale of spurious materials for the making of genuine Opaque Magic Mirrors by unscrupulous dealers who will be anxious to supply you after the publication and circulation of this message, you should write Messrs. de Laurence, Scott & Co., direct and they will advise you by return mail whether your dealer is obtaining his materials from them or not, or whether he is imposing upon you.

They also sell, at a small cost, an excellent sphere or Crystal, which no Mystic or Adept ever thinks of being without. See pages <page 306>-309.

A Mystic or real Adept would be in no better shape to carry on Occult or Mystical work without his Rock Crystal or "Hindu Beryl," or an imported "Astral Sphere," than would a man who tried to write with no ink in his pen. Messrs. de Laurence, Scott & Co. have on exhibition in their offices a genuine Rock Crystal or Hindu Beryl--imported Astral Sphere-- value of which is $150.00, the same being the personal property of Dr. L. W. de Laurence, who has repeatedly refused $500 cash for it.

Students and Mystics as well as others owe much to this progressive firm, whose business has increased so rapidly that they have been compelled to move in larger quarters, and there is a possibility that they may be compelled to erect their own building as their business is increasing daily.

This firm imports from the Orient and Europe and in turn exports books and other goods to every country in the world. Dr. L. W. de Laurence's name is as well known in South Africa, Gold Coast Africa, India and British West Indies as it is in Europe and the United States. After a careful canvass and checking up of sales it was found that there was not a city nor town in the United States but what sheltered one or more who had purchased and studied this famous man's books.

Another thing students have this firm to thank for is their bold manner of stopping dealers in charging exorbitant prices for official books and materials necessary to carry on Occult work.

A case in point is their recent publication of a fine edition of that famous book sold in London entitled, "The Mysteries of Magic," by Eliphas Levi. Importers and London dealers sold this book at $3.75, prepaid, cheaply gotten up; de Laurence, Scott & Co obtained a copy, set their typesetters, their platemakers, their printers and binders to work, and published a modern edition of this excellent work on Occultism and Magic, bound it in red silk and stamped it in pure gold and sold it all over the world for $2.00, prepaid, thereby saving sincere students $1.75 on this one book.

Still another case: "India's Hood Unveiled," "Spirit Sight At Will," written by a native of South India, was being sold from India at a high price, published in paper covers.

Today de Laurence, Scott & Co. have their own exclusive edition of this work on the market for $2.00, prepaid, finely bound.

Dr. L. W. de Laurence has given to the world, with the sole

object of forming "The Congress of the Ancient Divine Mental Christian Masters," to date, five grand "Text Books," namely: First, "The Imminence of God"--"Know Thyself"; Second, "God the Bible Truth and Christian Theology"; Third, "Zoroaster, the Great Persian"; Fourth, "A Question of Miracles"; Fifth, "Superstition in All Ages."

These works are having an unprecedented sale and edition after edition is rolling from the presses.

When these works get well into circulation they will be the foundation and credentials for the greatest Congress and Brotherhood ever known.

However, not wishing to digress too far from the subject matter in our message to you, we will return, but then it's well for you to know these things, which are true, for no man in the world today can produce the results that Dr. de Laurence has. He has written and published and put into circulation a larger number of standard Occult works than any man who has ever lived before in the world, and it is unlikely that any one man ever will equal this great master in this respect.

"The Great Book of Magical Art," Hindu Magic and East India Occultism, a large volume weighing six pounds, was issued ten years ago by him. All admit that this work is the only reliable and standard work on this subject in print. The first edition, owing to the great cost of publishing, were sold for $12.00 per copy. Dealers in rare books bought this work through their puppets and resold it for $25.00, $50.00 and $150.00 a copy.

Dr. de Laurence immediately stopped its publication for three years, being greatly displeased at this.

Messrs. de Laurence, Scott & Co. now sell this celebrated volume, bound in full cloth, for $6.75, prepaid.

This of course killed the rare-book dealers' little game. It is needless to say that any work which has sold day in and day out for ten years and is still enjoying a large sale is a Standard work.

HOW TO CONSTRUCT AND USE A MAGIC MIRROR.

Part Two.

MESSAGE PART TWO: The turpentine, which you are to obtain where you live, you are to use to thoroughly clean your brush and convexo concave glass with. The bituminiferous substance, with which you are to coat the Magic Mirror so as to make it opaque, you will receive from Messrs. de Laurence, Scott & Co., ready mixed, and will not need diluting unless it should be too thick; in this event, mix a little turpentine into it.

The brush MUST be new, as must be all the materials used in the construction of your opaque Magic Mirror.

The box, which you are to obtain where you reside, may be of wood, but new. The cloth, which you are to obtain where you reside, should be of purple or blue, and of goods very agreeable to your touch and sight. If you cannot obtain blue or purple, get green or white, but under no circumstances use red. Wrap your Magic Mirror in the cloth when not in use and keep it in the box.

With all materials ready you are to pass into a room by yourself when all conditions are agreeable, and proceed as hereinafter instructed. With a piece of new cloth (a small piece will do) clean the concave glass of dust after dipping the cloth in turpentine. This will cause the bituminiferous substance to adhere to the glass when you apply it. Dip your brush also into the turpentine, wipe it off, then proceed to paint or coat the convex side of the glass with the bituminiferous substance.

The outside of the glass is the convex side and is the side to coat. Don't coat the concave or inside. Start coating at one end of glass and proceed slowly until you reach the other end. Apply the bituminiferous substance smoothly and as evenly as possibly, not resting for any other purpose until you have entirely finished your work. You must not go back over the glass, as any imperfection or streak in the coating can be remedied by the next coat you are to apply on another day. You are to apply three coats, as above, which will be necessary to make this specially prepared convexo-concave superior transparent glass Opaque, on three different days.

HOW TO MAGNETIZE A MAGIC MIRROR.

After you have prepared the convexo-concave glass as above, allow it to dry while you are washing your hands, etc. Next proceed to infuse into it the particular individual virtues of your own aura and magnetism. This is accomplished as follows: Pass the right hand, palm down, in a circular motion over the Mirror after each coating--your hand being about two inches above it. Repeat with the left hand. Then operate as above, with both hands at once. You should, however, make any kind of a motion over the glass that you feel impressed to make. Do all this with confidence, as it certainly pertains to your own individuality. You should make no fancy motions for effect, but should keep your mind solemnly on your task. Let your movements be deliberate and regular. See to it that the palms pass close to both sides of the glass. At times allow the hands to stop near both ends of the glass. It is not the movements of your hands, of course, that infuses and magnetizes the bituminiferous substance. It is your aura, which you have projected and transmitted into it. This bituminiferous substance is of such a nature that it readily absorbs your vital Aura and magnetism. It is the only substance known that will do this so well, and the secret of its preparation is known only to Dr. L. W. de Laurence, who has received it direct from the unseen Mystics. Some may scoff at this, however--be that as it may--it is true, nevertheless, and you should not be influenced by any sort of sophistry.

Be sure that you give this bituminiferous substance ample time to take on and absorb your Astral Aura so that it becomes thoroughly infused and well impregnated with it while you are in a perfectly quiet mental state of deep meditation, all the while keeping before you the ideal Mystic life you have decided upon living.

After you feel that you have about exhausted your Aura and that it has been absorbed by the substance on the Mirror you should stop. Before and during the process of making your Magic Mirror let yourself be prompted only by high aspirations and pure desires. Drive out all worry and thought of self and earthly desires by meditating on your work and the purpose for which you have made your Mirror. Read and re-read this message before you begin this work. After you have prepared the Magic Mirror then lay it upon a piece of heavy paper or cardboard, the coated side up; place it in the box to dry, some place where it will not be disturbed and the atmosphere is of an even temperature, or nearly so.

Allow the cardboard to remain under the glass until you have on three different days recoated and re-infused or magnetized it. You now have a Magic Mirror whose opaqueness will be perfect, and it will be ready for use three days after you apply the last coat. These are the only complete instructions ever given out to the world in print for this work, and it is given without thought or desire for pay--it being our desire and request that it be given free to all who are far enough advanced to appreciate their great value.

The entire cost of printing and mailing this information to you will be paid personally by Dr. L. W. de Laurence. The amount is not a small one, as you know when you consider that we have directed it to be mailed to 25,000 people, and as you are one of these, we trust that you will realize that our only object is to show you that we have recognized you as a brother-sister and comrade.

After you have finished the first, second and last coating, clean your brush with turpentine and put it aside for future use. Also cork up your bituminiferous substance tightly, as it is a rare and very expensive preparation.

* * * * * * *

Once started, keep steadily on living your ideal Mystical life, as near as your conditions and family, if you be married, affairs will allow. Examine yourself at the end of each day and resolve to do better the next. Try and avoid lapses. Live a life that each hour, each week, each month and each year makes you better morally and stronger physically. Help those who are worthy and need assistance.

This kind of a life will surely bring you health, peace of soul, and the inspiration to do good will become stronger, as will your desire for truth and goodness. If you do this you will really feel yourself getting stronger and better. You will feel your Astral and spiritual self unfolding. As you perfect yourself and succeed in Astral attainments so will you attract to yourself by your Aura higher and purer forces and aspirations. With these there will come to you, and be added unto you, Astral and Mystical powers that will well repay you for your efforts--the power that will make you a power and a Mystic. Remember, Brother and Sister, that each should give to his or her ability and will receive according to his or her capacity.

This development, this inspiration, this Astral unfoldment, this progress, these powers--all these--and more--must come from within--for, remember, "The Kingdom of God Is Within You." Without this unfoldment of your Astral self all the spirits and Astral Powers in the Universe might be ready to help you and obey your invocation, but no results would follow their ministrations. You must unfold. Astral Powers, Astral Sight, and, Spirit Sight Must unfold from within you.

You can blindly follow the childish instructions and methods of the so-called professors and mediums and surface writers and so-called authors until you are sore tired, heartbroken and discouraged, and you will never even be able to receive intelligently an Astral or mental impression from the unseen World, let alone being able to co-ordinate and enter into intelligent communication.

With a heart destitute of selfishness, with your soul on fire for humanity, and a mind desiring and aspiring for help and truth, always desiring to engage in good Occult works--all these the fruits of a good life--you will need and shall have our help and companionship.

Once your Magic Mirror has been constructed strictly according to our direction in this message it will be necessary of course for you to give us an opportunity to materialize and also communicate with you.

This can only be accomplished by your conforming to certain conditions as hereinafter indicated.

The first essential is regular sittings or periods of meditation, when you must get mentally and physically quiet, so as to completely bring about a condition of receptivity to external psychic and astral forces. You should go into silent and secret meditation at certain specified times and observe that you attend well this duty, always endeavoring to bring about a state of introspection.

You will observe we have advised that these sittings be secret. This of course is for your own welfare and protection. Keep it from the curious and we do here admonish you in this beginning to be secret, and neither teach nor manifest to anyone this work, or place, or time, nor your desire, or will, except it be to a true companion, brother Mystic or Master of this work, who likewise should be faithful, discreet, silent, and dignified by nature, education and conduct.

Never are you to expose or reveal them to unworthy or unscrupulous persons; but reveal them only to faithful, discreet and chosen friends, for your association with a prating companion, whose misbelief, doubting, questioning, and, lastly, unworthiness, hinders and disturbs the effect and result of every Magical and Occult operation, consequently, and, in consideration of what has been said in the forepart of this message, about the undesirable astral Auras some people carry around with them, you should not seek the companionship of those who are unworthy.

Set a given time for your meditation period and development in the use of your Magic Mirror. Arrange these sittings at a convenient hour, then allow nothing to interfere except sickness or something beyond your power to prevent.

You should also procure unto yourself an Incense Burner of good ventilation and some Imported TEMPLE INCENSE and burn the same as directed on pages 310, 311, 312, 313.

Burn a small amount of this compound at every sitting with a Magic Mirror or a Crystal. One imported package will do for fifty or more sittings. This "Soul-Vision" and "Astral-Light," inducing subtle, fragrant compound, should always be burned in a special Incense Burner procurable of Messrs. de Laurence, Scott & Co.

Once you begin these sittings, be regular; do not disappoint us unless you wish to disappoint yourself.

Four times a week is often enough. Once a week will do if you cannot sit oftener. Sit from forty-five minutes to an hour, or an hour and a half, always commencing at the same time of day or night.

Have a quiet, neat room, where you can be alone. Be composed, be patient, and, above all, be faithful--believe there is more in life than the demoralized material world around you on the earth plane.

Have the room dark so you will not be able to see the Magic Mirror, though you are all the time gazing into it. Sit quiet and hold the Magic Mirror in both hands by placing them against the ends.

Just as soon as you start this you will be visited by members of our Occult Organization and Brotherhood from spirit life, and all necessary data regarding your desires and personality secured.

Your condition, capacity, ability, surroundings, vibratory forces, Astral Auras, time of sitting, and all necessary information carefully noted.

A report is then made and all data about you will be recorded. To successfully establish intelligent communication with you we must then proceed to find some brother or sister in the spirit world whose vibration, forces and Astral Aura will coordinate with you, and who will volunteer to be a companion to you so as to establish communication with you at given intervals.

Of course it may at times seem long before we succeed in securing the right companion for you.

However, if you are faithful, patient and regular you may rest assured the Brotherhood is interested in you and will not see you sit in vain.

Many, many, times you will be visited by those of us who would like to talk with you but cannot owing to some peculiar Astral or physical condition. Of course, we note these adverse conditions and set about overcoming them and to help bring you, into direct communication with us.

Once a brother is found whose vibratory forces coordinate with your own and he volunteers to become your companion results come quickly, and will be instantly noted on your OPAQUE CONVEXO-CONCAVE MAGIC MIRROR.

First, you will see all around the room bright lights like little stars snapping into life; while across the Black Opaque face of your Magic Mirror will pass an emulsive luminous film, which will be phosphorescent--without heat--of a white, cloudy appearance. This is the usual manifestation of the presence of Astral forces.

After the luminous film has passed away a little star may be seen to pass across the firmament of the MAGIC MIRROR. This is the first indication of real advancement and success upon your part.

However, you should keep quiet at this your initial phenomena, eliminating all quixotic thoughts from your mind.

Do not be too anxious for results or the advancement of your development. If you heed this advice you will act as have all ci-devant Mystics, and all others who are wise, quo ad hoc.

Once Astral phenomena and psychic results come you may be assured that we are around you; that we have a true gauge on you; and if you persevere, your ideas will undergo a complete transfiguration as far as Mysticism and true pneumatology is concerned.

In short, the veil of Osiris, if your efforts are not mediocre, will be raised before your admiring gaze.

Once you have learned from us, by this message, how to make a real, genuine Opaque Convexo-Concave Magic Mirror and other details which we have given here regarding Astral Vision and Magnetic Aura, it is our request that you interest any worthy brother or sister in this work and make them a Magic Mirror should they desire you to do so.

As the subject is of vital and universal interest to humanity, it may be hoped you will avoid all selfishness, as hereinbefore mentioned, and obtain as many brothers and sisters as you can.

They can either have you make them a Magic Mirror or send for materials to make one and thereby become a member of our Brotherhood of Mystics.

It your plain duty to do this, especially should they be influenced or inclined to apply to you by their Astral influence and not as the direct result of printed matter or advertisement.

In constructing an Opaque Convexo-Concave Magic Mirror for another who wishes to become a Mystic, take just as much care with it as if it were your own and deliver it to him or her, as the case may be, no matter if you have become greatly attached to it yourself. Your charge should not exceed $5.00, or less if you feel disposed.

Admonish the one who receives it never to let anyone else handle it. Try to become a trained psychic, seer and Mystic by studying and using the Opaque Magic Mirror and studying official and standard works that treat on this subject.

An excellent book for assisting you in the use of a Mirror and Crystal is The Mystic Test Book of "The Hindu Occult Chambers," Hindu and Egyptian Crystal Gazing, together with the Wonders of the Magic Mirror. This work teaches the original and true science of Hindu Seership and "Spirit-and-Astral-Sight-at-Will," as it was taught by the old Masters and mystics. See Order No. 12; Catalogue Page No. 36. If you would then know the initiations and disciples of the Mystic Brotherhood and understand the inner psychic and Astral nature of yourself and the spiritual basis of human Auras we beckon you, true brother and sister, to join our Mystic Brotherhood and no longer remain in ignorance regarding your Astral or Sidereal self.

You will then understand every system of Astral personality and be able to determine the primary fund and nature of Astral and psychic forces, and their nature, and their results, and their aptitudes in dominating industrial life and personal destiny.

It is not our purpose to here consider elaborately the nature and substance which compose, and the laws which govern, the Astral personality of humanity, or why the nature and destiny of a person is, and can be specifically influenced in one direction more than another by them.

This may seem strange. However, if you will consider for a moment the great contention of Occult and Astral Forces that are struggling for supremacy in the psychic or Astral regions around and in you, and into which you were born, and which wero born into you, and the fact that, even from a physical viewpoint, the volume, direction and effect of these Astral forces and Auras are forever varying; surging; overcoming; and again equalizing each other with your every change of thought and varying mental attitude and divers physical conditions, it should be easily understood and realized that they may and really do influence mentality destiny and results.

It would certainly cause a sensation in all social, domestic and commercial life, and would undoubtedly change a tentative art as medicine into an exact science, if the nature and laws that underlie Astral and Occult forces were universally understood.

It does not disprove our claims, as contained herein, nor place them subject to ridicule, because many are not initiated into their use or nature; else must many arts and sciences suffer the same results.

All Sages, Seers, and Mystics, and members of all Standard and proficient Occult organizations know by experience that Astral and psychic Auras and forces do influence and control the psychical and physical nature of men, women and children, and, in short, all active life.

The Astral and psychic sight and the intuitions of all Ancient and Modern Mystics is perfect.

Results are as a rule more regular in Occultism than those said to be obtained from the unmeasured phases of religion; ethics; morality and some other branches of so-called human knowledge and physical or material sciences.

People are fast giving up orthodoxy and religion and the more advanced of mankind are working out the solutions regarding the Astral or inner self.

Indisputable facts manifesting the Astral and mental forces are attested to by great and fearless Mystics and men of research all over the world.

The near future will be devoted to the solution of man's inner or Astral self. People are beginning to greatly desire Astral vision and to understand the silent, ever-pulsating forces of the unseen world.

Interesting, valuable and wonderful revelations are being secured by many today.

Dr. L. W. de Laurence, who we have honored as being the medium and instrument through which this message is given to humanity, is well trained for Astral sight and Psychic vision, and to this great and fearless Mystic and Seer and his wonderful publications we desire to call your special attention in this message.

He has written, published, and even given to his fellow brothers and sisters and his disciples the very information they needed to become a Mystic and Seer.

A supplemental and full record of the life of this great man and Mystic is now being written daily in the unseen world by an eyewitness, and will be given to the world after his death through the mediumship of a certain brother Mystic who has no personal knowledge of Dr. de Laurence, his early manhood, his travels in Oriental countries, his steadfastness, his trials, his initiations while a chela (disciple) into the greatest Occult organization existing today.

Dr. de Laurence has a mission to perform in Europe, America, West Indies, Africa, etc.; his mission is teaching "THE IMMANENCE OF GOD". in contest with Orthodoxy and the so-called Christian church, as well as true Occultism and Magic.

Dr. de Laurence is a man well advanced in life, although strong and capable as a man of twenty-five.

His intention is to live one hundred and fifty years, so as to give to the world such information and help as it may need regarding man's Astral, Mental and Psychic forces.

Many Mystics and advanced students have developed Astral and Spiritual consciousness by studying his works.

The alchemy of life, Telepathy and Intuition, Dream and Trance states, wider states of mental plane and consciousness of Astral Vision, Inherent Vibrant Astral force, higher Auras, Stages of Clairvoyance, Psychic Vibrations, which control the emotional and mental nature of men and women and children, and interpenetrate the physical body for health or disease, are fully and most intelligently treated by him. The very fact that his books have been simultaneously accepted as Standard and official by all the leading Spiritualists and Occult students has convinced us, as well as his record as a successful Mystic and Seer, that he was the proper one for us to select as our Medium to give this message to you. Again, he has more correspondents than any other teacher, besides being in the best position to circulate it properly.

Regarding the personal character and ability of Dr. de Laurence as an author, compiler and publisher, we, as well as his thousands of students and all who know him personally, have the utmost respect. However, there are some who will seek to belittle him, for they belong to a class of mental deformities who are attempting to build up their own interests by speaking ill of others. Dr. de Laurence is known to be a man who will not utter an ill word about any one, and those who have made themselves conspicuous in complaining about bis radical methods of cutting book prices and other business methods simply have shown that they possess a low grade of mentality, desiring to rise by pulling down a good man.

THE IMMANENCE OF GOD, KNOW THYSELF.

The publication of "The Immanence of God, Know Thyself," "God, the Bible, Truth and Christian Theology" and "Zoroaster, the Great Persian" have come like a boom among church officials, ministers and priests. These works have shocked Theology and Orthodoxy to its very foundation. Books that will follow in time will do even more. So mental underlings, and the "pocket edition" kind of an individual can sneer because that is their breed, and they must do it or their soul will corrode--the ministers and priests may shrug their shoulders and show their sneering natures by ignoring, but they cannot gainsay the truth of these books.

Our work and teaching will go out to the intelligent world in spite of all the critics and underlings. We care not for creed, color or clime, and this message will be read in Africa, India and America, as well as in Judea and Galilee, Japan and China.

We have sincere brothers and sisters in all climes. All are WELCOME to test their psychic qualities, or investigate the dynamic and psychic world, so that they may thereby obtain a better, fuller and clearer conception of the possibilities, faculties, nature and qualities of their inner or Astral self and the world of vibratory forces around them.

You need not ask if whether or no you are a Mystic. Every soul contains within itself the attributes of divinity. They may be repressed and crucified to the loss of the soul, or they may be made to bloom, like the lotus, to a beauty and power that may set the more inferior limitations of existence at any length.

Are you selfish? This is the question you should ask yourself. This is the deep, underlying condition we must combat. Can you lay this selfish instinct aside to work for the good of all in place of the aggrandizement of self I If so, then we welcome you to our Brotherhood. We reach out to you a hand over the

N infinite spaces, from the dim, forgotten centuries, and recognize you as brother and comrade.

Before the truth of our Brotherhood the bonds and shackles of mankind are destined to melt as snow beneath the Sun of Aries.

www.ingramcontent.com/pod-product-compliance
Lightning Source LLC
Chambersburg PA
CBHW060319050426
42449CB00011B/2555